CLIENT-CENTERED
COUNSELING:
A RENEWAL

Angelo V. Boy
University of New Hampshire
Durham, New Hampshire

and

Gerald J. Pine
Oakland University
Rochester, Michigan

Allyn and Bacon, Inc.
Boston • London • Sydney • Toronto

Library of Congress Cataloging in Publication Data

Boy, Angelo V.
  Client-centered counseling.

  Includes index.
  1. Client-centered psychotherapy. 2. Counseling.
I. Pine, Gerald J. II. Title.
RC481.B69   616-89'14   81-10900
ISBN 0-205-07639-4   AACR2

Printed in the United States of America.

10 9 8 7 6 5 4 3 2 1   87 86 85 84 83 82

CONTENTS

PREFACE

Client-centered counseling began as a process that was essentially applied to individuals and small groups. From its inception in 1942, with the landmark book *Counseling and Psychotherapy* (Houghton Mifflin) by Carl Rogers, client-centered counseling has evolved into a person-centered view with a wider range of applications. Today person-centeredness is being applied in teaching, administration, organizational behavior, marriage and its alternatives, parenting, race relations, the building of community, conflict resolution, social action, and interpersonal relations in general.

We are elated with this evolvement. Our expectation is that person-centeredness will be applied in even more interpersonal areas in the decades ahead. Indeed, the preservation of the dignity and worth of the person, in an increasingly depersonalized and technological world, requires a sustained commitment to the empathic attitudes and behaviors that are the core of person-centeredness.

Although we are deeply supportive of the wider applications of the person-centered viewpoint, and participate in that expansion ourselves, we are also disappointed that current person-centered theorists and practitioners are paying little attention to the basic process that nurtured the person-centered movement; namely, the process of client-centered individual and group counseling. This book represents our contribution to reestablishing the importance and necessity of this process within the person-centered movement.

While the person-centered movement is committed to issues and relationships that go beyond individual and group counseling, we want to reaffirm our commitment to client-centered counseling as an effective process for influencing attitudinal and behavioral change among troubled persons. While beneficial person-centered concepts are being implemented we want to be sure that the traditional counseling needs of individuals are also being met through a humanly sensitive process. These needs exist and must be attended to by those in the front lines of organizations and agencies that are expected to provide qualitative counseling services. While person-centeredness nurtures the generic development of human caring within society as a whole, client-centered counseling must also maintain its special sense of responsibility to troubled individuals within that society.

Our hope is that this book provides the reader with a reenergized interest in applying client-centered counseling. Our renewed concept of client-centered counseling is synergistic. We join established concepts of client-centered counseling with eclectic concepts so that each enriches and expands the other and makes the other more effective. We desire that client-centered counseling be renewed with a synergistic freshness and vigor that makes it applicable to a widening range of client needs.

In the renewed concept of client-centered counseling contained in this book we desire to accomplish the following:

Present our rationale for a renewed concept of client-centered counseling

Reestablish the importance of counseling theory as the foundation for the counseling process

Reinforce the influence of the self-concept on personality and behavior

Validate the importance of values and their influence on the counseling relationship

Provide an expanded concept of the modern client-centered counselor's role

Affirm the essential characteristics of a client-centered counseling relationship

Present a transcription of a renewed client-centered counseling relationship

Review the group counseling movement from its turbulent period to its current stability and provide a renewed client-centered perspective on its process components

Examine the difficulties and opportunities surrounding accountability and evaluation

Provide a student-centered perspective on the process of preparing a person to become a counselor

Indicate self-expanding therapeutic opportunities that are available outside the field of counseling.

Most important, we hope that this book contributes to an improvement in the human condition by members of the helping professions who read it and apply its contents in their work with clients. If clients are the ultimate beneficiaries of the viewpoint presented in this book, it will have served its purpose.

A. V. B.
G. J. P.

Chapter 1

CLIENT-CENTERED COUNSELING: A REFINEMENT

We have been identified with the client-centered literature of counseling since 1963 (Boy & Pine, 1963). We have functioned as full-time professional counselors for a combined period of 14 years and have had a collaborative involvement with the field of counseling for over 40 years. Our deep commitment to client-centered counseling has not only been a visceral commitment but the intellectual depth of the client-centered viewpoint has been reinforced in our own experience as counselors, by the human goals of the approach, the face validity of the process, and the objective research evidence that supports the effectiveness of client-centered counseling. Client-centeredness has been, personally and professionally, an enriching journey for us; but like other journeys, we have not yet reached our destination. It is the purpose of this book to continue that journey and to formulate a more applicable approach to client-centered counseling. Hopefully, our current viewpoint will attract the intellectual interests of theoreticians, the application interests of counselors, and the curiosity of researchers.

We are now involved in the momentum of a transition from a traditional interpretation of client-centeredness to a refined conceptualization of the client-centered viewpoint. This transition does not mean that we have abandoned the traditional philosophic values of client-centeredness; these values are enduring. But like all values that are subjected to the scrutiny of new experiences, these values evolve toward becoming more universal and more applicable to a wider range of clients with expanding human needs.

An effective theory of counseling must have a reach that exceeds its grasp. We shall attempt to move client-centered counseling theory a notch forward with this book and we realize that what we develop may not be the full outcome that we seek, but only another stopover in our journey.

Client-centered counseling was founded and developed by Carl R. Rogers (1942, 1951, 1954, 1961, 1967, 1969, 1970, 1972, 1973, 1974, 1975, 1977, 1980). What began as a viewpoint that was only applicable to one-to-one counseling has become expanded to an ever widening range of situations in which better interpersonal relations are crucial: Teaching, organizational behavior, families, parenting, groups, marriage and its alternatives, leadership, pastoring, and interpersonal relationships in general. The impact of the Rogerian view has been immense in enabling a person to become self-actualizing and thereby influencing the emergence of a self-actualizing behavior in others.

Hart (1970, pp. 3–22) identifies three historic periods in the development of client-centered counseling:

Period 1 (1940–1950): The nondirective period in which the counselor essentially formed a relationship with the client based upon acceptance and clarification.

Period 2 (1950–1957): The reflective period in which the counselor essentially responded to the client's feelings by reflecting those feelings back to the client.

Period 3 (1957–present): The experiential period in which the counselor goes beyond reflecting the client's feelings and engages in a wider range of responses in order to meet the needs of the client.

This book attempts to develop a view that incorporates the major emphasis within the three periods in an effort to identify a more effective and expanded application of client-centered theory.

We are essentially adding an energized dimension to the long-standing tradition of client-centered counseling. Rogers (Rogers and Wood, 1974, p. 213) never intended that the client-centered viewpoint be fixed and immobile. He indicates that a fundamental thrust of client-centered counseling has been its: ". . . willingness to change, an openness to experience and to research data has been one of the most distinctive features of client-centered therapy. The incorporation of this element of changingness has set it apart, almost more than anything else I know, from other orientations to therapy."

Corsini (1973, p. 123) indicates the evolving nature of client-centered counseling when he states that: "The changing character of client-centered therapy is due to Rogers' consistent insistence on looking at the facts and altering the methods and theory whenever experience and research so dictated."

Wexler and Rice (1974, p.9) indicate that a rigid interpretation of client-centered counseling would be in contradiction to the developmental nature of both Rogers and the theory: "Fortunately there has not grown up around Rogers the kind of orthodoxy that would require his formulations to be the last word on any issue. Rogers certainly would not welcome this kind of blind devotion, and would in fact view it as a failure in actualization."

Corey (1977, p. 56) also acknowledges client-centered counseling as a viewpoint that is still in the state of emergence: "Rogers has not presented the client-centered theory as a fixed and completed approach to therapy. He has hoped that others would view his theory as a set of tentative principles relating to how the therapy process develops and not as dogma."

Our client-centered approach to counseling accommodates the viewpoints of existentialism, humanism, and theology since certain aspects of these viewpoints contribute important parallel concepts regarding human nature, behavior, and the goals of existence that are congruent with client-centeredness. The client-centered viewpoint has traditionally dealt with human freedom, self-actualization, the necessity of a congruence between the ideal self and the actual self, acceptance, openness, socialization, the internal locus of evaluation, genuineness, nonpossessive love, and empathy. Viewpoints regarding the preceding have also emerged from existentialism, humanism, and theology in their treatment of free will, humanity's desire for peace and good will, personal honesty and responsibility, respect for the dignity and worth of others, the desired congruence between a person's personal and social consciousness, the person's natural inclination to transcend the self, and guidelines for moral behavior that sustains the self and serves others.

Client-centered counseling is the core of our viewpoint but existentialism, humanism, and theology can be viewed as enriching and expanding that core. We choose to have a primary identification with the client-centered viewpoint because it fulfills the requirements of a valid theory of counseling (Burks & Stefflre, 1979, pp. 7–9), has a substantive theory of personality that undergirds its application (Rogers, 1951), has an established and effective process model with enough range so that it can be translated into practice in a wide variety of settings, possesses both qualitative and quantitative research evidence supporting its effectiveness, and has been confirmed in our own experience as persons and as professional counselors.

AN EXPANSION OF THE CLIENT-CENTERED VIEWPOINT

We propose that there are two basic phases to an effective client-centered counseling relationship. In Phase One, the counselor becomes involved in building a therapeutic, facilitative, and substantive relationship with the client. Building such a relationship is the foundation from which future interactions with the client can be productive. When a counselor has an authentic caring relationship with a client, that client responds to the relationship by becoming fully involved in the counseling process. Because the client's relationship with the counselor is deep and real, the client moves toward belief and trust in the counselor and the counseling process. The counselor's credibility with the client becomes the catalyst for the client's positive movement in the counseling process (Egan, 1975; Patton & Griffin, 1974).

If the counselor has been effective in the relationship-building first phase of counseling, then what the counselor says or does in the second phase of counseling tends to produce a positive reaction on the part of the client. What is done in Phase Two, then, becomes effective essentially because the client has trust in the counselor; a trust that was initiated and developed by the counselor in the Phase One process of relationship building. Therefore, if the counselor concentrates on first building a relationship with the client, and if Phase Two of counseling centers on the needs of the client, then the outcomes of counseling should tend toward the positive.

Assertive theories of counseling are more effective when the counselor delays the implementation of strategies and interventions until after the relationship with the client has been established. Often these approaches to counseling are "too much too soon" for the client to accept and absorb. Counselors diminish the potential effectiveness of assertive approaches when they tend to apply them too quickly; the typical client is not ready to accept a counselor who is overly aggressive or assertive in the beginning phase of counseling. Initially, the client more typically desires to be received as a person; accepted and understood on the client's terms and from the client's internal frame of reference.

More assertive theories of counseling yield more positive results when they are founded upon the existence of a close, human, and empathic relationship with the client. It is the existence of such a relationship that enhances the effectiveness of any process applied in the second phase of counseling.

When the practicing counselor has developed a substantive relationship with a client, that counselor is able to implement any Phase Two approach that is appropriate to the needs of the client. Without the relationship and resulting counselor credibility, the counselor's effectiveness is greatly diminished in the second phase of counseling.

Clients respond to counselors who are persons. When the counselor is able to establish an affective bond with the client in the first phase of counseling, it is the credibility of the counselor's personhood that enables the second phase to be effective. Many novice counselors abandon an assertive approach to counseling when it is resisted by the client and has no impact upon the client's behavior. If these counselors *first* apply the fundamentals of relationship building, they would increase the potential of their assertive approach having a positive effect upon client behavior.

The development of an affective relationship requires that the counselor possess identifiable positive attitudes that can be communicated to clients through the counselor's verbal and nonverbal behavior. A modeling of these attitudes by the counselor to the client will influence the development of a substantive relationship, so crucial in the first phase of counseling. Without the demonstrated possession of these attitudes, the counselor cannot expect the second phase of counseling to be productive.

Relationship building between the client and counselor is one beneficial outcome of Phase One. Another equally valuable outcome is the full and accurate assimilation of the client by the counselor. By assimilating or absorbing the totality of the client's personality, attitudes, values, and behavior, the counselor is able to gain a full and accurate representation of the client's hopes, fears, desires, life style, self-concept, defenses, and essence as a person. Such a full and accurate representation of the client enables the counselor to more accurately understand which approach will yield the best results with a particular client during Phase Two. Far too many counselors proceed with therapeutic procedures that are based upon only a partial awareness of the client's personality, attitudes, values, and behavior; there appears to be little synchronization between the existential qualities of the client and the approach of the counselor. Phase One of counseling enables the counselor to assimilate the totality of the client; and such an assimilation results in the counselor judging more accurately which approach eventually benefits a particular client most during Phase Two.

Through assimilation, the counselor develops a more accurate approach for assisting a particular client because of the counselor's more sharpened and focused understanding of the client's full range of attitudes, values, and behaviors. Without this level of understanding, the counselor often makes the mistake of dealing with the client's presenting problem while deeper and more incapacitating problems go unattended; they were never identified by either the client or the counselor because of the superficiality of their relationship. Superficial relationships with clients are usually established when counselors do not take the necessary time to penetrate and absorb the inner, deep, and more influencing dimensions of the client's personality, attitudes, values, and behavior.

Therefore, two distinct advantages of Phase One are that it provides the counselor with a meaningful vehicle for building a therapeutic relationship with a client while also enabling the counselor to more deeply and accurately assimilate the full range of the client's personality, attitudes, values, and behavior; and a deep and accurate assimilation of the client contributes significantly to the counselor's ability to accurately meet the needs of the client in Phase Two.

The evidence currently available indicates that clients still respond to traditional Rogerian counseling. This is a confirmation that most clients desire to be treated as human beings rather than as objects. They respond positively when they have an equalized relationship with a counselor who is empathic, acceptant, genuine, liberating, involved, and a sensitive listener. These relationship-building counselor attitudes have proven to be effective in establishing the foundation for a productive counseling relationship. Indeed, for many clients these attitudes are sufficient to positively affect attitudinal and behavioral changes.

For many other clients, however, client-centeredness doesn't seem to be enough. Clients respond well to the client-centered attitudes of the counselor but often they also need to move toward a more concrete counseling process so that their individualized needs can be realistically met. Counselors in the mainstream have economic, political, social, and psychological strengths that they have inherited or earned and frequently take for granted. Clients outside the mainstream often need more than the caring attitudes of counselors. They often need the intervention of counselors to achieve a basic need: an artificial limb, a job, access to governmental agencies, adequate housing, etc.; and they desire a fair share of the psycho-social benefits of the American dream.

These are clients who have seldom crossed the thresholds of counseling offices in decades past. Their hierarchy of needs require fulfilling at the basic survival levels before they can devote the time and energy to becoming self-actualizing.

It is important to receive clients with the human fullness of the Rogerian attitude. Phase Two of our renewed approach enables the counselor to be more flexible and concrete in meeting client needs once the Phase One relationship has been established through the traditional process model of client-centered counseling.

The following Phase One counselor attitudes are fundamental: (1) They need to be present in Phase One of counseling if Phase Two is to be successful. (2) They are basic and need to be identified and actualized so that the counselor can reinforce the attitudes necessary for an effective counseling relationship to occur. (3) In a society that insists on becoming more hurried, mechanical, and superficial, they give definition to a human attitude that needs to be preserved by those committed to effective person-centered counseling.

PHASE ONE COUNSELOR ATTITUDES

Empathy

Empathy occurs when the counselor is emotionally congruent with the feelings of a client (Bergin & Garfield, 1971; Egan, 1973; Rogers, 1975). Empathy essentially means that the counselor is in full emotional contact with the client and feels the pain, the sorrow, the disgrace, the rejection that the client has felt and is expressing in the counseling session. The placing of one human spirit within another so that there is emotional congruence can sometimes be difficult. The counselor must be selfless enough not to allow his or her life and problems to encroach upon the counseling relationship. The more selfless the counselor is, the deeper the empathy. The empathic counselor is able to enter the client's being so that, in some way, the counselor is the client. Instead of sitting back sifting the rights and wrongs of the client's feelings, the counselor experiences, however imperfectly, the same emotions and feelings as the client. One client said to a counselor after an empathic counseling session, "You're me! It's unbelievable but you're me . . . you've felt everything that I've felt." To be emotionally close to clients is an enriching experience for a counselor. This empathic relationship is not academic jargon; it is something a counselor can deeply feel and the counselor realizes that it can occur again and again provided the counselor is willing to fully give the self when entering the inner perceptual world of the client.

When counselors empathize with troubled clients, they realize that this is the core of a substantive counseling relationship. The counselor's awareness of the client's feelings enables the client to see inside the self more accurately. Only a person highly sensitive to the thoughts and feelings of others can achieve empathy. Counselors develop the ability to be empathic when they diminish and eventually eliminate the intrusion of counselor values when communicating with clients in the first phase of counseling.

This giving of self by the counselor is perhaps the most significant quality a client senses and can respond to in a substantive relationship. The counselor who sublimates the self, and who deeply penetrates the emotional existence of another person, stands in a position to be of the greatest value to a troubled individual. The client desires to be fully understood and the counselor who gives the client the needed human response is the counselor who is selfless enough to be empathic.

Acceptance

The counselor's acceptance of the client is another facilitating characteristic of a substantive relationship (Polster & Polster, 1973; Rogers, 1977). Acceptance means many things to many counselors, and even within a counselor it varies in degree. For one counselor, acceptance may mean that as part of the counselor's work a certain number of clients have to be seen; this counselor accepts clients just as an accountant accepts numbers as part of the accounting function.

For another counselor, acceptance means that the counselor is in a full respectful contact with the client. This counselor does not feel that the client is just another person. The client is an individual, unique among all others, and carrying a very special problem. The counselor receives whatever the client says without judgment. The counselor indicates to the client that no barriers exist between them simply by the felt warmth of the counselor's attitude. The client can sense this counselor's acceptance, and, in turn, is willing to accept the counselor as someone who may be in a position to be of assistance.

Too often we think of acceptance as just emanating from the counselor to be absorbed by the client. But acceptance blossoms in the reciprocal giving between counselor and client. The client indicates a reciprocal acceptance by responding to the counselor's acceptant attitude.

True acceptance is unaffected by any attitudinal or behavioral deviations in the client. It is unconditional. It does not depend upon the client's behaving or communicating in a certain way, upon the client's background, religion, life style, economic status, or intelligence. It is not dependent upon the client's meeting certain moral, ethical, or behavioral criteria. It is complete.

For effective counselors, total acceptance is not difficult. They have seen something of life and realize that not everyone can fit into their personalized concepts of what people should be. These counselors have come to believe in this simple principle and to realize that life cannot have value and meaning unless one can be genuinely acceptant of others. Such acceptance has great depth and can be felt by the client in a substantive counseling relationship. An acceptant counselor realizes that in order to be close to clients, he or she must selflessly provide clients with the opportunity to be themselves, on their own terms.

Genuineness

A client is unable to move toward more personally satisfying attitudes and behavior until the client comes to grips with the genuineness of the self. The counselor cannot assist the client in such an evolvement unless the counselor is genuine in the helping relationship (Arbuckle, 1975; Lucas & Lucas, 1977). Genuineness must be achieved by both the client and the counselor if the client is to move toward more personally enriching attitudes and behavior. Therefore, the counselor must be authentic in developing a substantive relationship with the client for the degree of client authenticity is proportionate to the degree of authenticity demonstrated by the counselor (Boy & Pine, 1968, pp. 60–64).

When a client enters the counseling relationship, the client is typically unauthentic in that the self is obscured or not consciously known. Counseling is the process of uncovering the self and moving away from unauthentic self-statements and moving toward more genuine self-statements. Troubled clients live in a world where they have learned to engage in unauthentic patterns of response. They learn to speak the words that others expect to hear rather than to genuinely express feelings and attitudes. Such clients have some difficulty in the beginning of a counseling relationship because there is a tendency to be personally evasive rather than honest.

The client's search for genuineness is characteristic of movement in counseling. The client moves from an obscured self-concept to a clearer and more authentic self. The counseling atmosphere provides the client with the safety necessary to take a free and introspective look at the self. The counselor's authenticity is a quality that enables the client to move toward a more supportive self-concept, and to behave with a higher degree of personal satisfaction.

The counselor's genuineness is imperative if the client is to achieve genuineness. If the counselor is truly genuine, he or she engages in counseling attitudes and behaviors that influence clients to be genuine. The authentic counselor feels compelled to be involved in facilitative behaviors that have meaning and relevance for clients rather than to adopt superficial and mechanical behaviors that have little or no value.

For many counselors, a movement toward genuineness means discarding attitudes and behaviors that tend to be hollow; for if one takes a close look at the meaning of authenticity, one becomes involved in process-ing out irrelevant behaviors. Philosopher Wild (1965, p. 77) indicates this when he says:

> Authentic action is the expression of a very finite freedom. But it does not enslave us to norms that are externally imposed, since it takes them over, and lifts them up into a world of meaning that we have thought through and authorized for ourselves. There is a real sense in which these meaningful acts are mine. But they have not been laid down by an arbitrary decree, since they take account of the facts and make them meaningful precisely as they stand. Acts demanded of me by external norms, which I do not understand, are not mine. I am not the author of them. Hence they are unauthentic. Meanings which fail to take account of real conditions and existent facts make lasting action impossible. Hence they also are unauthentic—a hollow pretense and a sham.

Rogers (1962, p. 375) views the counselor's behavior as essentially the expression of personal authenticity. The counselor provides a substantive counseling relationship in which the counselor is genuine (internally con-sistent), acceptant (prizing the client as a person of worth), and empathi-cally understanding of the client's private world of feelings and attitudes.

Liberality

Liberality is another requisite of an effective counseling relationship if the client is to make any worthwhile progress. The client must feel free enough to reveal innermost feelings without fear of contradiction or reprisal from the counselor. In a truly liberal atmosphere the client can ex-plore innermost feelings, sift them, accept them, or reject them. The client can run the gamut of human emotions without the counselor interfering in any way.

The counselor does not create this liberal atmosphere by telling the client that freedom of expression exists. The counselor does it by not limit-ing the client's free expression. If the client goes into a tirade against the counselor's values, condemning them from several angles, the counselor does not interfere with the client's expression of these feelings. The counseling relationship is, after all, for the counselee's benefit, not for the counselor's defense of personal ideologies. In a liberating atmosphere a client is not afraid to explore, and it is only through such free exploration that the client can know the self more accurately.

Counselors inhibit the client's self-exploration by resorting to questions that may appear important to them but are totally irrelevant to the client. The counselor may also steer the counseling session in a direction the counselor thinks is best for the client rather than allowing the client the freedom to choose the topical direction. If we accept the principle that each person knows the self better than anyone else, and is therefore in the best position to explore, expose, and understand the self, we see that counselor direction of a counseling session is nonproductive. A counseling relationship that is restrictive will produce some superficial results, but often they only make sense to the counselor and have little real meaning for the client.

The client senses a liberating atmosphere and responds by exploring personal behavior with a depth and ease that may not have been previously experienced. In a substantive counseling relationship, clients often have their first experience in gaining some awareness of themselves and why they behave in a particular way. Our cultural standards are such that many people have been conditioned to hide their inner feelings. This seems to be a safer way to exist.

Without a liberating atmosphere the client reacts in a superficial manner, which is often less threatening for the counselor but does little in yielding results for the client. The degree to which a counselor creates a liberating atmosphere is directly related to the degree of counselor security. The secure counselor enables clients to engage in freedom of expression because the counselor is not threatened by what they may say or do. Less secure counselors may inhibit the client's free expression, not just by words, but by a generally restrictive attitude. If the counselor is restless, embarrassed, angered, moralistic, or judgmental, the counselee will be inhibited to disclose inner feelings.

A tightly guarded value system will often make the counselor insensitive to clients whose values are quite different from those of the counselor. The mark of an effective counselor is not his or her ability to deal with clients who come from the same value system as the counselor, but rather his or her ability to communicate with persons who have values that are vastly different from those of the counselor. The counselor must prize the client's right *to be* before the counselor can become involved in a process that will encourage their becoming.

Involvement

The counselor's sense of presence is essentially a cognitive and visceral different from those of the counselor. The counselor must prize the clients' private perceptual world and with the client's struggle to become a more adequately functioning individual. As Strasser (1970, p. 306) has said, "When I am present to the other, no distance exists."

The counselor who achieves a sense of involvement is able to enter the client's attitudinal and behavioral life (Bugental, 1978). This means more than sitting waiting for the client to pause so that the counselor may interject a judgment or moralization. It means to be attuned to the client's feelings, hopes, desires, frustrations, fears, defenses, anxieties – those attitudes and behaviors that make the client a unique individual. This type of involvement demands a giving of self – a putting aside of one's egocentric tendencies so that the counseling session exists for the evolvement and development of the client.

The ineffective counselor is unable to achieve a sense of existential involvement. Such a counselor introduces information from an external frame of reference, makes suggestions, supports or criticizes the client's attitudes or behavior, or may ask irrelevant questions. Each of these responses is a dilution of the counselor's involvement. Whenever the counselor engages in such responses, the counselor diminishes the possibility of involvement; a bonding of the counselor's existential self with the existential self of the client. An existential involvement does not include superficial responses. Instead, the counselor deeply responds to the client's feelings and attitudes, and such a level of involvement makes the use of rehearsed and superficial remarks impossible. In Phase One of counseling, when the counselor is deeply present in the client's inner world and is not threatened about being there, it is existentially impossible to retreat into a pattern of routine questioning and information gathering. To do so would indicate that the counselor is not really involved. When the counselor is deeply communicating with the client, the counselor's own needs are all but lost because of the deep involvement with the needs of the client.

Becoming involved requires that the counselor attain such a deep level of communication that his or her own values and opinions are put aside and replaced with an absorption in the client's values and self-opinions. Such a giving of self by the counselor is difficult because life has often taught us to be more interested in listening to ourselves than in being fully involved with another person. We tend to be more involved in judging and devaluing others than in understanding and internalizing another person's views. We tend to think that client growth can be achieved only if it is guided by the omniscience of the counselor. Such evaluative attitudes by the counselor make it difficult to be involved because they necessitate an identification with the counselor's judgments rather than the needs of the client. In relationship building, when the counselor assumes an evaluative attitude, the counselor is in effect diminishing the possibility of receiving communication from the client, since evaluation requires that the counselor assume a judgmental attitude toward the client. A sensitive counselor finds it impossible to be existentially involved with a client while at the same time evaluating the client. In a sense, the counselor attempting to do both communicates to the client that neither is taking place. Either the counselor is involved or the counselor is distant from the client because of the different requirements of an evaluative attitude. Client discomfort and early termination of the counseling relationship occurs when the client senses that the counselor has lost a sense of involvement. Such a loss occurs for the counselor whose counseling behavior goes from the client's internal frame of reference to the counselor's evaluative or external frame of reference.

Sensitive Listening

The counselor's ability to listen is often taken for granted. Certainly, a person who is considered to be an effective counselor should be a good listener. But the effects of *sensitive listening* are often underestimated. Sensitive listening is nonevaluative listening. Listening to a news broadcast or a lecture is often partial listening; we are listening with one ear, as it were, while at the same time thinking about something else or structuring our opinion about what is being said. But sensitive listening enables the counselor to feel the client's emotions with the client and it must be total if empathy is to develop (Larson, 1971; Suauki, 1970). Marcel (1963, p. 40) indicates this when he says: ". . . there is a way of listening which is a way of giving and a way of listening which is a way of refusing."

In describing the effective counselor, Maslow (1965, p. 182) indicates his awareness to sensitive listening when he indicates that the counselor: ". . . must be able to listen in the receiving rather than in the taking sense in order to hear what is actually said rather than what he expects to hear or demands to hear. He must not impose himself but rather let the words flow in upon him. Only so can their own shape and pattern be assimilated. Otherwise one hears only one's theories and expectations."

The kind of listening we do while engaged in conversation with acquaintances and colleagues is often very superficial. We listen in a way, but we don't get the full message because we are still involved with ourselves. We all have encountered persons who look over our shoulder or glance around as we talk. They are indulging in social listening, which would have no value in a counseling relationship. The client wants the counselor's complete attention. A counselor who half listens, only waiting until the client takes a deep breath so that the counselor can get a point across, is not really listening; the counselor is tolerating the client's verbalizations. The troubled client is aware of this shortcoming and usually won't bother to continue the relationship.

Clients who consider the counselor a poor listener, more interested in selfish interests and the rendering of a personal opinion than in them, will terminate the association unless, as in some situations, the counselor insists that the fruitless relationship continue. Too often this is the case. If the counselor has some sort of vested authority, the client continues the relationship, fearful that terminating it will have an adverse effect.

Sensitive listening demands that the counselor be super-sensitive, not only to the client's words but to the emotional tones in which they are spoken. The words are important but the emotional tones and underlying feelings that accompany them should be the focal point for the sensitive listener. Listening indicates to the client that the counselor cares and the caring counselor will be recognized and valued by the client.

Rogers (1980, p. 10) captures the deep impact of being heard: "Almost always, when a person realizes he has been deeply heard, his eyes moisten. I think in some real sense he is weeping for joy. It is as though he were saying 'Thank God, somebody heard me. Someone knows what it's like to be me.' "

Equalizing

Equalizing is the process whereby any human relationship is made more equal. That is, the relationship is brought into balance, accord, parity, or mutuality. Any human relationship that is equalized has the potential to be productive; any human relationship that is unequalized has the potential to be nonproductive (Boy & Pine, 1976). An equalized counseling relationship is one in which the counselor is not dominant. The counselor and client engage each other as equals.

An effective marriage is basically equalized. Both marriage partners equally share rights and responsibilities and have developed an intuition regarding the process whereby the relationship is kept in balance. When this balance is struck, the marriage is a personally rewarding and positive experience for both partners. When the relationship is not balanced, the groundword is laid for the deterioration of that marriage.

When the relationship between labor and management is equalized, the work incentive and level of productivity is higher than when the relationship is unequalized. Both labor and management behave productively when there is a balance between the groups in their trust, positive regard, and concepts of justice.

When the relationship between and among nations is equalized there is a tendency toward peaceful coexistence. When the relationship between and among nations is not equalized there is a tendency toward distrust which eventually leads to war. When nations are economically, territorially, politically, and militarily equalized, they possess the psychological security to deal with each other in an atmosphere of improved mutual trust.

In any human relationship, then, the equalizing principle is of paramount importance in the development of that relationship. Whether the relationship is between friends, worker and supervisor, marriage partners, client and counselor, or nations, it is the equalizing principle that prompts the relationship to move toward becoming substantive.

Within any human relationship the process of equalization is the undergirding factor that serves as the catalyst for a substantive relationship. This concept is especially true in the counseling relationship. When clients sense that their relationships with counselors are equalized, they can invest themselves in those relationships. This occurs because clients sense that they are respected coparticipants in the process of counseling. The client feels accepted, understood, free, trusted, and motivated to communicate honestly and identify those aspects of the self or behavior that need to be modified or changed. The counselor is perceived as someone who is equally involved in the process and outcomes of the relationship. Since the counselor is perceived as an equal, the client senses a coownership of the relationship and there is no need to be evasive, defensive, or vague.

Once the counselor internalizes the importance of equalizing the counseling relationship, he or she can identify with the following *pre-counseling procedures* that contribute to equalizing that relationship.

Develop an Orientation to Counseling

Before a client enters a counseling relationship there is a desire to have an awareness of what to expect from that relationship. This is a very human attitude. Persons desire to know what they're getting into before they move ahead with any experience; and the counseling profession has an obligation to satisfy the client's right-to-know.

Satisfying the client's right-to-know can be achieved by counselors who develop a program that orients potential clients to what transpires in a counseling relationship. Through such an orientation, the client is able to gain a vicarious sense of what sort of attitudes and behaviors to expect from the counselor. When clients are able to sense and internalize the equalizing dimensions of the counseling relationship, they will feel more comfortable with the counseling process. No client wants to be controlled by the counselor. Clients desire to be involved in an equalized counseling relationship in which their human rights and integrity as persons are respected. In such a relationship, clients sense more personal power and the opportunity to exercise their unique rights. This is a most human inclination for anyone involved in any experience.

Involve Clients Voluntarily

An equalized counseling relationship can more easily occur if the client is voluntarily involved. When clients make the decision to voluntarily enter a counseling relationship, their personal sense of being an equal to the counselor is enhanced. A voluntary client is not cast into a role that is subservient to the counselor; the role is equalized since the client retains personal rights in such a voluntary relationship than one in which the client is required to engage in counseling. In required counseling relationships, the client is usually antagonistic toward the counselor because the client does not own the decision regarding whether or not to enter counseling. For the client, an involuntary association with the counselor will lead to an unequalized and nonproductive relationship with the counselor in the second phase of counseling.

Forming voluntary relationships with clients has become more difficult in an era in which the rate of referrals to counselors is increasing. This increase is due, in part, to the bureaucratizing of human services. The counselor must counterbalance this tendency by developing creative and person-centered processes whereby clients will be drawn to the voluntary use of a counseling service while their problems are still in the formative stages.

Demystify Counseling

If potential clients perceive counseling to be a deep, dark, and mysterious experience with an authority figure, and if the counselor's attitude and behavior reinforces such perceptions, then any hope of equalizing the counseling relationship will be lost.

Through orientation to counseling, clients should perceive counseling for what it is—an equalized human relationship between persons who each invest themselves in the process of solving or resolving a human problem. Counseling is an understandable process and should be represented as such to potential clients so that they will see that counseling is not a threatening human relationship filled with counselor intrigue and power over the client. The psychoanalytic parenthood of the counseling profession has certainly contributed to the evolvement of the public's myths about counseling. Today's counselor needs to attack historical myths about counseling so that potential clients will see counseling as a vibrant human relationship in which their personhood will be treated with dignity because of the equalized nature of the relationship.

Develop a Positive Image of the Counselor

Clients want to associate with counselors who possess human attitudes that contribute to the progress of the client. Clients feel more equalized with a counselor who is sensed as a facilitative person who can assist the client.

In the name of professionalism, some counselors have inhibited the feeling of equalization on the part of the client. They have been bureaucratic in their attitudes and behaviors and have been perceived by clients as the gatekeepers of institutional policy. Clients do not feel that they can have an equalized relationship with such a counselor.

Own Human Attitudes and Behaviors

Some counselors assume too much power and perceive themselves as being in the best position to determine the client's attitudes and behavioral goals. Such counselors make the client defensive because the balance of power is decidedly tipped toward the counselor. When a counselor behaves this way, there is little hope that an equalized counseling relationship can develop.

Clients, covertly or overtly, rebel against such a counselor because they sense that their personal rights and power are being eroded. They sense that they really can't communicate with the counselor because the counselor has a preconceived concept about how human beings should and should not behave.

In such an unequalized relationship, the client engages in a struggle to resist the counselor's power. When both the client and counselor engage in such a power struggle, they place themselves in a win-lose position and the potential for a positive outcome for the client becomes lost in the struggle.

The counselor needs to keep in sight the importance of creating an equalized relationship with the client if the relationship-building phase of counseling is to be productive; the counselor contributes to this equalization if he or she owns human attitudes and behaviors that the client can perceive.

PHASE ONE COMMUNICATION

The counselor's basic response pattern in developing a substantive relationship with the client in Phase One is *reflection of feelings*. Unless a substantive relationship exists with the client, the counselor cannot expect to positively effect the behavior of the client in the second phase of counseling.

Clients expect to be understood, accepted, and able to reveal feelings and attitudes in a liberating atmosphere; they expect the counselor to be empathic, a sensitive listener, authentic, have a sense of presence in the relationship, equalize that relationship, and create a pattern of communication that will encourage the emergence of the client as a person. Clients want the counselor to be a receiving person; one who is able to absorb the client, as a person, and on the client's terms.

Counselor attitudes and behaviors that hinder relationship building in Phase One occur when the counselor functions as a moralist ("Living according to these values will only cause you to suffer"), advisor ("The best thing you can do is find another job"), judge ("I think it was a poor decision"), guide ("Why don't you try living in another community"), questioner ("How many times has it happened?"), and diagnostician ("This current behavior is related to your past inability to accept parental authority"). When the client hears such statements coming from the counselor, the client clearly understands that the counselor is not really interested in developing a relationship in which the client has the right to be.

Reflection of the client's feelings enables the counselor to enter the client's private perceptual world; to understand and empathize with what it means to be *this* client, with *this* background, undergoing *this* set of experiences, with *this* certain array of resulting attitudes, feelings, and behaviors. When the counselor communicates empathy to the client through reflection of feeling, the client experiences the emergence of previously hidden or denied feelings. The client expands personal awareness in this process and identifies closely with the counselor who enables this self-awareness to occur. The client realizes a sense of trust for the counselor and develops an ever increasing feeling of closeness to the counselor's personhood and caring energy. This is a supportive feeling for the client because, finally, in a fast moving and technological existence, there is someone who cares enough to listen and to empathize from the client's set of perceptions and feelings. This is an expanding and enriching personal evolvement for the client and the client develops a bond with the counselor who enables it to occur; and the counselor enables the client to experience this bond by reflecting the client's feelings – not the words, but the inner feelings beneath the words.

In reflecting the client's feelings, the counselor assumes the internal frame of reference of the client, perceives experiences as the client perceives them, and identifies with the feelings that undergird the experiences. When the counselor makes this existential identification with the feelings of the client, the counselor then translates that identification into words that accurately represent the feelings of the client; and mirrors back to the client those feelings so that the client may become aware of them, internalize them, and draw meaning from them.

When the counselor accurately identifies with the feelings of the client and wants to transmit to the client an awareness of those feelings, the counselor prefixes the reflection of feeling with such phrases as:

You are saying . . .

You feel . . .

If I understand you correctly . . .

I'm not sure I follow you, but is this it . . .

I gather that you mean . . .

Let's see if I really understand that . . .

Some counselors so deeply identify with the feelings of a client that their reflections of feelings gradually move from saying, "You feel that . . ." to "*I feel that* . . . ." This kind of transition takes place when the counselor develops such a deep and empathic identification with the feelings of the client that it becomes more natural to use "I feel . . ." rather than "You feel . . ." when identifying with client feelings. Using "I" rather than "You" is a quantum step forward for the counselor reflecting the feelings of the client; but when the step is taken, it occurs in a natural manner when the counselor feels so closely drawn to the feelings of the client that the most communicative response possible involves the use of "I."

The following reflections of feelings *by counselors* convey the depth of identification that can occur when responding to the feelings of clients by the use of "I":

I never could speak to her . . . I was always afraid that I'd be criticized.

It's difficult to be me . . . I want to but I never seem able to simply say what's on my mind.

I wish I could get angry . . . but somehow I just don't think that my anger would be heard or accepted.

I feel myself moving toward becoming a more confident person and it's exciting!

I wish that I could stop being my own worst enemy . . . sometimes I feel that if I could like me then things would begin to improve.

I'm confused . . . I was never in this kind of position . . . before I seemed to have a sense of what to do.

If I could only do it then maybe my anxiety and loneliness wouldn't be so crippling.

There are times when I don't even understand myself . . . times when about all I know about me is my name.

Once again, the preceding statements are *counselor responses* to the feelings of clients. They represent reflections of deep client feelings; they are responses counselors comfortably give after they accurately absorb and internalize the feelings of clients. Such a response pattern is the foundation of building a substantive counseling relationship with a client; without such a pattern of responses, the counselor cannot expect significant results in the second phase of counseling. Phase One must be qualitative if Phase Two is to be effective.

If the counselor makes the personal investment in the first phase of counseling, then what follows in the second phase will be naturally developed by the counselor and accepted by the client. In Phase Two of counseling, the counselor bases the transaction with the client upon what is clearly identified as client needs; and these needs are clearly known by the counselor as an outcome of the first phase of counseling.

The Transition from Phase One to Phase Two

Thus far, we have essentially presented the traditional elements of client-centered counseling which characterized its development through the first two periods of its history, from 1940 through 1957 (Hart, 1970, pp. 4–22). In the first historic period, the client-centered counselor essentially focused on developing the relationship with the client. In the second historic period, the counselor stimulated the development of that relationship by reflecting the client's feelings back to the client. These two historic periods are still viable and effective and correspond to Phase One of our current approach to client-centered counseling.

Our modification from the model of client-centered counseling depicted in the first two periods of its historic development occurs in Phase Two of our current approach to client-centered counseling; and our Phase Two still corresponds to the experiential third period in the development of client-centered counseling. Phase Two is experiential in that it enables the client-centered counselor to respond to the client in a variety of ways rather than being restricted to reflecting the client's feelings. In Phase Two the counselor adopts any pattern of responses that serve to meet the unique needs of the individual client. When the counselor has the flexibility to respond to the needs of different clients in different ways, the counseling process becomes individualized and client-centered counseling becomes enriched, expanded, and more accurate by being congruent with the particular needs of different clients. It becomes more accurate by being congruent with the needs of the client rather than the needs of the theory.

The identification of client needs in Phase One enables the counselor to determine which specific process will best assist the client in Phase Two. Without an investment in the necessary components of relationship building in Phase One, the counselor is unable to know what clearly has to be done in Phase Two. Phase One of counseling develops a mutuality and cohesion between the client and counselor; and this mutuality and cohesion sets the stage for Phase Two and enables it to be effective.

In Phase Two the counselor has a number of process alternatives available and a particular alternative must be matched with, and congruent with, the needs of the client. These process alternatives available in Phase Two of counseling are the attitudes, techniques, and approaches inherent in, and available from, *all other* existing theories of counseling as well as a logical and natural eclectic process.

This essentially means that in Phase Two the counselor can continue with the client-centered approach started in Phase One because this approach best meets the needs of *this* particular client, or the counselor can incorporate another approach to counseling because *it* best meets the needs of another client. In Phase Two of counseling the counselor has full flexibility to use a counseling approach that best meets the needs of particular clients.

If the counselor determines that a more confrontative approach would better meet the needs of the client in Phase Two, and if the needs of the client have been clearly identified in Phase One as a result of a substantive relationship existing between the client and counselor, then what the counselor proceeds to do in Phase Two will be *heard, internalized, and acted upon by the client.* The counselor increases the possibility of such a response coming from the client in Phase Two if the relationship-building components of Phase One have been adequately established. Counselors who are inclined toward more confrontative approaches to counseling desire that what they say to clients be heard, internalized, and acted upon by those clients. Such counselors will have a greater assurance that clients will respond to them if they have made a full investment in building a substantive Phase One relationship with clients. Persons hear and respond to friends, not strangers. This simple relationship principle indicates that a more confrontative counselor must first achieve an affective bond with the client in Phase One if the counselor's confrontations are to have any influence upon the attitude and behavior of the client in Phase Two.

The length of time that it takes a counselor to build a Phase One substantive relationship with a client varies according to the credibility and relationship-building ability of the counselor. Counselors with a high degree of credibility and relationship-building ability can achieve a Phase One substantive relationship with a client in a relatively short period of time. Other counselors may have to invest in several or more Phase One relationship-building counseling sessions, especially if the counselor has not yet achieved a high enough level of credibility or if the client is inclined to be distrustful of the human qualities emerging from the counselor.

The counselor knows that the relationship objectives of Phase One have been achieved when the client:

1. Has achieved an emotional catharsis and is no longer overwhelmed by incapacitating feelings
2. Is more open and honest in assessing the self and the attitudes and behaviors that constitute the self
3. Shows a movement from emotionally-based communication to rationally-based communication
4. Is motivated and is willing to energize the self toward solving or resolving a problem.

Phase Two Guidelines

Before the counselor actually reaches the Phase Two point of meeting the specific needs of an individual client, the counselor needs to make the previously cited transition from Phase One to Phase Two. The transition necessitates making a sound judgment about which Phase Two process should be incorporated to accurately meet the needs of *this* client with *this* problem. The success of the second phase depends upon both the effectiveness of Phase One and the accuracy of the counselor's judgment regarding which approach will be most beneficial for the client in Phase Two.

This transitional judgment is not difficult for the counselor because the judgment is not made in a vacuum. The judgment is based upon the counselor's deep assimilation of the client's attitudes and behavior during Phase One. The more adequate this assimilation, the more accurate is the counselor's judgment regarding which counseling approach best meets the needs of the client in Phase Two. If the counselor has only acquired a superficial assimilation of the client during Phase One, then that counselor is not in a position to make an accurate judgment about what process will be best for the client in Phase Two.

Flexibility in responding to the client is crucial if Phase Two is to be effective. Corey (1977, p. 69) indicates that if client-centered counselors limit their range of responses to clients to listening and reflecting feelings, then their ability to influence behavioral change is limited. Carkhuff and Berenson (1967, p. 30) also indicate that the empathic, genuine, and acceptant attitudes of the client-centered counselor are necessary components of establishing a relationship, but that the counselor must go beyond these attitudes if counseling is to be effective. They suggest that the counselor also needs to be *concrete* since such concreteness "encourages the client to attend to specific problem areas." This concreteness enables the counselor to offer a wider range of responses to clients and frees the counselor to more accurately meet client needs. The need for counselor flexibility in responding to the client has also been reinforced in the writings of Van Kaam (1966), Hansen, Stevic, and Warner (1972), Rosenblatt (1975), and Egan (1975).

When the counselor has only a limited and partial awareness of the client's personality, attitudes, values, and behavior, the counselor does not move ahead with Phase Two. In such a circumstance, moving ahead is detrimental to the client because the counselor has only a limited and partial reservoir of client information upon which to base a Phase Two process judgment. In such a case, the counselor needs to stay in Phase One for a longer period of time until a sufficient informational base has been developed upon which to make a sound judgment regarding which Phase Two process will be best for the client.

The process used with the client in Phase Two is not a guess. It is a sound and calculated judgment based upon a full awareness of the client's personality and behavior acquired through the assimilation process during the first phase.

Assuming that the counselor has had an effective Phase One with a client, the counselor now moves toward making an accurate judgment regarding which Phase Two process will be most beneficial for the client. The basis for this judgment must always be the therapeutic needs of the client; that is, which process will yield *the highest therapeutic gain for the client*.

The needs of the client must always remain paramount in Phase Two. When constructing a Phase Two approach that can affect the client's attitude and behavior, the counselor must be certain that the Phase Two approach will meet the needs of the client. During this phase the counselor is faced with the temptation of meeting his or her own needs rather than the needs of the client. The counselor may have a process bias that incorporates only one way of working with all clients during Phase Two. If the counselor succumbs to such a bias, the counselor will lose sight of the needs of *this* client, in *this* situation, with *this* particular configuration of needs.

The objectivity established in Phase One of counseling must not be lost in Phase Two. Phase One, if it is well implemented by the counselor, has a built-in opportunity for the counselor to widen and deepen the desired objectivity regarding the client. This objectivity must be continued into Phase Two so that the counselor focuses on the needs of the client rather than allowing the counselor's idiosyncratic process needs to intrude. Being objective requires a high level of self-discipline on the part of the counselor; being objective means that the counselor has a higher respect for the needs of the client than for the process needs of the counselor.

The client's progress in Phase Two is proportionably related to the counselor's investment and success in Phase One. Phase Two of counseling is not automatically productive. It is productive only in proportion to the counselor's effectiveness during the first phase. If it was an enriching experience for the client and resulted in the desired relationship and assimilation, then the stage is set for Phase Two to be an effective experience for the client. If Phase One had little positive effect upon either the client or counselor, then the stage is set for Phase Two to be ineffective. There is a clear and influencing proportional relationship between both phases.

The counselor must be flexible in Phase Two and not impose one approach on all clients. If a counselor is committed to, for example, confrontation and also sees the usefulness and desirability of Phase One, that counselor must not lie-in-wait for clients to come out of the Phase One woods so that the counselor can confront all clients. *Some* clients may need confrontation in Phase Two, but not *all* clients. The counselor needs to be flexible so that the approach used with a *particular* client meets the *unique* needs of *this* client.

Counselors who are bound by one set of process chains will have difficulty in being flexible and effective in Phase Two because the bonds of loyalty to only one process will constrict the counselor during Phase Two; and it is only the flexible counselor who is able to accurately meet the different needs of different clients.

Being effective in Phase Two requires that the counselor be operationally flexible in order to meet the needs of individual clients. Such flexibility requires counselors to become more knowledgeable regarding the different processes that might be used in Phase Two to meet the needs of individual clients.

Counselor preparation programs need to be prepared to expand the student-counselor's knowledge of the process models of different counseling theories if the prospective counselor is to be successful in attending to the individualized needs of clients.

The counselor must be prepared to go back to Phase One relationship building if the Phase Two approach is not producing results. If carefully considered and constructed, Phase Two generally tends to meet the needs of a client. If the evidence of the client's behavior, however, indicates that the Phase Two approach being utilized does not meet the needs of the client, then a reassessment of the client's needs is required. This is best accomplished by going back to the Phase One communication fundamentals that were earlier identified in this chapter. By returning to these fundamentals the counselor gains a more accurate and deeper understanding of the values, motives, goals, feelings, and attitudes that influence the client's behavior.

Counselors whose Phase Two approach does not yield results will often find that the necessary assimilation of the client, required in Phase One, did not occur deeply or well. Therefore, instead of struggling through the second phase with a process that is proving to be ineffective, the counselor's return to the first phase will result in a more accurate assimilation of the client and reestablish the relationship.

Anyone lost in the complexity of any behavior clarifies that behavior by returning to a much more simple and understandable form of that behavior. This simple principle of human experiencing is most appropriate when the counselor's Phase Two approach is not yielding results. By returning to Phase One, the counselor acquires the additional information necessary to make a more accurate judgment regarding a more appropriate Phase Two process.

The counselor's Phase Two approach must be based upon an accurate assimilation of client needs in Phase One. Phase Two will be productive if the counselor's approach is based upon an accurate assimilation of the client during Phase One. Phase Two becomes effective because the counselor has taken the time necessary, in Phase One, for the client's personality, attitudes, values, and behavior to become absorbed by the counselor. When the client has fully amplified the various dimensions of the self in Phase One, and the counselor has fully assimilated the client, then an accurate assessment of the client's needs becomes possible. Such an accurate assimilation of the client can only occur in proportion to the accuracy of the client's self-disclosure; and the accuracy of the client's self-disclosure will largely depend upon the counselor's ability to create a Phase One counseling relationship in which the client is open and honest regarding the self.

Phase Two can include a noncounseling approach if it more accurately meets the needs of the client. Some client-centered counselors see therapeutic benefits occuring only within the context of a person-to-person talk centering counseling relationship. Some behavior modification counselors see therapeutic benefits occurring only outside of the counseling relationship in behavioral experiences that are concretized for the client.

Which is generally the more effective approach is not a valid issue. The basic issue is which is the better approach for *this* client, in *this* relationship, with *this* identified set of needs. For one client, the talking out process may be the best mode for influencing behavioral change. For another client, the talking out process yields little and this client will change behavior only as a result of being involved in concrete and understandable actions that influence the development of positive behavior.

Knowing which approach is better for a particular client can only occur after the counselor has assimilated the client in Phase One, but Phase Two is an unknown quantity and only becomes a known quantity when we consider what would be an appropriate and effective Phase Two approach for *this* client; and Phase Two for some clients may not include the traditional person-to-person mode of counseling but may include noncounseling experiences that are useful in helping to change the behavior of *this* client.

Regardless of which approach is used in Phase Two, there should be evidence that client behavior has improved. Having clients feel good about themselves is a desirable and primary goal of counseling. Having counselors feel good about the effectiveness of their work is another desirable, but secondary, goal of counseling. But if feeling good about oneself were the only goal of counseling we would be in trouble as a profession since there may be less expensive, less involved, and more simple ways of helping people feel good about themselves.

Feeling good about oneself is essentially having a congruence between what a person, behaviorally, is, and what that person would, behaviorally, like to be. But for the self to feel fully good, positive self-referent words must be matched with self-enhancing behavior and there should be observable evidence that the self-enhancing behavior exists. A client's improved self-concept must be represented by observable behavior that affirms the existence of an improved self-concept (Ellis, 1973; Penn, 1977; Wrenn, 1973).

The emotionality or rationality of the client will determine which Phase Two approach is best for the client. An important aspect of the counselor's judgment about the most appropriate approach for the client in Phase Two is the client's tendency to respond best to either a rationally-based approach or an affectively-based approach.

Some clients engage in maladaptive behavior because the intellectual processing of information is a certain and definite influence in the formation of that behavior. With such a client, since rational influences play such a central role in the causality of maladaptive behavior, the rational process can be harnessed for the resolution of the problem. With some clients, a clearly rational approach to the solution of a problem influences the client to change the behavior.

Other clients engage in maladaptive behavior because their affective functioning is a greater influence in the formation of maladaptive behavior. These clients intellectually know the difference between behaviors that enhance or diminish the self, but they affectively and viscerally feel compelled to move toward and engage in maladaptive behavior. With such clients, the influences of emotions is so compelling in causing maladaptive behavior that the resolution of the client's problem lies in the counselor utilizing an affective approach in Phase Two.

Therefore, in Phase Two the counselor must recognize whether a rational or affective approach will best meet the needs of a particular client; and this judgment rests upon which was the greater influence in causing the client's problem and then using a matching approach that has potential for resolving the client's problem.

A client inclined to be abstract will respond best to an existential approach; a client inclined to be concrete will respond best to a more specific approach. Some clients see answers to their problems in abstract terms. If they can develop a set of unified abstract constructs in order to identify a solution to their problems, such abstracting is the first requirement of a personally relevant solution. Other clients see answers to their problems in concrete terms and must develop a set of concrete realities that provide a realistic solution to a problem.

The counselor working with an abstracting client needs to have the inclination and patience to follow the client into the various caverns of abstraction. This is not easy for the reality-based counselor, but such a counselor will need to develop this ability in order to promote behavioral change in a client whose primary mode of feeling and understanding is the process of abstraction.

The counselor working with a client who is concrete needs to have the ability to penetrate the importance of concreteness for this particular client. This is not easy for the counselor who is abstractly inclined, but such a counselor will need to develop the ability to see the viability of concrete solutions in order to facilitate behavioral change in a client whose primary mode of feeling and understanding is in concrete terms.

Penetrating and understanding the abstract world of some clients and the concrete world of others will require a high degree of insight and flexibility on the part of the counselor.

A refined concept of client-centered counseling is applicable to both individual and group counseling. The Phase One and Phase Two components of counseling are applicable to both group and individual counseling.

In group counseling, the Phase One combined processes of relationship building and the assimilation of group members sets the stage for the process of accommodating individual and group needs in Phase Two. During Phase One the group facilitator attempts to build relationships between and among group members and also assimilates the group's *raison d'etre*, motives, processes, and goals. By engaging in Phase One, the group facilitator identifies and develops the linking communication network whereby group members share attitudes, feelings, experiences, and personal observations.

During Phase Two, the group facilitator accommodates the needs of the group, and individuals within the group, by engaging in processes designed to meet the specific needs of a particular group and individuals within the group. The group facilitator also harnesses the natural and spontaneous therapeutic behaviors that exist among group members and enables other group members to sort out which of those therapeutic behaviors are particularly helpful. Therefore, in Phase Two the group facilitator shares the counseling role with group members and creates opportunities for group members to function as counselors for each other.

Phase Two can accommodate the counselor assisting the client with a process that is logical, natural, spontaneous, and eclectic. The last guideline for Phase Two is by no means the least important. In fact, it may be the most important. Sometimes a counselor can become too complex in attempting to identify a Phase Two process that will best meet the needs of a client. Often, after an accurate Phase One assimilation of the client, the most therapeutic process for the client will be that which emerges from the counselor in a logical, natural, and spontaneous eclecticism. If the counselor is attitudinally client-centered and has learned to trust the human, genuine, and empathic qualities of the self, the counselor needs only to engage the self in a process of responding to the client in a logical, natural, spontaneous way. This logical, natural, spontaneous, and eclectic process of responding to the client in Phase Two has great therapeutic potential, but its power has been lost by counselors who have buried it with wooden and mechanical techniques.

RENEWED CLIENT-CENTERED COUNSELING: SOME BASIC CONSTRUCTS

Phase One Constructs

The client expects . . .

to be voluntarily involved in counseling
to be given the opportunity to explore and clarify feelings and attitudes
to be respected as a person
to be treated with justice
to have an equalized relationship with the counselor
to be heard and understood
to develop a trust relationship with the counselor
to possess the opportunity for self-actualization

Phase Two Constructs

Many clients . . .

desire to solve or resolve their own problem
know themselves better than anyone else and are, therefore, in the best position to solve or resolve a problem
possess the ability to develop self-determined solutions
can achieve self-actualized behavior
can solve specific problems because of an improved self-concept
desire to be sensitive to the causes that prompt certain behaviors
are inclined to be introspective

Other clients . . .

desire counselor assistance and/or intervention in solving a problem
have limited self-knowledge
are unable to develop self-determined solutions

have difficulty in becoming self-actualized

develop an improved self-concept based upon their ability to solve specific problems

desire to change a behavior without any concern for the causes that induced the behavior

are inclined to be concrete

RENEWED CLIENT-CENTERED COUNSELING:
SOME PROPORTIONAL EFFECTS

1. Counseling will be effective *in proportion to* the qualitative *assimilation* of the client's personhood in Phase One and the accurate *accommodation* of the client's needs in Phase Two.
2. Phase One will have *a proportional influence* on Phase Two. If Phase One was successful then Phase Two will be successful; if Phase One was ineffective then Phase Two will be ineffective.
3. Phase Two cannot stand alone; it *is proportionately dependent* upon the existence of Phase One.
4. The client's progress in counseling *is proportionately related* to the therapeutic credibility of the counselor. If the counselor possesses therapeutic credibility then the client will make progress; if the counselor does not posses therapeutic credibility then the client will not make progress.
5. Clients will make progress *in proportion to* their trust for the counselor. Clients who trust the counselor will make progress; clients who have little or no trust in the counselor will make little or no progress.
6. The progress of a client *is proportionately related* to the voluntarism of the relationship. The client who voluntarily enters the counseling relationship will make progress; the client who is coerced into the counseling relationship will make little or no progress.
7. The success of counseling *is proportionately related* to the quality of the counselor as a person. Counseling is successful when incorporated by a person of quality; it is unsuccessful when the counselor possesses minimal human qualities.
8. Counseling is effective *in proportion to* the degree of administrative responsibility possessed by the counselor. The counselor with no administrative authority will have equalized relationships with clients that will tend to be effective; the counselor with administrative authority will have unequalized relationships with clients that will tend to be ineffective.
9. Counseling is effective *in proportion to* the intelligence of the counselor; and intelligence is considered as a venturesome adaptability on the part of the counselor and has been defined as follows (Kagan and Havemann, 1972, p. 472): "Intelligence is the ability to

profit from experience, to learn new information, and to adjust to new situations."

In the following chapters we shall deal with traditional and emerging issues that face client-centered counselors. Some of these issues have been addressed in the existing literature of client-centered counseling while others have not. Some of these issues deal directly with the counseling relationship while others are external to that relationship but affect its quality. Some of our observations regarding these issues will be consistent with the traditions of the client-centered view while other observations will reflect our refinements of client-centered counseling.

REFERENCES

Arbuckle, D. S. *Counseling and psychotherapy: An existential-humanistic view.* Boston: Allyn and Bacon, 1975, 85–86.

Bergin, A., & Garfield, S. *Psychotherapy and behavior change.* New York: John Wiley and Sons, 1971, 313.

Boy, A. V., & Pine, G. J. *Client-centered counseling in the secondary school.* Boston: Houghton Mifflin, 1963.

Boy, A. V., & Pine, G. J. *The counselor in the schools: A reconceptualization.* Boston: Houghton Mifflin, 1968.

Boy, A. V., & Pine, G. J. Equalizing the counseling relationship. *Psychotherapy: Theory, Research, and Practice,* 1976, *13,* 20–25.

Bugental, J. F. T. *Psychotherapy and process: The fundamentals of an existential-humanistic approach.* Cambridge: Addison-Wesley, 1978, 37.

Burks, M. M., Jr. & Stefflre, B. *Theories of counseling.* New York: McGraw-Hill, 1979.

Carkhuff, R. R., & Berenson, B. G. *Beyond counseling and therapy.* New York: Holt, Rinehart and Winston, 1967.

Corey, G. *Theory and practice in counseling and psychotherapy.* Monterey, Calif.: Brooks/Cole, 1977, 56, 59.

Corsini, R. *Current psychotherapies.* Itasca, Ill.: F. E. Peacock, 1973.

Egan, G. *Face to face.* Monterey, Calif.: Brooks/Cole, 1973, 91.

Egan, G. *The skilled helper.* Monterey, Calif.: Brooks/Cole, 1975.

Ellis, A. *Humanistic psychotherapy.* New York: McGraw-Hill, 1973, 145.

Hansen, J. C., Stevic, R. R. & Warner, R. W., Jr. *Counseling: Theory and process.* Boston: Allyn and Bacon, 1972, 177.

Hart, J. The development of client-centered therapy. In J. T. Hart & T. M. Tomlinson (Eds.), *New directions in client-centered therapy.* Boston: Houghton Mifflin, 1970, 3-22.

Kagan, J., & Havemann, E. *Psychology: An Introduction.* New York: Harcourt, Brace, Jovanovich, 1972, 477.

Larson, E. *Why don't you listen?* Liguori, Mo.: Liguori Publishers, 1971, 55.

Lukas, M., & Lukas, E. *Theilhard: The man, the priest, the scientist.* New York: Doubleday, 1977, 134.

Marcel, G. *The philosophy of existentialism.* New York: Citadel Press, 1963.

Maslow, A. Cognition of being in the peak experiences. In D. E. Hamachek (Ed.), *The self in growth: Teaching and learning.* Englewood Cliffs, N.J.: Prentice-Hall, 1965, 182.

Patton, B., & Griffin, K. *Interpersonal communication in action.* New York: Harper and Row, 1974.

Penn, R. A dollar's worth of counseling and a lifetime guarantee. *The Personnel and Guidance Journal,* 1977, *56,* 204–205.

Polster, I., & Polster, M. *Gestalt therapy integrated.* New York: Vintage, 1973, 53.

Rogers, C. R. *Counseling and psychotherapy.* Boston: Houghton Mifflin, 1942.

Rogers, C. R. *Client-centered therapy.* Boston: Houghton Mifflin, 1951 (renewed 1979), 483–522.

Rogers, C. R. *On becoming a person.* Boston: Houghton Mifflin, 1961.

Rogers, C. R. The conditions of change from a client-centered viewpoint. In B. Berenson & R. Carkhuff (Eds.), *Sources of gain in counseling and psychotherapy.* New York: Holt, Rinehart and Winston, 1967.

Rogers, C. R. *Freedom to learn.* Columbus, Ohio: Merrill, 1969.

Rogers, C. R. *On encounter groups.* New York: Harper and Row, 1970.

Rogers, C. R. *Becoming partners: Marriage and its alternatives.* New York: Delacorte, 1972.

Rogers, C. R. Empathic: An unappreciated way of being. *The Counseling Psychologist,* 1975, *5,* 2–10.

Rogers, C. R. *On personal power.* New York: Delacorte, 1977.

Rogers, C. R. *A way of being.* Boston: Houghton Mifflin, 1980.

Rogers, C. R., & Dymond, R. F. *Psychotherapy and personality change.* Chicago: University of Chicago Press, 1954.

Rogers, C. R., & Meador, B. Client-centered therapy. In R. Corsini (Ed.), *Current psychotherapies.* Itasca, Ill.: F. E. Peacock, 1973.

Rogers, C. R., & Wood, J. Client-centered theory: Carl Rogers. In A. Burton (Ed.), *Operational theories of personality.* New York: Bruner/Mazel, 1974.

Rosenblatt, D. *Opening doors: What happens in Gestalt therapy.* New York: Harper and Row, 1975, 7.

Strasser, S. Feeling as a basis of knowing the other as an ego. In M. Arnold (Ed.), *Feelings and emotions.* New York: Academic Press, 1970.

Suauki, S. *Zen mind, beginner's mind.* New York: Weatherhill, 1970, 87.

Van Kaam, A. *The art of existential counseling.* Denville, N.J.: Dimension Books, 1966, 140.

Wexler, D. A., & Rice, L. N. (Eds.). *Innovations in client-centered therapy.* New York: John Wiley and Sons, 1974.

Wild, J. *An invitation to phenomenology.* (J. M. Edle, Ed.). Chicago: Quadrangle books, 1965.

Wrenn, C. G. *The world of the contemporary counselor.* Boston: Houghton Mifflin, 1973, 256–257.

Chapter 2

THE IMPLICATIONS
OF COUNSELING
THEORY

Theory has little or no practical value for some counselors who tend to diminish the utility of theory and separate theory from practice. Often counselors become upset with the amount of literature that focuses on theoretical concepts. They prefer that the literature of counseling focus on practical issues. The assumption underlying a negative attitude toward theory is that theory can be separated from practice, but theory and practice cannot be this easily separated; they are inextricably intertwined. No matter how many times ones attempts to separate the two, one inevitably finds that practice is founded upon theory. The counselor may not have developed a formal and systematic theoretical position as a foundation for practice, and indeed may not be aware that what is done each day as a counselor is based upon theory, but nevertheless the counselor does operate from a theoretical base. This is pointed out by Hansen, Stevic, and Warner (1977, pp. 16, 20), who go on to indicate that there is a danger in using a vague and implicit approach:

> To try to function without theory is to operate in chaos, for without placing events in some order it is impossible to function in a meaningful manner. Those who claim that they can operate without theory are generally operating on some vague and implicit assumptions about the nature of events. In reality they are working from a theoretical frame of reference.
>
> . . . The danger in this approach is that a implicit or hidden theory is subject to the interjection of personal biases into an individual's interpretation of experience. . . . To state a theory in explicit terms, while it runs the risk of being dogmatic, tends to minimize the problem of personal bias.

Dimick and Huff (1970, p. 57) also indicate that even when a counselor feels that no explicit theory of counseling is followed in practice, the counselor still has an implicit operational identification with some sort of theory:

> . . . each person operates from a theory, his own, although he may not have it well defined or be able to verbalize it. Nevertheless, some sort of theory is

implied in his beliefs and behaviors. It is also our belief that the task of the counselor is made more complicated and his potential for effectiveness reduced when his theory has not been made explicit. Often implicit and unexamined theories contain incongruities which may result in inconsistent and unpredictable counselor behavior. From evidence that is available, inconsistency may be the single, most frustrating factor that an individual can bring to a relationship.

THE UTILITY OF THEORY

Through the examination and evaluation of a counseling theory, the counselor may find how practical theory can be. Polster and Polster (1973) indicate that a counseling theory must have utility in order to have credibility as a theory.

The counselor seeks generalizations to account for a wide range of client attitudes and behaviors. These generalizations serve as areas of understanding in helping clients to modify their attitudes and behaviors. These are very practical concerns, for, if the counselor cannot profit from previous experiences with clients, and if each client in turn is a new experience, then the counselor has little justification for status as a specialist in human affairs (Boy & Pine, 1968, pp. 97–98).

It is essential that the counselor develop a theoretical rationale to undergird professional behavior. Without a theoretical foundation, counseling lacks breadth and depth. A counselor without a theory becomes more interested in the mechanics of guiding than in the art of counseling.

The utility of a counseling theory is essential if we expect the counselor to make use of a theory. The practitioner desires to incorporate a theory that produces results. As Brammer and Shostrom (1977, p. 28) point out, a good theory of counseling has practical value in that:

Theory helps to explain what happens in a counseling relationship and assists the counselor in predicting, evaluating, and improving results. Theory provides a framework for making scientific observations about counseling. Theorizing encourages the coherence of ideas about counseling and the production of new ideas. Hence, counseling theory can be very practical by helping to make sense out of the counselor's observations.

Krause and Hendrickson (1972, p. 20) indicate that the practical demension of a counseling theory is the theory's ability to affect a client's behavior and attain the goals of counseling:

Theories are related to practice or technique in that a theory's quality of predictability and structure forms the foundation and the means to create a change or modification in a counselor's behavior. Briefly, a theoretical position enables the counselor to derive clues as to what technique is the most effective in obtaining the goals of the counseling experience.

Combs, Avila, and Purkey (1971, p. 37) state that utilizing a theory has a useful function because a theory: ". . . provides the worker with guides to action and makes his behavior more likely to be consistent and efficient."

Shertzer and Stone (1974) reinforce the importance of a theory being useful in their identification of a theory's major functions. They state that a theory:

1. Synthesizes a particular body of knowledge
2. Increases the understanding of a particular body of knowledge
3. Provides the tools by which predictions can be made
4. Encourages further research into the area.

Through the careful examination and evaluation of a counseling theory one can appreciate how practical and valuable theory is. Theory has a number of useful functions:

1. *Theory helps us to find relatedness, or some degree of unity, among diverse observations and experiences of human existence particularly as these occur in counseling and living situations.* Counselors working with clients who are changing their behavior can bring unity to their counseling if they are able to identify those counselor attitudes that influence behavioral change. These counselor attitudes serve to enrich the counseling relationship so that there is a bond between the counselor's approach and the client's behavioral responses. But counselors who desire to attitudinally link themselves with clients must expend full effort in identifying the theoretical constructs that enable such an attitudinal linkage to take place.

2. *Theory compels us to observe relationships that we had previously overlooked.* When counselors feel that a theoretical base for counseling is unimportant, each day is merely a series of unrelated events. Sally cried, Ted shouted, Henry became more withdrawn, Debbie was more evasive, Ann was anxious again. Counselors who possess a theoretical base see these events as having a relationship to each other because theory enables one to grasp the wholeness and interrelated meaning of these observations regarding human behavior.

3. *Theory provides operational guidelines that help us in making provisional evaluations of the directions and desirability of our development as counselors.* Counselors who possess a theoretical base for their counseling move themselves toward decisions and solutions that are logical outcomes of their theory. They rarely find themselves in a blind alley in the decision-making process. They realize that one's theory will guide a particular decision if that theory is given an opportunity to function. The practical solution will eventually be known if the theoretical base guiding that solution is given an opportunity to become energized.

4. *Theory focuses our attention on relevant data by telling us what to look for.* Counselors who function from a theoretical base address themselves

to primary and substantive facts in order to develop an approach to counseling. Because these counselors think conceptually, they are able to see the wholeness of a problem as well as the necessity of assisting the client in developing a whole solution. They are able to conceptualize and behave in wholes because their theoretical base is whole.

5. *Theory provides us with guidelines for helping clients modify their behavior more effectively.* Counselors who function from a theoretical base are, intellectually and attitudinally, deeply involved. They are always seeking out better motivations, better approaches, and better results. They look upon their counseling behavior as a tentative solution for assisting clients because they are always aware that better solutions loom over the horizon. The better they expand their theoretical base the better will be their practical solutions in the process of assisting clients.

6. *Theory helps us to constuct new approaches to counseling and point to ways of evaluating old ones.* Counselors who possess a theoretical base possess an enlarged awareness of the impact of their counseling behavior. They are more free to be creative in their counseling behavior because their theory prompts them to be always seeking rather than being static and content. They either discard or revitalize old approaches because as their theoretical base expands and evolves their practical behavior is also influenced to expand and evolve.

Kelley (1963, p. 22) has pointed out that a theory provides a basis for the development of a functional freedom for assessing events:

> Theories are the thinking of men who seek freedom amid swirling events. The theories comprise prior assumptions about certain realms of these events. To the extent that the events may, from these prior assumptions, be constructed, predicted, and their relative courses charted, men may exercise control and gain freedom for themselves in the process.

JUDGING A THEORY OF COUNSELING

When does an approach or concept of counseling possess enough substance to be legitimately classified as a theory? Should a counselor utilize a theory just because the counselor has an idiosyncratic idea regarding the best way to counsel clients? If a counselor counsels from a purely subjective base, how does the counselor objectively justify such a personalized process?

A professional in any field must go beyond a personal bias in selecting and applying a theory. One of the behaviors characterizing any professional is the professional's sense of personal responsibility and public accountability in selecting and applying a theory. Certainly, we would not want a physician to treat us according to personal biases or hunches. We would instead want that physician to engage in a medical procedure that is based upon a set of objective standards that go beyond personal bias. We would want a physician to base treatment on a theory or set of procedures for which there is objective evidence indicating its effectiveness.

Experimentation in all fields is crucial if there is to be an advancement of knowledge. But experimentation must confine itself to experimental settings and proceedings before it is publicly applied. All professions possess the obligation to be certain that a theory or process has a reasonable chance of working before publicly applying it; and during an experimental period, there must be an adherence to standards and procedures so that the well being of persons participating in the experimentation will be protected (American Psychological Association, 1973).

Therefore, the professional counselor is obligated to apply a theory of counseling that meets the criteria for being a theory, rather than engaging in the practice of applying a personal bias. Counseling is both an art and a science and although the effective counselor pays full attention to the artful dimensions of counseling that rely on the counselor's personhood, the effective counselor also pays attention to the scientific dimensions of counseling. Science rests on objectivity, and the effective counselor proceeds beyond selfish needs and identifies objective criteria that will enable the selection and application of a legitimate theory.

What are the criteria that will enable a counselor to know when a theory is legitimate and has the potential to be successfully applied? Stefflre and Grant (1972, pp. 4–7) offer the following criteria for judging whether or not a counseling theory has legitimacy as a theory. A theory should possess:

1. Assumptions regarding the nature of man
2. Beliefs regarding learning theory and changes in behavior
3. A commitment to certain goals of counseling
4. A definition of the role of the counselor
5. Research evidence supporting the theory.

Patterson (1973, pp. xv–xvi) identifies the following criteria for judging whether or not a counseling theory can be classified as a bona fide theory. A bona fide theory would possess:

1. Importance
2. Preciseness and clarity
3. Simplicity
4. Comprehensiveness
5. The ability to be applied
6. Empirical validity or verifiability
7. A stimulating substance.

Hansen et al. (1977, p. 20) focus on the following criteria for ascertaining the credibility of a counseling theory. They state that a theory must:

1. Be clear
2. Be comprehensive
3. Be stated in terms that are explicit enough to generate research

4. Relate means to desired outcomes
5. Have utility.

A legitimate theory of counseling should meet certain criteria but no theory should lock the counselor into a fixed and mechanical set of procedures and responses. Although the counselor fits the general framework of a particular theory and operates within it, a theory should also enable the counselor to possess individuality and flexibility so that process judgments can be made that meet the individualized needs of clients. Dimick and Huff (1970, p. 59) reinforce the view that a theory should provide individuality and flexibility for the counselor: "A useful theory is molded for the individual and is well thought out, practical, and consistent with the behavior of the individual counselor. A the same time it is flexible enough to incorporate change by the individual counselor."

THE DEVELOPMENT OF A .
COUNSELING.THEORY

The counselor's attitude toward the self and others is the cornerstone of the counselor's philosophy of life (Boy & Pine, 1968, pp. 100–103). Counseling is a process that reflects the counselor's philosophy of existence; in other words, counseling is not a mechanical technique but a way of living (Dimick and Huff, 1970, p. 242). Each counselor must resolve certain basic questions regarding human nature before the counselor can communicate effectively with clients. Hart (1970b, p. 566) indicates that we must first come to grips with fundamental philosophic concepts that have recurred in every era: evil, God, truth, knowledge, justice, and beauty.

The importance of a philosophical foundation for counseling has been brought out by Williamson (1965, pp. 154–157) who stated that counselors, in order to be effective in helping clients to realize their potential, must continuously examine (perhaps for a lifetime) five basic philosophic questions:

1. What is the nature of human nature?
2. What is the nature of human development?
3. What is the nature of the "good life" and the "good"?
4. What is the nature of the determination of the "good life"?
    Who determines what is "good"?
5. What is the nature of the universe and what is man's relationship to that universe?

From a philosophy of human nature an applicable theory of counseling emerges. The counselor moves toward a theory of counseling that provides an understanding of the process or practical dimensions of counseling.

Once the counselor can see the bridge between theory and practice, the counselor can begin to form an explicit theoretical framework for counseling. From such a framework the counselor begins to derive some meaning from each day's involvement with clients. The counselor finds a point of reference for each counseling session and can function more consistently in the different kinds of relationships in which he or she becomes involved. There is no searching for ways of working with new clients because theory enables the counselor to react and respond to clients with an effective degree of consistency. Although the counselor is not able to perfectly translate theory into practice, theory, nevertheless, is able to provide worthwhile goals for our professional behavior. The more the counselor implements a theory, the more the counselor develops an integration between theory and practice.

Tolbert (1972, p. 90) indicates that there are three fundamental approaches for examining philosophic questions:

1. Ontology. What is real?
2. Epistemology. What is true?
3. Axiology. What is good?

Once again, before implementing a theory of counseling, the counselor must first deal with the self and those philosophic views that influence his or her personal life style, values, and behaviors and how they, in turn, influence the counselor's counseling attitude and behavior. By first taking an introspective and philosophic view from within, the counselor will be able to make a connection with a theory that amplifies and makes applicable those personal philosophic views. When the counselor is able to do this, there is a vibrancy and relevancy in the application of a counseling theory because that theory is a reflection of a more basic personal philosophy. The counselor must be prepared to introspect and deal with the questions of what is real? what is true? and what is good? and how these questions and their answers are related to one's theory of counseling.

INTEGRATING THE SELF WITH A THEORY

A counselor's theory need not be a carbon copy of someone else's theory. Each counselor engaged in the development of a theoretical foundation adopts a theory tentatively and subjects it to the test of practice. From such testing evolves a tempered theory, refined and modified in the light of the counselor's personal philosophy. This means that, in purely objective terms, there is no such person as a client-centered counselor or a behavioral counselor. If counselor Mary Smith adopts client-centered theory, she adopts it in her own unique and personalized way, and is "Smithian" in her counseling approach. And if counselor John Jones adopts a behavior modification approach, he may be more accurately perceived as "Jonesian" in his approach. It is the personalization of a theory that makes it meaningful to the counselor and enables the counselor to put it into practice effectively.

This personalized implementation of a theory does not imply by any means that one learns a set of rules and techniques and then applies these mechanically in the counseling relationship. As Tolbert (1972, p. 95) has said: "A counselor might read about counseling, talk about it, and adopt a theory and use it with work with others, without having a feeling for what takes place in counseling or a real investment in a counseling relationship. The approach does not reflect the counselor as a person; it is more or less a mechanical process operating at a techniques level."

A counselor's theory of counseling is a reflection of the counselor as a person; that is, what the counselor *is* as a person is demonstrated in his or her application of a theory. Lewis (1970, p. 61) indicates that there should be a congruence between the counselor as a person and the counselor's theory. If this congruence exists, the application of the theory becomes more effective: "The experienced counselor has made his approach a part of himself and he can therefore present it honestly and convincingly to his clients."

Dimick and Huff (1970, p. 59) state that there should be a blending of the counselor's personhood with a theory and that when this occurs: "Counseling is a way of being, a way of behaving, a way of living. The counselor attempts to affect human growth potentialities whether inside the counselor's office or on the street corner. The truly facilitative person is facilitative regardless of the setting."

The application of counseling theory is quite different from the application of theory in the physical sciences. Physical theories can be applied with little regard for the element of human interaction, but counseling theory, which is applied in the give and take between and among persons, must be integrated into the counselor's philosophy and personality. To apply theory in counseling as one applies it in the physical sciences would result in a view of oneself and the client as objects, with the consequent loss of the human element so essential to the success of a counseling relationship.

The competent counselor is sensitive to the need for a sound theory to support the practice of counseling. The degree of criticism of an organization's counseling service appears to be in proportion to the extent to which that service has a rationale underlying its visible functions. If a counseling program does certain things to and for its clientele, these functions should be defensible in terms of an underlying theory. If they are not, perhaps the criticism is justifiable.

The counselor's counseling procedure is not a conglomeration of methods used because they *appear* to be the best techniques on hand. Rather, the counselor's counseling approach is based on philosophical and theoretical hypotheses that enable the counselor to confront, with a reasonable degree of confidence and security, the daily and ever pressing problems of counseling. Because the counselor knows the "why" of counseling, the "how" of counseling is handled with greater facility and more effectiveness. The functional aspects of counseling do not constitute a problem for the counselor who has developed a congruence between counseling theory and practice.

Today's client-centered counselor has high regard and respect for legitimate theories of counseling. There is no blind clinging to client-centered theory while ignoring other views. The client-centered counselor is a positive person, and puts into practice a theory to which there is a deep commitment, but there is also a willingness to grow and develop in light of new evidence in the process and outcomes of counseling; there is a personal sensitivity to what is believed and why it is believed.

The client-centered counselor is sensitive to the fact that any theoretical commitment is based on hypotheses that are provisional and tentative in nature and does not consider any theory to be absolute. A theory is not dogma—it consists of the changeable. It has changed, is changing, and will continue to change. As new evidence and clinical data become known, the hypotheses of any theory of counseling will be refined, modified, reformulated, and serve as an impetus for the generation of new hypotheses. Rogers (1951) has historically emphasized the tentativeness of his own theory and has spurred research to test established hypotheses and to develop new theoretical constructs. He defines very clearly the mutability of client-centered theory in emphasizing that the central hypotheses of client-centered therapy are capable of proof or disproof and hence offer a hope of progress, rather than the stagnation of dogma. This quality of development, reformulation, and change appears to be one of the salient characteristics of the client-centered approach.

Theoretical Identification

The client-centered counselor is effective when there is a personalized identification with the client-centered theory; a link is formed between the theory and the self. From this integration the counselor's personal and professional behaviors take on a unity. A theory is not something the counselor leaves at work. Rather, it serves as an attitudinal basis for *all* the counselor's relationships. The counselor knows that personal and professional functioning is most cohesive when there is a high degree of congruence between what the counselor is as a person and how the counselor counsels.

A client-centered counselor is sensitive to the limitations of theory. Although the counselor is theory-oriented, the counselor is not theory-bound. There is an awareness that a single theory allegiance can blind us to the individuality of the client and that we can be tempted to force the client to fit on the procrustean bed of an inflexible theory. The client-centered counselor realizes that such an application of a theory negates the theory and makes the counselor anything but open in perceiving the client.

A number of counselors have been unable to translate counseling theory into practice because they have failed to integrate into their own personalities the philosophical and psychological nutrients of a particular theory. Without such an integration, counselors have mired themselves in a morass of literal translation and purity of technique—the quicksand of theory application. Counselors should be sensitive to this possibility and not become theoretically encapsulated. They should respect their counseling theory to the degree that it can be reasonably translated into the cold reality of a work setting. They should be sensitive to the fact that the most successful practitioners are theorists—and the most successful theorists are practical persons.

Theoretical Openness

There is the tendency for the client-centered counselor to look upon the behavior modification counselor as autocratic, dogmatic, coercive, and insensitive. The behavior modification counselor, on the other hand, has a tendency to view the Rogerian counselor as passive, laissez-faire, sentimental and generally sitting on a nondirective backside. Actually, both counselors should realize that the opposite they are describing in no way represents the reality of professional counseling. The opposites whom both describe are, in fact, nonprofessional counselors whose functioning is not substantiated in the professional literature.

The client-centered counselor sees no need to be ideologically defensive when discussing theoretical viewpoints in counseling. Such a counselor possesses a personal openness to theory that enables the counselor to learn instead of being bound by a dogmatic viewpoint which, in reality, is often a defense of personal values rather than a clarification of the theoretical viewpoint. Kemp (1962, p. 9), in attempting to determine the effect of counselor open-mindedness upon the counselor's behavior in the counseling relationship, found that counselors with a high Dogmatism Scale score (closed-mindedness) responded to the client with significantly more evaluative, interpretive, probing, and diagnostic responses than did open-minded counselors, and that understanding and supportive responses were significantly less frequent for the closed-minded counselor.

Counselors who are loyal to a single theory may in reality be displaying a personal anxiety when confronted with different hypotheses and propositions that are inconsistent with personal values. Such anxieties may indeed limit the degree to which opposite points of view can be understood and assimilated. It appears that feelings of anxiety serve to narrow perception and that such narrowing is reflected in a reduction of the number of choices that an anxious individual employs in dealing with an issue.

Personal Needs and Theory Selection

When a client fails to make progress in counseling, the counselor usually attempts to find a reason, or reasons, why such progress has not occurred. The counselor may look toward the client's marriage partner as a causal factor, feeling that the client's stoic spouse has inhibited the client's progress in counseling. For another client, the counselor may feel that the barrier preventing progress may be the bureaucratic attitude of the client's work environment. For still another client, the counselor might feel that overly protective peers are preventing the client from making progress in counseling. Another counselor may blame the unrealistic propositions of a particular counseling theory.

These factors *may* have some influence on a client's progress, but the prime influencing factor is often the counselor *as a person* – the counselor's ability to marshal humanistic attitudes that result in the creation of a counseling relationship that is helpful to the client. A counselor's theory of counseling is essentially a reflection of the counselor's humanism, not a self-protective excuse that insists on blaming the client for a lack of progress in counseling.

King (1972) has suggested that the theoretical allegiance of the counselor can often interfere with the effectiveness of the counseling relationship when the counselor tends to perceive client problems only in terms of their relationship to the counselor's own theory. As an example, take the counselor who perceives most counselees as being unhappy because of vocational maladjustment or the analytically trained counselor who feels that trouble on the job is invariably linked to the counselee's maladaptive childhood experiences. A counselor's behavior in the process of counseling is often so closely entwined with his or her theory that we cannot discuss one without including the other.

The self of the counselor is the most influencing factor that a counselor brings to a counseling relationship. As a person, the counselor is the instrument for affecting client progress; and the counselor needs to realize this and refine and improve this instrument. No amount of verbalization can replace the crucial impact of the counselor's very being upon the client's progress.

An openness to theory is an openness to self. When the counselor is able to achieve a nondefensive openness to self, the counselor is able to look at theories and realize the degree to which personal values influence the tendency toward one theory rather than another.

The involvement of the self in a counselor's selection of a theory has led some counselors to believe that the desired goal in developing a theoretical viewpoint is the personal comfort of the counselor. In other words, the counselor should utilize a theory of counseling that enables him or her to be personally comfortable in the counseling relationship. Certainly, counselor comfort with a counseling theory is important, but this cannot be the sole criterion by which a counselor determines which counseling approach will be used. A counseling approach should not be judged in terms of the comfort of the counselor but rather in terms of *its effect on the client*.

Effective counselors follow a theory of counseling with which they have a personal comfort, but the criteria of personal comfort is secondary to the needs of the client. Sometimes, in the name of personal comfort, some counselors adopt theories that make them feel good but have very little effect upon the behavior of clients.

Selecting an appropriate theory of counseling does require an enormous amount of effort, but if the counselor becomes involved in the task the result will be: (1) the development of a consistent process for helping clients, (2) the establishment of a model against which one's practice can be evaluated, (3) an ability to judge other theories because of the possession of a basic theoretical frame of reference, (4) the identification of a model against which the counselor can compare personal and professional behaviors, (5) a clearer concept of the counselor's role, and (6) a frame of reference for conducting research designed to measure the effectiveness of counseling. Ultimately, however, the counselor must *own* the theory; it must be a personal theory. Krause and Hendrickson (1972, p. 20) indicate that the success or failure of counselors hinges on their development of such a personalized theory of counseling: "We feel that the success or failure of those of us in the counseling profession evolves not only around techniques, but primarily around our having developed, modified, and implemented a personal theory of counseling."

ISSUES THAT INFLUENCE THE EFFECTIVENESS OF A COUNSELING THEORY

A counselor's theory serves as the foundation upon which the counselor's decisions and behaviors with clients are built. It serves as the roots from which all the branches and leaves of professional behavior receive their nourishment. It is as basic to the work of the counselor as the Constitution is to the functions of the legislative, executive, and judicial branches of our government.

Although there is general acceptance of the basic concept that a counselor's professional behavior and functions should be governed by an identified theory (Arbuckle, 1975), little attention has been given to determining why a theory, any theory, does or does not produce the desired results. This is a neglected area of investigation essentially because of the complexities involved. It is difficult enough to determine *why* a certain theory of counseling produces the desired results without becoming involved in the additional confusion of determining *why* a theory does not yield results. The counseling profession has evidence of the positive results of counseling but little or no indications regarding *why* a certain theory of counseling appears to work and even less evidence regarding *why* it or another theory of counseling does not work.

It is the purpose of this section to investigate why a counseling theory, any theory, may or may not produce the desired results. By doing this, we hope to create an awareness of certain factors that are fundamental to the success of any counseling theory. That is, the success of any theory of counseling does not occur by chance, but is related to more fundamental issues that will affect the success of *any* theory of counseling.

We identify the following issues that will influence any theory of counseling to be effective or ineffective. These issues can exert a positive or negative influence upon a counseling theory when they are considered individually, as a whole, or in clusters.

The Counselor's Relationship with the Client

No theory of counseling can be applied in a vacuum. Some theories of counseling describe the desired process, goals, and outcomes of counseling and assume that if a certain set of techniques are applied then the behavior of the client will tend to be positive. A theory of counseling cannot be isolated from the counselor who practices it; and any experienced counselor realizes that a particular theory of counseling is only as effective as the substance of the relationship with a client.

A theory of counseling tends to produce positive results because it is applied within the context of a positive therapeutic relationship between the counselor and client (Boy & Pine, 1978). Such a relationship will influence any reasonable theory of counseling to produce positive results; and conversely, when a theory of counseling tends to produce few or no results, we can look toward the quality of the relationship between the counselor and client as being a vital contributor to the ineffectiveness of the theory.

We often credit the positive outcomes of counseling to a particular theory but a significant portion of the credit should go to the quality of the relationship between the counselor and the client. A qualitative relationship influences the client to be receptive, to listen, to cooperate, and to invest the self in behavioral change. Without a substantive relationship, a theory of counseling will tend to be ineffective.

The Client's Perception of Counseling

If a client perceives the relationship with a counselor to be equalized, then the client will make a deeper commitment to the process and outcomes of that relationship (Boy & Pine, 1976a, p. 13):

> When clients sense that their relationships with counselors are equalized, they can invest themselves in moving toward more positive behavior. This movement occurs because clients sense that they are co-participants in the process of counseling. The client feels accepted, understood, free, trusted, and motivated to communicate honestly and identify those aspects of personal behavior which need to be modified or changed. The counselor is perceived as someone who is equally involved in the process and outcomes of the relationship. Since the counselor is perceived as an equal, the client senses a coownership of the relationship and there is no need to be evasive, defensive, or vague.

When the client perceives the counseling relationship as one in which the interactive and manipulative power is in the hands of the counselor, the client reacts by being uninvolved, passive, and generally uncooperative. Clients who are referred to a counselor often respond to the relationship in this manner. They feel that the control of the relationship, the decision regarding whether or not to participate in counseling, and the purpose and need of the relationship are all outside their control. They respond to such unequalized relationship by interfering with and diminishing the potential effectiveness of that relationship.

The counselor's theory of counseling may be professionally appropriate but the client's negative perception of the counseling relationship prevents that theory from being applied and being potentially effective.

The Counselor's Intellectual Knowledge Regarding a Theory

Because some counselors are superficial in the process of selecting an appropriate theory of counseling, they do not possess the necessary intellectual and objective knowledge regarding the process, goals, and outcomes of that theory. They apply a theory that the intellect has only partially absorbed and when they find themselves between a hard place and a rock, they become confused. Such a confusion would not occur if the counselor made the necessary intellectual investment to fully comprehend the depth and range of a theory.

If a theory of counseling is substantive, it contains the answers necessary for the counselor to solve or resolve issues related to the process, goals, and outcomes of counseling. If the theory does not furnish the counselor with clear insights and answers, then either the theory is inadequate or the counselor's intellectual understanding of the theory is inadequate. Most theories of counseling are adequate enough to contain the answers to a wide range of issues. The answers exist within a theory for the counselor who has made the intellectual investment necessary to fully comprehend the theory.

A theory will often yield few or marginal results not because the theory itself is inadequate but because the counselor applying the theory has only a partial intellectual understanding of the theory. Therefore, the intellectual investment of deeply understanding a theory will enable that theory to be more effectively applied.

The Counselor's Attitudinal Identification with a Theory

A counselor's intellectual understanding of a theory is closely entwined with his or her attitudinal commitment to the theory. When a counselor is both intellectually and attitudinally committed to a theory, we find that the theory will tend to be effective because of the balanced influences of both the counselor's intellect and attitude. Whether one commits oneself to an idea, religion, marriage partner, or cause, we realize that the commitment is full when it is both intellectual and attitudinal.

When a counselor is just intellectually committed to a theory, then that theory will lose a large portion of its potential effectiveness. When a counselor is just attitudinally committed to a theory, then that theory will lose a large portion of its potential effectiveness. But when a counselor is *both* intellectually and attitudinally committed to a theory, the theory takes on a unified and synergistic strength that enables it to be more effective. The intellectual and attitudinal influences serve to deepen and widen the counselor's investment in the theory and this level of commitment will exert a positive influence on the credibility and outcomes of the theory. As Lewis (1970, p. 62) has said: "One of the major reasons for the counselor's positive expectations with a new client is his faith in the theoretical approach which he employs."

The Counselor's Role

Often the role of the counselor works against the success of a counseling theory. Most theories of counseling conceive the role of the counselor in pure terms; that is, they perceive the counselor as being essentially a counseling professional who spends the greatest portion of each working day in actual individual and group counseling relationships with clients. These theories also postulate that actual and potential clients see the counselor in exactly the same way; as a caring person who is committed to the well being and development of the client. All theories of counseling basically conceive the counselor as being deeply immersed in a pure and unencumbered counseling role.

In the reality of the counseling profession, few counselors have a pure counseling role. Many counselors are more involved in administrative activities, environmental manipulations, meetings, record keeping, and the coordination of institutional loose ends. Such noncounseling involvement will certainly leave the counselor with a cluttered mind that is not focused on the human needs of clients who are occasionally counseled. This kind of noncounseling involvement by the counselor will also be sensed by the client and the therapeutic potential of the counseling relationship will be eroded.

In order for any theory of counseling to have the potential for being effective, it must be practiced by a counselor whose counseling role is pure enough for the theory to be applied. No theory can be filtered through a counselor whose role is cluttered with administrative and managerial requirements; any theory applied by such an administratively overloaded counselor is bound to be ineffective (Boy & Pine, 1976b).

The Theory and Institutional Needs

A theory of counseling tends to be ineffective when it is not coordinated with institutional needs (Boy & Pine, 1978). For example, a theory of counseling may require that a counselor establish nonevaluative and nonjudgmental counseling relationships while an institution may instead require that the counselor be evaluative and judgmental regarding clients so that the institution can make accurate administrative decisions about those clients. A counselor in this bind will often abandon the theory because of the superficial judgment that it is ineffective. In reality, however, the theory maintains its ability to be effective but its potential to be effective is diminished because of the evaluative needs of the institution. Therefore, the culprit is not the theory but institutional needs that prevent the theory from being applied. The counselor, however, does not sense or respond to the blockage of the theory because of institutional needs but simply dismisses the theory as being ineffective. In order for any theory of counseling to be effective, institutional goals and needs must be reasonably congruent with the theory.

WHY CLIENT-CENTERED COUNSELING?

A churchgoer who participates only in the rituals of a religion never really knows what is believed or why it is believed. This person's religious participation is often social and the whole matter of belief becomes a mixture of mysticism, auctions, bean suppers, incense, and sweet-smelling flowers. The practices of a person's religion become confused unless that religion is based upon some objective and subjective beliefs that give substance to its practice. *Something* has to serve as a rationale for one's religion, otherwise the practice of a religion becomes a hollow experience.

A religion that bases itself upon superficialities cannot hope to retain the commitment and belief of its members over an extended period of time, because people need more than superficialities in order to achieve an *internal* feeling of belief. They need a spiritual awareness that enables them to deal with the fundamentals of life long after the sweet scents and appetizing foods have become the victims of nature.

A counselor's adherence to a theory of counseling is very similar to a person's adherence to a religion. Some counselors believe only in superficialities, techniques, and rituals, while others believe because of the interplay of objective and subjective judgments that give substance and depth to the belief and make it translatable and operational in one's work and life.

In this section, we will attempt to identify those objective and subjective reasons that have influenced us to support the theory and practice of client-centered counseling, in both its traditional form and in our refined concept.

It possesses a positive philosophy of the person. Client-centered counseling views the person as having basic impulses of love, belonging, and security, which influence the person to be cooperative, constructive, trustworthy, forward moving, rational, socialized, and realistic. These human qualities tend to become actualized in environments that encourage their emergence and tend to be dormant in environments that inhibit their emergence. Counseling, then, is the process of liberating a capacity that is inherent to the individual but has been stifled because of environmental influences. The counselor enables this liberating to occur by genuinely owning attitudes toward the client that focus on respect, the individual's capacity and right to self-direction, and a prizing of the worth and significance of each individual (Patterson, 1973, pp. 380–381).

In our opinion, no other theory of counseling views the person in such substantive and positive terms, and since we share this view of the person and the counseling process that serves to liberate the person toward these positive qualities, we are congruent with the philosophic core of client-centered counseling.

It articulates propositions regarding human personality and behavior. These propositions regarding human personality and behavior (Rogers, 1951, pp. 483–524; Rogers, 1959, pp. 184–256) form and reflect the philosophic core of client-centered counseling and provide the counselor with a general conceptual framework for understanding human motivation. These propositions view the person as:

1. Being the best determiner of a personal reality
2. Behaving as an organized whole
3. Desiring to enhance the self
4. Goal directed in satisfying perceived needs
5. Being behaviorally influenced by feelings that affect rationality
6. Best able to perceive the self
7. Being able to be aware of the self
8. Valuing
9. Interested in maintaining a positive self-concept
10. Behaving in ways that are consistent with the self-concept
11. Not owning behavior that is inconsistent with the self-concept
12. Producing psychological freedom or tension by admitting or not admitting certain experiences into the self-concept
13. Responding to threat by becoming behaviorally rigid
14. Admitting into awareness experiences that are inconsistent with the self if the self is free from threat
15. Being more understanding of others if a well integrated self-concept exists
16. Moving from self-defeating values toward self-sustaining values.

We are attracted to client-centered counseling because we are congruent with its theory of human personality and behavior that serves as the foundation for the process of client-centered counseling and makes it understandable and applicable.

It possesses achievable human goals for client. The goals of client-centered counseling are very personalized and human goals *for the client* rather than being goals designed to simply support the theory, society, or its institutions; but in achieving these personalized goals, the client will behave in ways that contribute to the well being of society and its institutions. Although the goals of client-centered counseling are general, they are interpreted and translated by the individual client within the process of counseling and can become applicable to the client's life outside of counseling. Client-centered counseling is aimed at helping the client to:

1. Engage in behavior that liberates, actualizes, and enhances the self
2. Engage in the discovery of previously denied feelings and attitudes
3. Become more acceptant and trustful of the self
4. Engage in self-assessment
5. Engage in reorganizing the self
6. Become more self-reliant
7. Become more responsible for the self
8. Engage in self-determined choices, decisions, and solutions
9. Achieve individuality while being conscious of social responsibilities
10. Become sensitive to the process of becoming a person that involves a new and self-actualized way of being.

Our experience as counselors indicates that these client goals represent a process that can bring the client closer to an optimum level of psychological wholeness and stability. We have experienced clients achieving these goals in proportion to the quality of the client-centered counseling that was offered.

It possesses a definition of the counselor's role within the counseling relationship. The counselor's client-centered attitude toward the client finds its expression in the following behaviors. The counselor is understanding, liberal, acceptant, emphathic, a sensitive listener, authentic, and possesses a sense of involvement while equalizing the relationship.

We add the term *concrete* (Carkhuff and Berenson, 1967, p. 30) to the preceding desired counselor behaviors because in our refinement of the client-centered viewpoint, after the therapeutic relationship has been established with the client through the process of the counselor reflecting the client's feelings, the counselor is able to move toward nonreflective responses specifically related to the needs of the individual client. These nonreflective responses are more concrete and represent an individualization of the counseling process that coincides with the experiential third period (1957 to the present) in the historic evaluation of client-centered thinking (Corey, 1977, p. 64; Hart, 1970a, pp. 3–22).

While identifying the necessary counselor behaviors for effective counseling, the client-centered viewpoint also indicates counselor behaviors that must be avoided. The counselor is not a moralist, questioner, or diagnostician.

An enlightening aspect of client-centered counseling is that it defines the counselor's role in terms of attitudes and behaviors that will both facilitate and inhibit the client's progress in counseling. Our experience as counselors confirms that when we exhibited the desired counselor attitudes and behaviors our counseling was beneficial to clients, and when we exhibited undesirable attitudes and behaviors the outcome was to inhibit the client's movement toward improved behavior.

In the second phase of our refinement of client-centered counseling, the counselor tends to be more concrete and open to personal reactions to the client and is comfortable in expressing these reactions to the client; but these reactions are always focused on the person-centered needs of the client rather than being expressions of the needs of the counselor to be a moralist, questioner, or diagnostician.

It has research evidence supporting its effectiveness. Although client-centered counseling is more an art than a science, we feel that any theory of counseling must also satisfy the requirements of science by possessing both qualitative and quantitative research evidence that confirms the effectiveness of the theory. In this area, client-centered counseling does not let us down. It does possess the desired research evidence that supports its effectiveness. In fact, it goes far beyond the requirements in this area. As Patterson (1973, p. 412) has observed: ". . . it must be noted that the client-centered approach has led to, and is supported by, a greater amount of research than any other approach to counseling or psychotherapy."

Corey (1977, p. 57) also acknowledges the attention that has been paid to developing the research evidence that supports client-centered counseling: "Perhaps more than any other single approach to psychotherapy, client-centered theory has developed through research on the process and outcomes of therapy."

From our own investigations and research into the effectiveness of client-centered counseling (Arbuckle & Boy, 1961; Boy & Pine, 1963, 1968) and its application to learner-centered teaching (Pine & Boy, 1977), plus the far more voluminous investigations and research of others, we feel that client-centered counseling has more than met its obligation to have its effectiveness supported by research evidence.

It is comprehensive. Client-centered counseling has the needed substance to be applied beyond the one-to-one counseling relationship. The comprehensive nature of the client-centered view is seen in its application to teaching, organizational behavior, family relationships, parenting, groups, marriage and its alternatives, leadership, pastoring, and interpersonal relationships, in general.

Another indication of its comprehensiveness is that the same principles of client-centered counseling can be applied to all persons—"normals," "neurotics," and "psychotics" (Corey, 1977, p. 56). The comprehensiveness of client-centered counseling enables it to be applied by counselors in a variety of settings dealing with a wide range of human problems: mental health centers; elementary, middle, and high schools; colleges and universities; rehabilitation agencies; prisons and halfway houses; pastoral counseling centers; marriage and family centers; human development centers; employment service agencies; youth centers; religious seminaries; and professional schools of law, medicine, and dentistry.

From our experience, the depth and range of the client-centered view-point enables it to be applied in any agency that deals with human problems. We have been able to apply it to our individual and group counseling, consultation, staff relations, teaching, family living, friend-ships, administrative functions, interpersonal relationships, and recreational and spiritual experiences. Whenever it has been well applied we were in attitudinal and behavioral congruence with the philosophy and process of client-centered counseling. Whenever we stumbled or failed it was because we were attitudinally and behaviorally detached from its philosophic and process cores. We do sense, however, that the client-centered theory has the necessary comprehensiveness to be applied even further in interpersonal relations and encounters that have yet to be identified and experienced.

It can be applied.   Client-centered counseling is clear and precise enough so that it can be applied. At the process level, the counselor's reflections of the client's feelings is an understandable concept that is applicable in pro-portion to the counselor's grasp of why it is done and how such reflections contribute to the client's self-awareness and also enable the counselor to assimilate and accommodate the needs of the client. We see no difficulty in applying client-centered counseling *if* the counselor is *attitudinally* client-centered. When a counselor is not *attitudinally* client-centered, then that counselor has difficulty in intellectually absorbing and applying reflections of the client's feelings. Such a counselor typically reflects the surface content of what the client is saying rather than reflecting the feelings behind the surface content of the words the client is using. When the counselor does this the results are innocuous, bland, and ineffective, and the counselor gives up an inclination toward client-centered counseling. But this counselor doesn't give up a client-centered counseling theory because the counselor never applied it. What the counselor applied was a misin-terpretation of the client-centered approach rather than the approach itself.

To us, the process of reflecting feelings appears to be simple on the sur-face while actually being quite complex. A counselor's ability to accurately reflect feelings depends upon his or her ability to read and absorb those feelings, the ability to accurately represent those feelings back to the client, and a vocabulary range that can reflect a core feeling in a number of descriptive ways that penetrate the client's self-awareness. And once again, the quality and depth of a counselor's reflections are proportional to the degree to which the counselor is *attitudinally* client-centered.

The second phase of our refinement of client-centered counseling has utility in proportion to the quality of Phase One. If Phase One was a qualitative encounter between the client and the counselor, and if the rela-tionship between them is interpersonally solid and equalized, then Phase Two is a natural sequence of events. Phase Two flows easily and well from Phase One because Phase One was qualitative and effective.

The only danger in our concept of Phase Two is that the counselor's per-sonal needs for domination, moralization, or righteousness could impinge upon and influence the counselor's responses, and the result could be the creation of a forum for the counselor's expression of personal ideologies and needs rather than the development of a Phase Two which meets the needs of the client. But once again, this will not occur in Phase Two if the counselor is *attitudinally* client-centered.

Our experience in the preparation of counselors to work in a variety of settings dealing with a wide range of human problems indicates that our refined concept of client-centered counseling is both teachable and applicable, and becomes teachable and applicable only in proportion to the degree to which we are able to demonstrate and model the attitudes and behaviors that characterize both phases of client-centered counseling.

It has an expansive intellectual and attitudinal substance. Intellectually, client-centered counseling keeps us alert to better understand its philosophy, process, goals, and outcomes. On some days there are rays of intellectual insight that give a wholeness to the viewpoint, while on other days a personal experience, or the reading or experiencing of another very different viewpoint, cause us to wonder about the accuracy of client-centeredness. From these insights and uncertainties there emerges a clarity or synthesis that serves to energize our intellectual understanding of client-centeredness. We are always alert to, and challenged by, the ability of client-centeredness to be intellectually stimulating. It possesses an intellectual *gravitas* which can sometimes exceed our grasp but we appreciate the viewpoint's ability to keep our brain cells curious and electrified.

Another intellectually stimulating aspect of client-centeredness is its connection with other past and present systems of thought and the degree of congruence with these systems. The writings of existentialists, humanists, phenomenologists, theists, rationalists, and politicians take on a clarity because we have a point of reference – the client-centered viewpoint – from which to better understand these other views. Without this point of reference our understanding would be superficial, partial, and segmented.

Attitudinally, client-centeredness gives us a process structure by which our religious tendencies can be expressed. Those who possess a religious faith often have difficulty in identifying a career, role, or structure by which that faith can be expressed in the secular world. Client-centeredness appears to be the bridge that connects our religious tendencies to the real world of interpersonal relationships; it enables us to express those religious values that deal with truth, honesty, beauty, justice, love, human rights, and peace. The congruence between client-centered counseling and our religious tendencies gives us a feeling of unity and wholeness.

It focuses on the client as a person rather than on the client's problem. In terms of the philosophy, process, and goals of client-centered counseling, it has much to say about the person and the improvement of the human condition. It is person-centered rather than being technique-centered, process-centered, or counselor-centered. It focuses on *the client as a person* rather than on the client's problem, and this, to us, is where the focus should be.

When the counselor is able to assist a client to become a more adequate and better functioning person, this improvement in the personhood of the client will enable the client to solve and resolve current and future problems. When the person is psychologically whole, that person is able to deal with problems because that wholeness produces intellectual and attitudinal solutions. From a psychological wholeness there emerges insights and attitudes that prompt behaviors designed to deal with specific problems.

Other theories of counseling focus on the client's problem rather than the personhood of the client and produce a short-range and temporary solution to a problem while often neglecting to affect the cause of the problem – the client's personhood – that mixture of attitudes, values, and perceptions that contribute to the development of the problem.

Since client-centered counseling focuses on the person rather than the problem, it possesses a deeper potential for assisting a person to become more adequate, *as a person*, in dealing with a range of problems that we all have to face in life. The better the personhood of the client, the better able the client is to deal with, and find solutions to, specific problems.

It focuses on the attitudes of the counselor rather than on techniques. The counselor's facilitative attitudes all flow from the personhood of the counselor. If we desire clients to develop themselves as persons, then we must also expect the counselor to do the same if he or she is to be influential in affecting behavioral change among clients. We cannot expect the client to become a more adequate and better functioning person if the counselor does not model attitudes that enable these behaviors to emerge from the client.

The personhood of the counselor, when expressed through a qualitative counseling relationship, becomes the primary influence that prompts the client to move toward a more satisfying and sustaining behavior. The counseling profession has neglected to focus on the therapeutic influence of the counselor as a person but instead has given its attention to the development of mechanical techniques to induce behavioral change. These techniques can sometimes be useful (role playing, Gestalt empty chair, confrontation, goal identification) if they are used *as an adjunct* to the personhood of the counselor. In too many cases, however, such techniques are the core of the counseling process and the therapeutic influence of the *counselor as a person* is neglected.

If one listens to clients describe how a counselor has helped them, one will hear these clients describe the counselor's personhood as the *primary influence* rather than the techniques the counselor employed.

It provides the counselor with a systematic response pattern. Most theories of counseling make insightful statements regarding their philosophy, goals, process, and outcomes. Their philosophic, goal-oriented, and outcome statements are often noble and sometimes border on the poetic when describing the human condition and its improvement. But most counseling theories do not present the student-counselor or practitioner with a systematic response pattern whereby the counselor is able to assist the client in moving toward these philosophically insightful goals and outcomes. These theories address themselves to the "why" of counseling but provide the counselor with little regarding the process or "how" of counseling.

Client-centered counseling presents the most clear and well defined response pattern to guide the client-centered counselor in the process of counseling: reflecting the client's feelings. This response pattern enables the counselor to assimilate and absorb the client's perceptions, values, and attitudes and how these affect the client's behavior; it enables the client to develop an awareness of how these perceptions, values, and attitudes affect the client's behavior; it enables the client to perceive the counselor as a caring person who is able to penetrate and understand the client and the client's problem from the client's viewpoint; it serves to free the client to communicate values and attitudes that the client was not able to disclose in other interpersonal relationships; and it serves to establish a trustful bond between the client and the counselor.

Although reflecting the client's feelings may be sufficient and effective throughout a counseling relationship and has the potential to influence behavioral change on the part of the client, the second phase of our refined concepts of client-centered counseling enables the counselor to go beyond reflecting feelings *if such verbal behavior more adequately meets the needs of clients.* Further, if in this transition from Phase One to Phase Two results are not produced for the client, the counselor is able to return to reflecting the client's feelings in order to better clarify the client's perceptions, values, and attitudes, thereby developing a more accurate identification of the client's problem.

Reflecting the client's feelings, then, affords the counselor with a systematic response pattern that serves as the core of the counselor's responses in Phase One of our refined view of client-centered counseling but is not the only response pattern available to the counselor in Phase Two. The fact, however, that reflecting the client's feelings exists as a process concept gives the counselor an understandable and applicable foundation upon which to build an effective counseling relationship.

It provides flexibility for the counselor to go beyond reflection of feelings. In the first two historic periods of client-centered counseling, perhaps some client-centered counselors were in a verbal straight jacket when they only reflected the client's feelings. During these two periods, however, there were some other client-centered counselors who felt free and comfortable with reflecting the client's feelings and saw evidence that such a process was therapeutically effective.

We believe in, and have continually experienced, the therapeutic effectiveness of reflecting feelings. Reflecting the client's feelings does not have to be bland; the process can be lively, penetrating, and expanding in proportion to the counselor's ability to read the feelings of clients and the counselor's psychic investment in the process. A pure reflection of the client's feelings does possess therapeutic impact in that it prompts the client to investigate previously denied feelings and bring them into conscious awareness.

Reflecting the client's feelings also has another potential — it can incorporate what we have come to call "additives," a procedure that has been recently explored by Turock (1978) and has been found to have much potential. That is, a pure reflection of the client's feelings can be extended to include an additive that is confrontative, interpretive, or challenging. When well timed, such additives can serve to give the client an added dimension of self-awareness not typically included in a pure reflection of feeling. For example, a pure reflection of feelings by the counselor might be: "You feel depressed and lonely during this period of your life." A counselor additive that is confrontative would be: "You feel depressed and lonely during this period of your life *and have lost the courage to do something about it*." A counselor additive that is interpretive would be: "You feel depressed and lonely during this period of your life *and would feel much better if you only knew that your husband cared for you*." A counselor additive that is challenging would be: "You feel depressed and lonely during this period of your life *and you are content to stay this way*."

Reflecting the client's feelings can be done purely, without additives, or with a flexibility that enables the counselor to add something to the basic and pure reflection. A counselor additive can be used on certain occasions when such an additive serves to give the client a new insight that could not be achieved if the counselor's response was just a pure reflection.

In the third historic period of client-centered counseling, the experiential period extending from 1970 to the present, counselors have engaged in behaviors, mostly counselor self-disclosure, which have gone beyond just reflecting the client's feelings. In Phase Two of our refinement of client-centered counseling, the counselor has four choices: (1) the counselor can continue to engage in pure reflections of feelings if doing this best meets the therapeutic needs of the client, (2) the counselor can make additives to basic reflections of feelings if doing this best meets the therapeutic needs of the client, (3) the counselor can incorporate techniques from nonclient-centered theories of counseling if doing this best meets the therapeutic needs of the client, and (4) the counselor can make a natural and responsible judgment to do something natural, intuitive, and eclectic if this best meets the therapeutic needs of the client. As Rogers (1980, p. 15) has said, "sometimes a feeling rises up in me which seems to have no particular relationship to what is going on. Yet I have learned to accept and trust this feeling in my awareness and try communicate it to my client."

Client-centered counseling is not a set of static and hardened principles. It gives the client-centered counselor a high degree of flexibility if one is willing to absorb the implications of what it means to be *client-centered*. In our opinion, this means that the client-centered counselor's behavior is within the bounds of the theory when it is *client-centered* and meets the needs of the client, and the counselor's behavior is outside the bounds of the theory and is *counselor-centered* when it instead meets the needs of the counselor.

It can be individualized according to the particular needs of a client. Client-centered counseling's ability to be flexible enables it to more accurately meet the particular needs of clients. It should not be viewed as a fixed theory that does not have the malleability to be shaped toward a client's unique needs. Client-centeredness can be individualized to meet client needs and this is one of its inherent strengths.

Some clients can become manipulated by the constructs and requirements of a theory rather than having their needs met. If a theory requires that clients behave realistically, then clients must be molded to behave realistically; if a theory sees the problems of adulthood rooted in the experiences of childhood, then the client must be prompted to recall those inhibiting childhood experiences; and if a theory postulates that repressed anger is the cause of a client's problem, then the client must be confronted in order to release that anger. Counseling according to a narrow theoretical bias can result in a particular theory being thrust on all clients, regardless of their individualized needs or problems. The client whose problem is far from the need to be realistic is molded to be realistic; the client whose problem is situational and far removed from childhood is prompted to delve into childhood experiences; and the client whose problem is far removed from the need to express anger is confronted to release a nonexistent anger.

The flexibility of the client-centered approach enables it to be individualized according to the needs of the client. The theory has no grandiose message that the counselor has to deliver to clients. What the theory does require is the development of a relationship in which *the client* can identify the problem and a relationship in which *the client* can choose the behaviors that will enable the problem to be solved. A client-centered relationship is an open and flexible relationship because the client is the one who determines the scope, depth, and intensity of a problem, and once this recognition has occurred, the client is in the best position to determine the process through which the problem will be solved. Such an individualization of the counseling process enables client-centeredness to be a highly accurate approach in its ability to be directly congruent with client needs.

It enables client behavior to change in a natural sequence of events. A client who enters a counseling relationship typically has an interpersonal communication problem with a person or persons in their lives. The cause of the problem is usually that the client is unable to communicate with that person or persons and, as a result, has repressed a large number of negative feelings. Such a repression of feelings often produces tension, behavioral confusion, and physical symptoms.

In Phase One of our refinement of client-centered counseling, the counselor establishes a relationship with the client in which these repressed feelings can be released. The counselor accomplishes this essentially by reflecting whatever feelings the client may present. If the counselor's reflections are both accurate and penetrating, the client becomes more comfortable in the relationship and feels secure enough to go more deeply into these feelings and to explore new and previously denied feelings.

Once a client has fully expressed previously repressed feelings and feels released from the debilitating effects of having had to repress these feelings, the natural inclination is for the client to begin to seek a solution to the interpersonal conflict that initially brought the client to counseling. At this stage, because the client feels emotionally cleansed, the client moves away from emotionally based attitudes and reactions and toward a rational solution to the problem. Because the client is no longer in a subjective emotional knot the client can begin to work toward an objective rational solution. The resources of the client's intellect, clouded by emotions in the past, are now free to function and move toward a rational solution. All persons are both emotional and rational, and problems often develop because our emotions overpower our ability to think. Once we have released and tamed our emotions, we free our intellect to function clearly and bring us to a reasonable solution.

In our refinement of client-centered counseling the counselor can follow this natural sequence of events by basically reflecting the client's feelings in Phase One, and as the client becomes more rational the counselor can begin to respond to the client by using more rational and objective responses.

An important aspect of effective counseling, regardless of theory, is that a counselor should respond affectively to an emotionally burdened client and should respond rationally to a client who communicates rationally. Our refinement of client-centered counseling postulates that clients are generally emotional at the beginning and middle stages of counseling and are more rational during the later stages of counseling. Therefore, the counselor's response pattern should be congruent with the client's emotionality or rationality if effective communication is to take place.

It can draw from the process components of other theories of counseling and human development. As was indicated earlier in Phase Two of our refinement of client-centered counseling, the counselor has four basic response patterns for meeting the individualized needs of clients: (1) continuing to reflect the client's feelings started in Phase One, (2) making additives to reflections of feelings, (3) incorporating techniques from nonclient-centered theories of counseling, and (4) making a natural and responsible judgment to do something intuitive if this best meets the therapeutic needs of the client

We wish to emphasize that in Phase Two, the counselor can draw from nonclient-centered counseling theories those process components or techniques that possess potential for meeting the individualized and unique needs of clients. A client-centered counselor does not have to believe in the philosophy, theoretical constructs, and goals of another theory of counseling in order to use that theory's effective process techniques, just as a physician does not have to adopt communism if that physician utilizes an effective medical technique that was developed in Russia.

It appears that client-centered counseling has failed to develop such techniques because these techniques have been traditionally inamicable with the relationship-centered philosophy of client-centered counseling; namely, that the *relationship itself,* if it were of sufficient quality, could influence behavioral change on the part of the client and that such techniques were too superficial and mechanical to be accommodated within the purity of an effective relationship and would, in fact, interfere with that relationship.

Such closed-mindedness on the part of client-centered counselors has resulted in the theory not developing or possessing a usable set of techniques. The one exception is the counselor's reflecting of the client's feelings, which some do classify as a technique. Since the client-centered approach is basically without techniques and relies more on the counseling relationship itself as the vehicle for behavioral change on the part of the client, the counselor who is at Phase Two in our refinement of client-centered counseling must look to other theories in order to identify usable techniques such as role playing, fantasizing, desensitization, goal identification, modeling, encouragement, and confrontation. But if the client-centered relationship developed in Phase One is of sufficent quality, the counselor should be able to utilize modified versions of these techniques especially if they are more accurate processes for meeting the individualized needs of clients. Once again, the essential criterion in selecting a Phase Two technique is the degree to which the technique will be helpful in meeting the individualized needs of the client rather than being a technique that instead meets the needs of the counselor to dominate, control, manipulate, or proselytize.

In our Phase Two refinement of client-centered counseling the counselor is also able to make a natural and responsible judgment to do something intuitive if this best meets the therapeutic needs of the client. This judgment may prompt the counselor to utilize the techniques and process components of play therapy, art therapy, music therapy, or recreational therapy if techniques associated with these therapies can accomplish more in meeting the identified and individualized needs of clients.

The counselor's Phase Two natural and responsible judgment can also be concrete and based upon common sense as in the following illustration of a client-centered counselor's Phase Two decision. The counselor had counseled a female client on a weekly basis for about nine months. The client had a poor self-concept and felt that she was physically unattractive and unable to feel comfortable in her relationships with peers. The client became isolated, lonely, shy, and depressed. The counselor responded to her feelings by reflecting those feelings, and although the client felt close to the counselor and appreciated the counselor's genuineness and warmth, there was no improvement in her self-concept and, hence, no improvement in her behavior. As the counseling relationship developed, the counselor began to notice that the client had a mouthful of decayed and broken teeth and the client began to express negative feelings about the condition of her teeth. The counselor made an intuitive common sense judgment that her poor self-concept could be partially due to the condition of her teeth. Since the client had no finances and came from an economically deprived family, she felt that she was forever doomed to carry a negative self-concept and to become more introverted as a result.

The counselor decided to intervene by telephoning a local school of dentistry and inquiring about the possibility of free dental work for the client. The dental school was cooperative, and, with the client's consent, the counselor arranged a series of visits for the client to the school's dental clinic which was staffed by dental interns. After the client completed her dental work, which necessitated the removal of all existing teeth and replacing them with full upper and lower dental plates, there was a dramatic improvement in her self-concept. She became friendly and gregarious and was no longer isolated, shy, and depressed. Her new teeth gave her confidence in meeting people and she became confident and alive.

The client-centered counselor in this case could have complicated and inhibited the client's development of a positive self-concept by continuing to reflect her feelings, making additives to the reflections, or using a technique from another theory of counseling. The counselor chose not to do any of these in Phase Two, but instead made an intuitive common sense judgment that resulted in a dramatic improvement in the client's self-concept.

Such intuitive common sense judgments are available in Phase Two if the client-centered counselor is not theory bound, but instead is flexible enough to match the theory with the identified and individualized needs of clients.

In summary, we believe that an effective client-centered counselor both believes and doubts. Within the framework of the theory of client-centered counseling there is much that is applicable in the process of assisting clients; but there are certain other aspects of the theory we must be willing to doubt in order to shed new light not only on the theory itself but on the general process of counseling. A competent counselor is one who believes in a theory but also maintains a flexibility regarding the theory and its application. This flexibility is necessary in order to force a theory to meet the individualized needs of clients rather than forcing clients to meet the needs of a theory.

The flexibility needed by a counselor is aptly represented by the following two historic statements:

> No scientific investigation is final; it merely represents the most probable conclusion which can be drawn from the data at the disposal of the writer. A wider range of facts or more refined analysis, experiment, and observation

will lead to new formulas and new theories. This is the essence of scientific progress. (Pearson, 1897)

Knowledge progresses by stages, so that the theory one holds today must be provisional, as much a formulation of one's ignorance as anything else, to be used as long as it is useful and then discarded. Its function is to organize the available evidence. It is really a working assumption which the user may actively disbelieve. (Hebb, 1958)

REFERENCES

American Psychological Association, *Ethical standards for research with human subjects.* New York: 1973.

Arbuckle, D. W. *Counseling and psychotherapy: An existential-humanistic view.* Boston: Allyn and Bacon, 1975.

Arbuckle, D. S., & Boy, A. V. Client-centered therapy in counseling students with behavior problems. *Journal of Counseling Psychology,* 1961, *8,* 136–139.

Boy, A. V., & Pine, G. J. *Client-centered counseling in the secondary school.* Boston: Houghton Mifflin, 1963.

Boy, A. V., & Pine, G. J. *The counselor in the schools: A reconceptualization.* Boston: Houghton Mifflin, 1968.

Boy, A. V., & Pine, G. J. The rights of the client. *Counseling and Values,* 1974, *18,* 154–159.

Boy, A. V., & Pine, G. J. Equalizing the counseling relationship. *Psychotherapy: Theory, Research, and Practice,* 1976, *13,* 20. (a)

Boy, A. V., & Pine, G. J. The process of counselor advocacy. *Counseling and Values,* 1976, *20,* 112–118. (b)

Boy, A. V., & Pine, G. J. Effective counseling: Some proportional relationships. *Counselor Education and Supervision,* 1978, *18,* 137–143.

Brammer, L. M., & Shostrom, E. L. *Therapeutic psychology: Fundamentals of counseling and psychotherapy* (3rd ed.). Englewood Cliffs, N.J.: Prentice-Hall, 1977.

Carkhuff, R. R., & Berenson, B. G. *Beyond counseling and therapy.* New York: Holt, Rinehart and Winston, 1967.

Combs, A. W., Avila, D. L., & Purkey, W. W. *Helping relationships: Basic concepts for the helping professions* (2nd ed.). Boston: Allyn and Bacon, 1971.

Corey, G. *Theory and practice of counseling and psychotherapy.* Monterey, Calif.: Brooks/Cole, 1977, 56–65.

Dimick, K. M., & Huff, V. E. *Child counseling.* Dubuque, Iowa: Wm. C. Brown, 1970.

Hansen, J. C., Stevic, R. R., & Warner, R. W. *Counseling: Theory and process.* Boston: Allyn and Bacon, 1977.

Hart, J. The development of client-centered therapy. In J. T. Hart & T. M. Tomlinson (Eds.), *New directions in client-centered therapy.* Boston: Houghton Mifflin, 1970, 3–22. (a)

Hart, J. Beyond psychotherapy: The applied psychology of the future. In J. T. Hart & T. M. Tomlinson (Eds.), *New directions in client-centered therapy*. Boston: Houghton Mifflin, 1970.

Hebb, D. O. *A textbook of psychology*. Philadelphia: Saunders, 1958.

Kelley, G. A. *A theory of personality*. New York: Norton, 1963.

Kemp, C. G. Influence of dogmatism in the training of counselors. *Journal of Counseling Psychology*, 1962, 9, 155–157.

King, P. T. Psychoanalytic adaptations. In B. Stefflre and W. Grant (Eds.), *Theories of counseling*. New York: McGraw-Hill, 1972, 102.

Krause, F. H., & Hendrickson, D. E. *Counseling techniques with youth*. Columbus, Ohio: Merrill, 1972.

Lewis, E. C. *The pscyhology of counseling*. New York: Holt, Rinehart and Winston, 1970.

Patterson, C. H. *Theories of counseling and psychotherapy*. New York: Harper and Row, 1973.

Pearson, K. *The chance of death and other studies in evolution*. London: E. Arnold, 1897.

Pine, G. J., & Boy, A. V. *Learner-centered teaching: A humanistic view*. Denver: Love, 1977.

Polster, E., & Polster, M. *Gestalt therapy integrated: Contours of theory and practice*. New York: Bruner/Mazel, 1973.

Rogers, C. R. *Client-centered therapy*. Boston: Houghton Mifflin, 1951 (renewed 1979), 3–4.

Rogers, C. R. A theory of therapy, personality, and interpersonal relationships, as developed in the client-centered framework. In S. Koch (Ed.), *Psychology: A study of science*. Study I. *Conceptual and systematic*. Vol. 3. *Formulations of the person in the social context*. New York: McGraw-Hill, 1959.

Rogers, C. R. *A way of being*. Boston: Houghton Mifflin, 1980.

Shertzer, B., & Stone, S.C. *Fundamentals of counseling* (2nd ed.). Boston: Houghton Mifflin, 1974.

Stefflre, B., & Grant, W. (Eds.). *Theories of counseling* (2nd ed.). New York: McGraw-Hill, 1972.

Tolbert, E. L. *Introduction to counseling* (2nd ed.). New York: McGraw-Hill, 1972.

Turock A. Effective challenging through additive empathy. *The Personnel and Guidance Journal*, 1978, 57, 144–149.

Williamson, E. G. *Vocational counseling*. New York: McGraw-Hill, 1965.

Chapter 3

SELF-CONCEPT AND THEORY OF PERSONALITY AND BEHAVIOR

One central aspect of the client-centered view revolves around the person's self-concept and how it affects attitudes, feelings, motives, cognitions, and behaviors. Another central aspect is a theory of personality and behavior that enables the counselor to have an understanding of the causes of human behavior and serves to guide the counselor's attitude and pattern of responses in the counseling relationship. The first section of this chapter will deal with the self-concept, while the second part will be our annotated presentation of the theory of personality and behavior developed by Rogers (1951, pp. 483–524).

SELF-CONCEPT

In Pine's* review of self-concept theory (1977), she indicates that in the study of human behavior, many terms have been used to describe the phenomenon of the self. It is necessary to understand the meaning of the term *self-concept* vis-a-vis other terms related to self in order to develop a more adequate conceptual base for planning research, facilitating communication, and improving counseling practices. Perhaps the most common definition of the self-concept is that it is referent to the pronoun, "I" (Helper, 1955, pp. 184–189). However, others offer more specific definitions.

Perkins (1958, p. 226) defines the self-concept as those "perceptions, beliefs, feelings, attitudes and values which the individual views in describing himself." The individual's self-concept consists of the persisting ways the person sees the self in the life situations that one faces or might

---

*The first section of this chapter is adapted with permission, from Mary A. Pine, "Reading, Self Concept, and Informal Education," a chapter in Pine, G. J. & Boy, A. V., *Learner Centered Teaching: A Humanistic View.* Denver: Love Publishing Company, 1977.

face. McDonald (1967) suggests that the self-concept is an individual's conception of integral unity as one moves from role to role—the way one sees the self, the set of characteristics associated with the self, and the set of inferences drawn from self-observation in different situations that describe personally characteristic behavior patterns.

Most personality theorists consider the self-concept to be an important factor underlying the individual's behavior. Wylie (1961, p. 129) points out that "all the theories of personality which have been put forth within the last two decades assign importance to the phenomenal and/or nonphenomenal self-concept with cognitive and motivational attitudes."

As James (1890) pointed out many years ago, the individual has many selves. One might conceive of the self as one really believes it is, the self one aspires to be, the self one hopes exists now, and the self one fears exists now. According to Brownfrain (1952), the self-concept is a configuration of those and other possible self-definitions, and the stability of the self-concept is derived from the interrelations among these various ways of defining self. Allport (1937) says that the "proprium of personality," which is comprised of awareness of self and other activities, gives stability and consistency to evaluations, intentions, and attitudes.

Mead (1934) considers the self as an object of awareness. She states that the individual responds to the self with specific feelings and attitudes as others respond to that self. A person becomes aware through the way people react to one's self as an object. Lewin (1936) gives Mead's self a functional process of causality that is dynamically active, through what he calls the "life space." According to Lewin, the self-concept is represented by a life-space region that determines present beliefs about the self. The life space includes the individual's universe of personal experience. It is a complex internal mechanism that produces behavior. Lundholm's (1940) theory of the self is similar to Mead's, in that he believes the self is primarily an object of awareness. He makes no mention of the functional, motivational, or process dynamics of the self. The subjective self is mainly what a person comes to think about the personal self. Symonds (1951) incorporates the social philosophy of Mead. He sees the ego as a group of processes and the self as the manner in which the individual reacts to the personal self. Although the ego and self are distinct aspects of personality, there is considerable interaction between them.

Cattell (1950) conceives of the self both as an object and a process. He considers the self the principal organizing influence on the individual, giving the person stability and bringing order to personal behavior. The sentiment of self-regard is the most important influence. Cattell (1950, p. 161) states that sentiments are the "major acquired dynamic trait structures which cause their possessors to pay attention to certain objects, or class of objects, and to feel and react in a certain way with regard to them." Here he is discussing selective perception as it relates to self-concept. He also introduces the process of self-observation in describing the real self and the ideal self. Murphy (1947) expands the objectified self. He defines self as the individual as known to the individual. It is derived from a person's conceptions and perceptions of one's total being. He says that the major activities of the ego are to defend and enhance the self-concept.

Rogers (1951, p. 191) stresses the self-concept as the principal determiner of behavior. He believes in the discontinuity of the conscious and unconscious. People behave in terms of the ways in which they see themselves—a conscious activity. He allows for the probability of an unconscious, but implies that only when information about the self and the environment is "admissible to awareness" does it influence behavior: "As long as the self-Gestalt is firmly organized, and no contradictory material is even dimly perceived, then positive self-feelings may exist, the self may be seen as worthy and acceptable, and conscious tension is minimal. Behavior is consistent with the organized hypotheses and concepts of the self-structure." Rogers describes the self-concept in Wylie (1961, p. 174): "as an organized configuration of perceptions of one's characteristics and abilities; the percepts and concepts of the self in relation to others and to the environment; the value qualities which are perceived as associated with experiences and objects; the goals and ideals which are perceived as having positive or negative valence."

As interest in self-concept grew, more carefully defined and detailed thinking evolved. The work of Combs and Snygg (1959) is presently one of the clearest representations of self-concept theory. They describe the self-concept as the organization of all that the individual refers to as "I" or "me." It is the self from the self's point of view. The self-concept is not the sum of isolated concepts of self, but a patterned interrelationship of all these concepts. The self-concept has a degree of stability and consistency that gives predictability to an individual and to that individual's behavior. How a person behaves is the result of how that person perceives the situation and the personal self at the moment of action. Awareness directs behavior; how a person feels and thinks determines one's course of action.

Combs (1963, p. 470) states: "The self is composed of perceptions concerning the individual and this organization of perception in turn has vital and important effects upon the behavior of the individual."

Combs and Snygg (1959) give us a self that is both an object and a process, thereby avoiding semantic differences. The self-concept is an inference about the self. It is useful in helping us understand ourselves and it enables us to deal with a complex function that is not directly observable. The fact that it is an inference does not make it invalid. To the individual, perceptions of the self have the feeling of reality; one's self-concept seems to the person to be truly what one is.

The Relationship between Self-Concept and Behavior

Generally speaking, there are two aspects of self-concept theory that most social scientists appear to agree on:

1. An individual's self-perceptions include one's view of the self as compared to others, one's view of how others see the self, and one's view of how one wishes the self to be.
2. An individual's self-perceptions are largely based upon the experiences one has had with people who are important to the self.

A fundamental thesis of this perceptual point of view is that behavior is influenced not only by the accumulation of our past and present experiences but also by the personal meanings we attach to our perceptions of those experiences. In other words, our behavior is not only a function of what happens to us from the outside, it is also a function of how we feel on the inside.

The idea that behavior is an expression of the self-concept has been fully developed in the works of Combs and Snygg (1959), Maslow (1959), Kelley (1951), and Rogers (1951). In essence, they believe that the adequate person has an essentially positive view of self developed not only from many successful experiences but also from an inner feeling of self-worth and the ability to cope. The person of high self-concept looks on life and its challenges as an adventure. If such a person experiences failure, the experience is kept in perspective. Such a person recognizes failure in this particular instance, *but does not feel that the self is a failure.* This person continues to see the self as an able human being and confronts each new experience from this vantage point. Because this person feels the ability to cope, he or she generally does. Therefore, such a person accumulates many successes, and internal reactions to these successes support and enhance an already positive self-concept.

People who are relatively inadequate tend to view themselves quite negatively. Lacking a feeling of self-worth, they tend to perceive themselves as unliked, unwanted, and unable to cope with problems. Their tendency to focus on inadequacies causes them to lose touch with their strengths and abilities. When they encounter situations, they expect not only insurmountable difficulties but also failure. The self-fulfilling prophecy continues, each failure bringing about others, with the accompanying feelings of inadequacy, helplessness, and inferiority. The result is a further lowering of self-concept. Purkey (1970, p. 10) states:

> Perhaps the single most important assumption of modern theories about the self is that the maintenance and enhancement of the perceived self is the motive behind all behavior. Each of us constantly strives to maintain, protect, and enhance the self of which he is aware. It therefore follows that experience is perceived in its relevance to the self and that behavior is determined by these perceptions.

In a counseling relationship, the counselor must remain highly sensitive to the client's self-concept since it is the client's self-concept that influences behavior. A client typically enters counseling with a low self-concept. Such a low self-concept finds its expression in behaviors that tend to reinforce an already low self-concept. As the client progresses in counseling, the self is perceived as having more worth and this improving self-concept finds its expression in behaviors that tend to enhance an improving self-concept. In the final stages of counseling a client moves toward a positive self-concept, which expresses itself in positive behaviors that reinforce, enhance, and solidify a positive self-concept. The client's self-concept moves toward being more positively perceived in proportion to the counselor's ability to create a counseling relationship in which such movement can occur.

THEORY OF PERSONALITY AND BEHAVIOR

One of the cornerstones of client-centered counseling is the existence of a theory of personality and behavior that enables the counselor to understand the evolvement and development of those personality attributes that influence behavior. When Rogers developed a theory of personality and behavior (1951, pp. 483–524), it served to bolster interest in his evolving client-centered viewpoint. Practitioners became more attracted to client-centered counseling because the counselor's response pattern now had a *raison d'etre*. The counselor's response pattern became understandable and applicable because it was based on, and flowed from, a client-centered theory of personality and behavior.

Rogers (1951, pp. 483–524) presented his theory of personality and behavior in the form of nineteen propositions. We have annotated each of the propositions in order to furnish our perspective on their meaning.

Proposition 1: *Every individual exists in a continually changing world of which he is the center* (p. 483).

Counselors should realize that no two individuals who pass through the counseling process are ever alike and that the human personality is so complex that any diagnostic labeling of an individual is never accurate; after all, a person is a combination of many different experiences and may react to a given situation in a variety of ways. The uniqueness of the individual is such that it can be known, in any significant sense, only by the individual. That is, the causal factors that influence a person's behavior may or may not be part of that person's awareness. But if these factors are to be known, if a person's substantive essence is to be known in any meaningful way, then the person becomes the best source of perceptions about the self since he or she has been the center of an experiencing self since birth.

No amount of diagnostic labeling will accurately render the essence of an individual because, although such labels are simple and convenient symbols of a totality, they in no way express what a person is, since awareness is within the individual and cannot be rendered by the use of a convenient diagnostic word or phrase. The complexity of the person often defies the accurate categorization of that person. The categorization of individuals is subject to the variable of the observer, and observers may see different things often because of their needs rather than because their observation was fully objective. We tend to read meaning into things and situations essentially because the reading to which we subscribe is in conformity with our general needs or the needs of the moment.

Thus, the uncovering of the perceptual world of the client, if it is to be known in any real sense, must come from the client, who has been and is the center of an experiencing organism that has rejected and assimilated various experiences into the self-concept.

> Proposition 2:   *The organism reacts to the field as it is experienced and perceived. This perceptual field is, for the individual, reality* (p. 484).

Reality is often in the eyes of the beholder, and one's perception of reality is often closely related to what one *wants to perceive* in a given situation. Reality may be perceived in distinctly different ways by different clients in contact with the same reality situation. This is brought into sharp focus for the counselor when Client A describes Mr. Smith as a saint, while Client B describes the same Mr. Smith as a sinner. The logical question becomes: What is Mr. Smith in reality? Is the reality of Mr. Smith achieved by adding up the positive client reactions to Mr. Smith and then weighing these against the negative reactions? Will the majority opinion determine the reality that is Mr. Smith? Let's say that we can fully and completely know the essence of Mr. Smith, and we find him to be a most saintly individual. Could we then present this reality perception of Mr. Smith to a client who is antagonistic toward Mr. Smith and have the client assimilate this newer perception? Or will the client's perception of Mr. Smith significantly change only after the client has had the opportunity to fully examine the self-perception, and, finding it ill-founded, develop a more personally acceptant attitude toward Mr. Smith? The client's perception of reality will change only after the client has had the opportunity to examine these self-perceptions and decides that they need altering. Throughout all this, Mr. Smith may indeed be a consistently good, wholesome individual who was perceived as evil by a client's need to see reality in a self-serving manner.

> Proposition 3:   *The organism reacts as an organized whole to this phenomenal field* (p. 486).

Counselors generally tend to look upon the client as one who has many separate problems not concomitant upon each other. If a client is doing poorly at work, is constantly in conflict with peers, and is at sword's points with a parent regarding a decision, some counselors tend to see these behaviors as three separate problems with independent solutions.

Persons respond and react as total organisms. That is, the counselor who works with clients on problems that appear to be separate from each other will, perhaps, mend to a degree the client's malfunctioning. But this type of assistance affects only a fractional part of the client's functioning. Later on, the same client brings to the counselor similar kinds of problems, only within a different context.

Counselors must be sensitive to the fact that the person reacts as an organized whole, and an improvement in one remote aspect of a client's functioning has no great impact upon total functioning. Counselors must become more aware of the fact that when a client is able to exist in a counseling relationship in which the client's wholeness can respond, growth will occur in many aspects of the client's life. Therefore, instead of only dealing with the client's secondary problems, the counselor needs to create a counseling atmosphere in which the person can become involved in the process of becoming a better functioning total person. When the client becomes a better functioning total person, the secondary problems of functioning become alleviated. The client possesses a psychological strength that is capable of solving such problems. The more fully functioning person, who is self-actualized, will not only be better able to deal with current problems, but will be better able to handle future problems because of an increased belief in the strength of the self.

Proposition 4: *The organism has one basic tendency and striving—to actualize, maintain, and enhance the experiencing organism* (p. 487).

Because of the person's nature as a goal-directed human being, there are positive forces that move one toward actualizing the self. There is a general striving within the individual to transcend the self, to become a more positively functioning individual, to become more mature, to improve as a person. It is this basic human force that has resulted in the process of building a better civilization. Each generation builds upon the accomplishments of the previous one as persons collectively attempt to improve.

The counselor can look upon the person from a deterministic or fatalistic framework and see little good in human nature and little hope that the person can improve because certain forces can never be overcome. Or the counselor can view the person as involved in the process of improvement; as one who can be self-enhancing and goal-directed if one achieves the internal freedom and strength to become involved in this process.

If the counselor sees the person optimistically, sees the person as possessing the power to improve, the counselor's counseling will be more optimistic and dynamic. If the counselor sees the person as being powerless, the counselor's counseling will perhaps be one of patchwork, since the person is doomed never to overcome the forces of fate.

Proposition 5: *Behavior is basically the goal-directed attempt of the organism to satisfy its needs as experienced, in the field as perceived* (p. 491).

Behavior often is a reaction, not to objective reality, but to our perception of reality. What we perceive is often dependent upon our needs. If we didn't possess different needs, all reality would be objectively perceived in the same manner. But persons function according to personal needs and our needs influence our perception of reality.

Need fulfillment influences behavior. If the counselor ignores this issue, the counselor will become involved in the superficiality of looking at each client's behavior and judging it. The counselor must become involved in assimilating the client's needs and motives, which have influenced the client to behave in a particularly way. When the counselor is sensitive to these needs and motives and helps the client to develop an understanding of their existence and their effect upon behavior, the counselor assists the client to become more sensitive to how these needs can also influence future behavior.

Proposition 6:   *Emotion accompanies and in general facilitates such goal-directed behavior, the kind of emotion being related to the seeking versus the consummatory aspects of the behavior, and the intensity of the emotion being related to the perceived significance of the behavior for the maintenance and enhancement of the organism* (pp. 492–493).

The self can be threatened or enhanced in proportion to the emotionality one pours into a reaction. When the self is threatened and the threat is accompanied by a high degree of emotionality, the organism reacts negatively in a verbal or physical manner. This same emotionality can also work to assist one to become a more positive individual. That is, when a client feels unsatisfied with personal behavior and is emotionally committed to changing that behavior, a beneficial behavioral change occurs. Behavior changes only when the client changes.

A client who is persistently told what to do and who persistently proceeds to do just the opposite is not only insensitive to the needs that cause the behavior, but is also emotionally committed not to change. The client will change only when he or she perceives the behavior as being inappropriate and only after becoming emotionally committed to change.

Persuasion or coercion will not produce a behavior change that is significant or long term. When a client is internally motivated, emotionally and attitudinally drawn toward a behavior change, that change will occur. The counselor, then, in order to create a counseling atmosphere in which such change can occur, must be sensitive to the client's emotional or feeling level; must respond to and reflect the client's negative feelings so that the client can perceive them and their consequences; and must respond to the client's movement toward positive feelings so that the client is able to fully perceive their effect and influence.

Proposition 7:   *The best vantage point for understanding behavior is from the internal frame of reference of the individual himself* (p. 494).

Clients have often received positive or negative external evaluations that are often taken for granted as being true; but it is the client's perception of the self, the client's internal frame of reference, with which the counselor must become involved, rather than the external evaluations of the client. This self-picture taken from an internal frame of reference is the client's reality. The external frames of reference may be well intended attempts to describe a client but they are not accurate because they are not often part of the client's self-awareness.

The client-centered counselor works with the client's internal frame of reference, not only to penetrate the rationale of the client's attitudes and behavior but to present to the client a picture of the self that the client perceives and can begin to understand and accept. When the client is confronted with a self-picture that the client has structured, this picture has far more significance for the client than externally conceived pictures of the self.

Proposition 8: *A portion of the total perceptual field gradually becomes differentiated as the self* (p. 497).

A counselor who categorizes and stereotypes clients perhaps will never exhibit as much counseling ability as the counselor who is aware of the uniqueness of each person. The categorizing and stereotyping of clients may be an easy accomplishment for the counselor who has a narrow view of life. Such a counselor approaches each client with a preconception rather than an openness that will allow the counselor to discover the uniqueness, not only of the individual, but the particularized manner in which the client values and behaves. For the client in the process of identifying a personal uniqueness, it becomes imperative for the counselor to perceive this uniqueness. Unless the counselor assimilates this uniqueness, counseling will not provide the client with a feeling that the counselor has been able to sense this uniqueness. All clients are unique and desire to have that uniqueness recognized.

Proposition 9: *As a result of interaction with the environment, and particularly as a result of evaluational interaction with others, the structure of self is formed—an organized, fluid, but consistent conceptual pattern of perceptions of characteristics and relationships of the "I" or "me," together with values attached to the concepts* (p. 498).

Proposition 10: *The values attached to experiences, and the values which are part of the self-structure, in some instances are values experienced directly by the organism, and in some instances are values introjected or taken from others, but perceived in distorted fashion, as if they had been experienced directly* (p. 498).

The evaluational nature of the environment directly influences the development of the self-concept. When the environment is positive, it enables the person to develop a self-structure in which there is neither denial nor distortion of experience. In such an atmosphere the individual feels no need to protect the self, to be defensive, and can thus simply learn to develop the self and admit into awareness the positive and negative elements that comprise the self. The client who has blocked a threatening experience from awareness will be threatened by a similar experience unless the original experience is allowed into awareness and discussed.

Propositions 9 and 10 indicate that the self is formed and assimilates values only through an interactive relationship with the environment. The counselor interested in developing a facilitative counseling relationship must be nonevaluative so that the client can involve and invest the self in this free-flowing process of discovery.

> Proposition 11:   *As experiences occur in the life of the individual, they are either (a) symbolized, perceived, and organized into some relationship to the self, (b) ignored because there is no perceived relationship to the self-structure, (c) denied symbolization or given a distorted symbolization because the experience is inconsistent with the structure of the self* (p. 503).

It is difficult to allow the negative reactions of others into one's self-structure. There is a general ignoring of these negative reactions because they are perceived as being unrelated to the self. The person who is verbally threatened usually does not hear what is being said because there is an unwillingness to admit into a self-structure the threat of what is being said.

For the client to admit certain awareness into a self-structure, the client must be involved in a counseling relationship in which one can truly look at the self without the need to deny certain aspects of the self.

The client also becomes involved in giving distorted symbolization to an experience because of its inconsistency with the self-structure. Because of a sometimes natural defensiveness, and because of a negative evaluation that may be inconsistent with self, the client can either ignore or give a distorted symbolization to the experience.

The client-centered counselor reflects to the client these distorted symbolizations in order to assist the client in seeing the distortions. Many counselors take such symbolic distortions and attempt to point out to the client that they are distorted. Usually what results is that the client reinforces the distortion because of the threat presented by the counselor's attempt to point out "reality."

> Proposition 12:   *Most of the ways of behaving which are adopted by the organism are those which are consistent with the concept of self* (p. 507).

A negative self-concept produces behavior that is a reflection of that negative self-concept. When a person perceives the self as being depressed, then the person will engage in depressing behaviors that reinforce this self-picture. When a person perceives the self as being optimistic, then he or she will engage in optimistic behaviors that tend to enhance this self-picture.

We tend to behave as we perceive ourselves. Our behaviors reflect what we think of ourselves and how we evaluate ourselves. Our self-pictures tend to get played out as we interact with others and our environment. Our behaviors become a "self-fulfilling prophecy."

Client-centered counselors have an empathic understanding of the client's self-concept because of the realization that the client's self-concept will influence behavior. Client-centered counselors have faith in, and have observed, the client's ability to move from a negative to a positive self-concept. They know that when this movement occurs the client's behavior will become more positive as an outcome of a more positive self-concept.

Proposition 13: *Behavior may, in some instances, be brought about by organic experiences and needs which have not been symbolized. Such behavior may be inconsistent with the structure of the self, but in such instances the behavior is not "owned" by the individual* (p. 509).

Because the client is human, even the well counseled person will continue to have moments of distress, weakness, and uncertainty. The difference between a client's pre- and post-counseling behavior is that before counseling the client was not able to deal with certain aspects of the self. The terminated client is better able to cope with life because of a more positive self-structure that influences behavior. The person is subject to the frailties of being human, and as a human being the person sometimes has trouble managing the behavior that comes from the complexity of being human. Eventually, however, the person begins to accept such behaviors as being part of one's existence, but they are not usually assimilated into the person's self-concept. They exist but there is no ownership.

Proposition 14: *Psychological maladjustment exists when the organism denies to awareness significant sensory and visceral experiences, which consequently are not symbolized and organized into the gestalt of the self-structure. When this situation exists, there is a basic or potential psychological tension* (p. 510).

The person is often confronted with experiences and frames of reference which, because of their threatening nature, are not allowed admission into the self-picture. The person who feels good and honorable will reject the frames of reference that indicate that he or she is bad and untrustworthy. But if these exterior frames of reference have some quality of truth, or if they are close to the interior self-picture, this is when the person may seek out counseling assistance. When the environmental viewpoints of the person are clearly rejected by the person, the self-structure remains intact. When those exterior frames of reference penetrate the self, the person must have an opportunity to evaluate these experiences, through counseling, before he or she can clearly reject or assimilate them.

When a client rejects external perceptions of the self, group counseling may be one of the most significant experiences for the client. That is, if Mary's behavior has been characterized as extreme by others and she has denied this perception into awareness, she would be more willing to accept it when it comes from a peer within the context of group counseling. Mary can assimilate or reject this perception into her self-concept, but the chances are that she will be less defensive with a peer within the context of group counseling.

> Proposition 15:   *Psychological adjustment exists when the concept of self is such that all the sensory and visceral experiences of the organism are, or may be, assimilated on a symbolic level into a consistent relationship with the concept of self* (p. 513).

A self-protective attitude prevents the client from being open when evaluating the self. The self must be free enough to allow experiences to be assimilated. That is, the person must be psychologically free enough to absorb a day's experiences, and judge why certain experiences have been denied awareness and why such denial is necessary.

In a freeing atmosphere with an empathic counselor, the client is able to consider experiences and their personal meaning. There is an openness to explore one's experiences because it is only through such an exploration that the client is able to develop a relationship between those experiences and the self.

Counseling should be a process in which the client can honestly confront the self, instead of being selective and considering only those experiences that are self-protecting. When counselors attempt to control the client's self-expression by suggesting that only certain experiences be discussed, they influence the client to deal only with a designated and limited range of experiences.

In client-centered counseling, the client is free to communicate and open the self to the widest range of feelings, attitudes, and reactions. The client is able to give meaning to experiences instead of denying their occurrence, and is able to freely discuss a threatening relationship and the degree to which the experience is congruent with the self, instead of repressing the experience and finding that later such a repression is a contributor to personal malfunctioning.

> Proposition 16:   *Any experience which is inconsistent with the organization of the self-structure may be perceived as a threat, and the more of these perceptions there are, the more rigidly the self-structure is organized to maintain self* (p. 515).

The least threatening of all human services workers should be the counselor. The counselor must become involved in creating a counseling relationship in which the client feels that, because of a lack of counselor threat, the client is able to relax defenses and begin to discuss those aspects of behavior that have not been accepted by an environment. If the counselor poses more threat to such a client, the client's usual reaction is to become more rigid in order to protect the self.

The more pressure an organization places upon a client to meet the organization's rules and regulations, the more rigid that client becomes in noncompliance. Certainly, in order for society to function, it must function within a framework of reasonable orderliness, but when in the name of orderliness an organization insists on coercing clients, that organization must be willing to accept an increasing level of client discontent. The more threats to self imposed by an organization, the more that organization moves away from a helping concept in which the dignity and worth of the individual is respected.

The counselor who works with an organization that insists on dehumanizing the person, is obligated to do more than work with clients in counseling relationships. The counselor must also be involved in a consultative role with the organization in an effort to improve the organization's human climate and identify those aspects of the organization that are detrimental to the psychological well-being of the individual client. Impositions upon human dignity that are threatening to the selfhood of the individual require the counselor's involvement with both the client and the organizational context in which such threats are conceived and executed. Human services organizations must become places in which the ideals of democratic living are fully expressed in the attitudes of staff members.

Proposition 17: *Under certain conditions, involving primarily complete absence of any threat to the self-structure, experiences which are inconsistent with it may be perceived and examined, and the structure of self revised to assimilate and include such experiences* (p. 517).

In a nonthreatening counseling relationship, the client can begin to look at those experiences that previously were not explored because they posed a threat to the self. Instead of defending the self, the client gradually begins to investigate the degree to which he or she has contributed to the development of a problem. The client begins to acknowledge those aspects of behavior that were self-protective rather than self-enhancing. The client begins to assume responsibility for the consequences of one's behavior.

The typical client enters counseling defensively and sees the cause of personal malfunctioning as totally the fault of an environment. The client generally feels that the environment is insensitive to him or her as a person. As the client examines personal behavior, the client begins to develop a balance between the self and that environment. An increasing awareness occurs of the reciprocal relationship between the self and the environment. The client doesn't suddenly absolve someone else of all responsibility in an antagonistic relationship, instead he or she begins to examine the viewpoints of others and becomes more responsive to their meanings. The client communicates deeply about those experiences that previously were blocked out of awareness because they posed a threat to self.

The freer the client is from threat, the more the client is willing to discuss self-defeating behavior. The client begins to soften hardened attitudes because the counselor has created a receptive and nonjudgmental counseling relationship. Clients become unwilling to explore their behavior when the counselor finds it necessary to place a value judgment upon the merits of that behavior. The client who has difficulty expressing the dark sides of personal behavior usually does so because of the felt threat of the counselor's judgmental reaction.

Proposition 18: *When the individual perceives and accepts into one consistent and integrated system all his sensory and visceral experiences, then he is necessarily more understanding of others and is more understanding of others as separate individuals* (p. 520).

The acceptance of others begins with the acceptance of self. The well-functioning self first accepts the self and then extends beyond the self. It seeks to be in communication with others. It desires to heal rather than to remain dysfunctional; but the process of reaching beyond one's self begins with the self.

The client who achieves self-acceptance becomes involved with life. He or she begins to seek out communication with persons in the environment from whom isolation was previously sought. The client reaches beyond the self rather than building a protective wall around the self. The client's outreach behaviors are more comfortable because there is no need to be superficial or defensive. An emerging trust in others develops because the client senses a similar emergence coming from within.

The extension of self-acceptance into an acceptance of others appears to be a natural thrust of the human organism. At the beginning of a counseling relationship, the typical client sees little beyond the self and usually engages in self-serving statements while diminishing others. As the client begins to see the extent to which the self has contributed to a problem, there emerges a sensitivity to others—how *they* feel, how *they* respond. These persons become accepted as separate individuals whose reactions to the client can change because the client has changed. The counselor hears reports from clients that relationships that were previously filled with conflict have become more normal. Because of the client's more accepting attitude toward others, a reciprocal attitude of acceptance emerges from the environment. The well counseled client can affect both the self and the environment. Such a client no longer sees personal behavior determined by an environment but develops an understanding that one's positive behavior can influence an environment and the persons in that environment.

Proposition 19: *As the individual perceives and accepts into his self-structure more of his organic experiences, he finds that he is replacing his present value system—based so largely upon introjections which have been distortedly symbolized—with a continuing organismic valuing process* (p. 522).

Some organizations are involved in promoting certain values, the rationale being that if clients are exposed to certain values they will then assimilate these values as their own. Certainly organizations have a right to present values, but these values having personal meaning are those that are self-determined. The values of an organization are meaningless to a client because, although there may be a generalized and socialized acceptance of these values, they have not been internalized by the client—they have not emerged from within.

Some staff members do not encourage the emergence of personalized values among clients because of a fear that the emergence of individualized values among clients may eventually lead to anarchy. Such staff members are insensitive to the fact that a free person moves toward values designed to enhance both the self and others rather than toward values that are destructive to the self and to others. The person desires to enhance a personal existence but the person also recognizes a responsibility toward others. As Rogers (1951, p. 524) has stated: "Since all individuals have basically the same needs, including the need for acceptance by others, it appears that when each individual formulates his own values, in terms of his own direct experience, it is not anarchy which results, but a high degree of commonality and a genuinely socialized system of values."

External values have little meaning to the client unless these values have been personally absorbed because of their relevance to the client. The counselor who suggests appropriate behavioral values to clients may do so to avoid the repercussion of not being a perpetuator of an organization's values. But if the counselor makes a thoughtful investigation of how personally significant values emerge in individuals, the counselor discovers that they emerge from within rather than being infused by an external source.

Values that emerge from within affect behavior. The client who values peer acceptance will involve the self in behavior designed to gain that peer acceptance. When such a client becomes involved in processing personal values, the client has a natural inclination to move toward values that provide a balance between the self and one's society.

Rogers (1980, p. 134) indicates that although persons in a nurturing climate of human interaction are free to chose any values and behaviors, they actualize themselves through values and behaviors that are positive and constructive.

REFERENCES

Allport, G. W. *Personality: A psychological interpretation.* New York: Holt, Rinehart and Winston, 1937.

Brownfrain, J. Stability of the self concept as a dimension of personality. *Journal of Abnormal and Social Psychology,* 1952, *48,* 594–597.

Cattell, R. B. *Personality: A systematic, theoretical, and factual study.* New York: McGraw-Hill, 1950, 161.

Combs, A. W. Syngg and Combs' phenomenal self. In C. Hall, & G. Lindzey (Eds.), *Theories of personality.* New York: John Wiley and Sons, 1963, 470.

Combs, A. W., & Snygg, D. *Individual behavior: A perceptual approach to behavior* (2nd ed.). New York: Harper and Row, 1959.

Helper, M. Learning theory and the self concept. *Journal of Abnormal and Social Psychology,* 1955, *51,* 184–189.

James, W. *Principles of psychology.* New York: Holt, Rinehart and Winston, 1890.

Kelley, E. C. *Education for what is real.* New York: Harper and Brothers, 1951.

Lewin, K. *Principles of topological psychology.* New York: McGraw-Hill, 1936.

Lewin, K., et al. Level of aspiration. In J. M. Hunt (Ed.), *Personality and behavior disorders.* New York: Ronald Press, 1944.

Lundholm, H. Reflections on the nature of the psychological self. *Psychological Review,* 1940, *47,* 110–127.

Maslow, A. H. *Motivation and personality.* New York: Harper and Row, 1959.

McDonald, F. *Educational psychology.* Belmont, Calif.: Wadsworth Publishing, 1967.

Mead, G. H. *Mind, self, and society.* Chicago: University of Chicago Press, 1934.

Murphy, G. *Personality: A biosocial approach to origins and structure.* New York: Harper and Row, 1947.

Perkins, H. Factors influencing change in children's self concepts. *Childhood Development,* 1958, *29,* 226.

Pine, M. A. In G. J. Pine, & A. V. Boy, *Learner-centered teaching: A humanistic view.* Denver: Love Publishing, 1977, 143–148.

Purkey, W. W. *Self concept and school achievement.* Englewood Cliffs, N.J.: Prentice-Hall, 1970, 10.

Rogers, C. R. *Client-centered therapy.* Boston: Houghton Mifflin, 1951 (renewed 1979).

Rogers, C. R. *A way of being.* Boston: Houghton Mifflin, 1980.

Symbonds, P. M. *The ego and the self.* New York: Appleton-Century-Crofts, 1951.

Wylie, R. *The self concept.* Lincoln: University of Nebraska Press, 1961, 129, 174.

Chapter 4

VALUES IN COUNSELING

Humanity's search for appropriate values has always characterized civilization. If humanity were not searching for more meaningful values, progress would have been halted in the Stone Age. But people have always been compelled to ponder personal existence and to discover values that would better sustain the self. Humanity valued communication, so the prehistoric person began to scrawl upon the walls of caves and give meaning to the grunts that previously had characterized communication. Persons have historically sought out values that would enable them to enhance and enrich their existence (Boy & Pine, 1968, p. 21).

Mowrer (1964) indicates that a person develops a meaningful existence only when a commitment is made to values and morals, and that a society that ignores the existence of certain moral values will find itself victimized by a relativism that grants free license and makes moral *all* of behavior regardless of its effect upon others.

Allport (1968, p. 162) indicates the importance of values in our lives when he says:

Deep in our hearts we know, and most of the world knows, that our national values derived, of course, from Judeo-Christian ethics, are about the finest mankind has yet formulated. In no sense are these values out of date, nor will they go out of date in the world tomorrow. Yet many of them are badly rusted. Unless they are revitalized, however, our youth (indeed, humankind) may not have the personal fortitude and moral implements that the future will require.

There has generally been an aversion to the question of values on the basis that a counselor is on morally questionable ground when attempting to impose values on others. On this point there is little disagreement. But an avoidance of the issue of values has led some to assume that the counselor should not possess values. This is a highly questionable position since the mere fact of a counselor's existence indicates that the counselor values life over death. The counselor values food as he or she eats to sustain life. The counselor values the counseling relationship by virtue of the fact that he or she engages in counseling. The counselor values physical health when he or she makes an appointment with a physician. And, hopefully, the counselor values professional competence, the rights of the client, and ethical behavior.

Because of the fear that counselors would impose their values on others, the professional literature has not addressed itself adequately to the question of values on the basis that they are so highly relative that they cannot be discussed, let alone agreed upon. Yet, if one examines the characteristics of competent counselors, one would find a commonality of values undergirding their functioning. It this were not true, we could never hope to discover the common traits that characterize the effective counselor. As Arbuckel (1975, p. 302) has said, "I would assume that there would be certain values which would be part of an effective counselor while others would reflect an ineffective counselor." Any writing that presents the qualities of an effective counselor and an efficient counseling service is essentially a reflection of the values of the author, although there is a general aversion to the use of the word *values*. Even those who hold that values are illusory are expressing a value when they reject the existence of values!

Corey (1977, p. 222) points out that counselors have sometimes been influenced to avoid the issue of values in counseling:

> Therapists are sometimes taught that they should remain value neutral, that they should avoid passing value judgments on to their clients, and that they should keep their own values and philosophies of life separate from the therapeutic relationship. I maintain that we cannot exclude our values and beliefs from the relationships we establish with clients, unless we do routine and mechanical counseling.

Okun (1976, p. 183) reaffirms the preceding viewpoint when she indicates that:

> The traditional models of helping maintained that if helping relationships were objective, distant, and neutral, the helper's values would not contaminate the relationship. However, in recent years, we have recognized that in any interpersonal relationship, whether or not it is a helping relationship, values are transmitted either covertly or overtly between the participants.

The recognition of the importance of values in the counseling relationship has become more established in recent years:

> Values act as motivational forces, Values provide standards that do not momentarily arise in any given situation but offer direction in a variety of circumstances (Peterson, 1970, p. 53).

> Values clarification is a part of helping relationships in that the helper and helpee both take responsibility for their attitudes, beliefs, and values (Okun, 1976, p. 14).

The life of each individual reflects values. Counselors and clients demonstrate in action the quality and quantity of their values. The decisions each person makes, the activities of his or her life, and the goals which are established are reflections of values (Hansen et al., 1977, p. 514).

Smith and Peterson (1977) indicate that all members of the helping profession deal with value issues as they assist clients. They see values clarification as a crucial challenge to counselors that must be met if the profession is to develop a unified sense of mission.

Within the client there exists an array of values that influence the way the client acts and reacts in any given situation. These values often have their roots in a self-concept since a person's values are highly dependent upon how the person views the self. Values are a highly relevant key to the counselor who is attempting to understand a client's self-structure, since they are a reflection of the client's essence as a person. What clients say are often expressions of values emanating from a self-concept. Therefore, as the counselor responds to the client, the counselor is responding to an interwoven pattern of self and values. A sensitivity to the client's values will enable the counselor to become more closely attuned to the client's behavioral motives. The counselor cannot avoid coming to grips with personal values and those of clients, how these values affect each of them, and how values interact as the client and counselor become involved in a relationship.

Different and contradictory values are often in competition with each other within a client. It is when these contradictory values collide that the client often seeks out the assistance of a counselor. The client seeks to reinforce some values and eliminate others. The client desires to achieve an inner peace that will enable the client to formulate plans that will positively influence his or her behavior (Tolbert, 1974).

Values emanate from a knowledge of ourselves, and since persons are continually involved in the process of becoming, they are constantly reaching toward more meaningful values. If this were not true, societies would not develop, persons would not reach for more cohesion in their existence, and the counseling process would not be a consciousness expanding experience. The counselor's role has developed more professional meaning because, as counselors began to perceive themselves and their function, they became determined to move toward values that were professionally more appropriate and more beneficial to clients.

The existence of more relevant values has not only led to the emergence of a more professional role for the counselor, but to a closer examination of the influence of these values upon the client-counselor relationship, as well. A counselor's values will determine the extent to which the counselor attempts to control the direction and content of the counseling relationship.

THE SEARCH FOR VALUES

It is in the person's search for values that the person expands self-awareness. It is a search in which entire nations are involved when their representatives sit to discuss issues of peaceful coexistence. It is the undergirding factor when theologians meet to ponder civilization's moral behavior. It is the influencing dimension whenever any person meets with another in efforts to bring meaning to life. It is the inner struggle engaged in by clients when they become involved in a counseling relationship. It is a search engaged in by the sensitive counselor who is attempting to understand the self and how the counselor relates to clients. It is humanity's eternal struggle, the process whereby a person attempts to bring greater significance and meaning to the person's existence. To avoid the issue of values is to lead a hollow existence in which one's functioning doesn't really matter, since the person is predestined by fate to be cast in a role that cannot be enhanced or improved. The adoption of such a fatalistic view would leave the person immobile, unable to grow, develop, and improve personal existence. But the person, by nature, is searching for values. To exist is to be involved in this process. It is unavoidable, since the person inherently moves the self toward creating a more meaningful existence based upon the influence of a more appropriate set of values. A few years ago, Rogers (1964, p. 100) made this observation about humanity's search for values. This observation is still relevant today:

> There is a great deal of concern today with the problem of values. Youth, in almost every country, is deeply uncertain of its value orientation; the values associated with various religions have lost much of their influence; sophisticated individuals in every culture seem unsure and troubled as to the goals they hold in esteem. The reasons are not far to seek. The world culture, in all its aspects, seems increasingly scientific and relativistic, and the rigid, absolute views on values which come to us from the past appear anachronistic. Even more important, perhaps, is the fact that the modern individual is assailed from every angle by divergent and contradictory value claims. It is no longer possible, as it was in the not too distant historical past, to settle comfortably into the value system of one's forebears or one's community and live out one's life without ever examining the nature and the assumptions of that system.

It is the client's searching and processing of values that characterizes the client's involvement in counseling. The process of counseling essentially involves the client's search for the true self. As the client becomes involved in this search, he or she comes to grips with the values that have been assimilated and that influence behavior. The client processes these values into a hierarchy of importance that influence behavior (Wrenn, 1973).

As Curran (1976, p. 79) has said: "When people change in counseling and psychotherapy it appears to be not simply because someone has educated them, but because they have come to what is often a rediscovery of basic values."

When involved in counseling, the client is essentially engaged in talking about values that influence personal behavior. When the discovery is made that certain values are personally discomforting, the client is then in a position to reject them and move toward values that are personally more appropriate and enable the client to exist with less inner turmoil and with greater personal satisfaction.

If the client is to move toward more self-sustaining values, the client must first come to grips with those values that interfere with personal functioning. This is the process of self-discovery in counseling, the process whereby troublesome values are replaced by values that are more self-enriching and enable the client to relate to the environment with a higher degree of personal satisfaction.

Counseling, then, is a relationship in which the counselor provides the client with a communicating atmosphere that gives the client the opportunity to become involved in the discovering, processing, and synthesizing of values.

In the counseling profession, it is important that we identify values that will enable the counselor to counsel more effectively. There are overlapping values held in common by counselors who provide clients with effective counseling relationships. These are the values we are obligated to identify and discuss in the hope that we can bring a commonness of purpose to counseling and make it more effective. This is not to say that counselors must lose their individuality by developing a rigid set of values with which all must agree. It does indicate that we must become involved in identifying those values toward which we tend, individually and as a profession.

ATTITUDINAL VALUES

There is certainly agreement that each of us has a personal value system that influences our behavior. One has only to summarize one's behavior for today, and that person can determine the extent to which actions and reactions were based upon the influence of personal values.

As the individual is involved in various kinds of behavior, that behavior has a high degree of similarity to the behavior of other persons, and, in turn, that similarity in behavior is largely due to a convergence of values among groups of civilized persons. Granted that there are divergencies in values among some, but the existence of these divergent values is not alarming, since humanity is still, and will continue to be, involved in the process of value development. The fact that there are divergencies in values among some doesn't eliminate a commonality of values among many.

Values are part of a functioning counselor and developing a sensitivity to their existence and how they influence behavior is a necessary investigation for the counselor who desires to bring a greater meaning and awareness to the different dimensions of the counseling relationship. Such an investigation will not only enable the counselor to develop a greater awareness and understanding of the values that influence behavior among clients, it will also enable the counselor to develop a keener sensitivity to how the counselor's personal values can either help or hinder the behavioral development of clients.

Among client-centered counselors, there has been a movement away from value neutrality and a recognition that counselors must become more explicit regarding their values. Hart and Tomlinson (1970, p. 565) indicate this when they state that: "Within client-centered therapy, too, there has been a move away from insisting on a neutral value stand for the therapist toward an explicit recognition of the value commitments therapists must make."

General Attitudinal Values

The counselor who intends to be of service to clients, must value their integral worth as persons (Boy & Pine, 1968, p. 26). When a counselor values power, personal recognition, or a superiority over others, the counselor has difficulty in valuing anything beyond the self. The counselor must value others and their existence; value those qualities that comprise the human personality; value the basic goodness of others and the factors that make behavioral improvement difficult; and must sense in others attributes and tendencies that ennoble the person and make human life the highest form of existence.

When the counselor values others, the counselor will move toward developing a sensitivity to the problems of living and will develop an empathic quality toward others. Because the counselor cares, the counselor places the self in relationships that will enhance clients and not block their development. The counselor helps clients to become more aware of the self by providing a relationship in which the client can explore the self. Because the counselor values clients, he or she doesn't retreat behind defenses but is open to the self and how it affects client openness.

Without counselor respect for the dignity, worth, and integrity of the individual, the counselor can never hope to communicate at an empathic level. The counselor must welcome opportunities to assist others and provide clients with the therapeutic benefits of a truly warm and caring attitude.

Previously, the counselor was far more concerned with case histories, profiles, inventories, neat files, and jargon than with the client's struggle for identity. Today's counselors are beginning to move toward a greater valuing of persons and the quality of their existence.

The counselor who values the client has a fundamental respect for the client's freedom to know, shape, and determine personal attitudes and behavior. Clients have a human tendency to develop themselves toward a more self-enhancing existence (Boy & Pine, 1968, p. 28). If clients did not possess this quality, they would never have the capacity to overcome problems. Clients inherently visualize attitudes and behaviors that are more personally satisfying. Clients cannot eliminate this tendency, no matter how deep their discouragement or despair. When a client is pushed into the shadows of an emotional problem, the tendency is to move toward sunlight, toward a life that is more enriched and personally satisfying.

The human inclination is to project the self toward this more satisfying existence. The counselor who is pessimistic about the forward thrust of attitudes and behavior will have difficulty in being involved in a counseling relationship that respects this tendency and movement. This pessimistic attitude will foster counseling relationships in which the counselor feels a compulsion to control the client rather than trust the client's ability for self control and development. The creation of a liberating counseling relationship requires that the counselor not only have a fundamental belief in the client's tendency toward health, but that the counselor create a counseling atmosphere in which this tendency is nourished (Arbuckle, 1975; Rogers & Stevens, 1975).

A person's free functioning not only tends toward a development of the self; it also includes one's responsibility to other persons (Boy & Pine, 1968, p. 30). A person's social consciousness enhances personal existence and gives it a deeper meaning because the person defines existence, not just in terms of the self, but in relation to others (Glasser, 1965). At the beginning of a counseling experience, the client often thinks and talks, first and foremost, about the self. The client is usually only sensitive to a selfish view of meanings and is not typically aware of how the client's behavior affects others. As the client becomes more open and receptive to the self there is a lessening of self-referent statements and an increased receptivity to the social obligations of one's existence. The client becomes more acceptant of other persons, attempting to understand their perceptions, attitudes, and behavior. This does not mean that the client gives up individuality; the client certainly remains highly sensitive to the importance of individuality. But the client also goes beyond the self and develops a social consciousness; internalizing the concept that inner values, if they are to be personally appropriate, cannot be imposed upon others but must be in harmony with the well being of others (Glasser, 1972). There is a high degree of difference between doctrinaire individualism and socially conscious individuality. The healthy person tends toward an individuality that is sensitive to others and their individual rights; there is a valuing of the self but, because of a conjoined awareness, others are also valued.

Rogers (1964, p. 160) states that when a person chooses personally appropriate values it is characteristic for the human organism to move also toward socialized goals that acknowledge the well-being of others:

> I find it significant that when individuals are prized as persons, the values they select do not run the full gamut of possibilities. I do not find, in such a climate of freedom, that one person comes to value fraud and murder and thievery, while another values a life of self-sacrifice, and another values only money. Instead, there seems to be a deep and underlying thread of commonality. I believe that when the human being is inwardly free to choose whatever he deeply values, he tends to value those objects, experiences, and goals which make for his own survival, growth, and development, and for the survival and development of others. I hypothesize that it is *characteristic* of the

human organism to prefer such actualizing and socialized goals when he is exposed to a growth promoting climate.

Rogers (1964, p. 160) concludes with:

The psychologically mature person as I have described him has, I believe, the qualities which would cause him to value those experiences which would make for the survival and enhancement of the human race. He would be a worthy participant and guide in the process of human evolution.

Barnes (1962, pp. 182–183) indicates that before a person can come to respect and value the uniqueness of others, the person must first be self valuing:

Ultimately, of course, the meaningful life is one which includes others. Existentialists have written much about the *Mitsein* or being-with-others. But I think one must begin with the solitary individual. In any case, one will not get far with an unhappy client by pointing out to him his duty to think of others or by telling him he ought to feel a sentimental glow when reflecting on his close relationship with them. A person is not capable of thinking with or for other people until he has learned to value himself. Once he knows how to choose for himself the kind of life he can honestly feel to be significant, then he is free to realize the importance of the other person's uniqueness and to find that a wholly different way of life may be profoundly interesting to him without threatening him.

The counselor values genuineness; the counselor's genuine attitude is so deeply a part of the counselor that it can be sensed and responded to by those with whom the counselor has contact. It is the genuineness of the counselor that is often the difference between effective and ineffective counseling (Boy & Pine, 1968, p. 32). Clients react to counselor genuineness by communicating freely and openly. Genuineness can be sensed just as surely as one senses sunlight. Because of the counselor's genuineness the client is able to communicate with ease; the client is able to delve into various aspects of personal functioning because the client feels that the counselor is authentic in caring for the client as a person (Egan, 1975; Eysenck, 1972).

Counselor genuineness in the counseling process enables clients to feel that they can be themselves; that they can involve themselves in a relationship that is characterized by a free exploration of why one acts and reacts in a particular way.

Specific Attitudinal Values

The client possesses free will—he or she can be the determiner of a personal destiny. At the beginning of a counseling relationship, clients center on other persons and situations as the causes of their problems. The tendency to blame other persons or situations is certainly natural because when the cause of a problem can be projected toward someone else, the client can then escape the responsibility for personal behavior. Such clients begin counseling with statements like, "I can never change because my wife won't allow me the freedom to change"; "The antiquated attitudes of society do not allow me personal freedom"; "I'll never feel comfortable unless my neighbor stops harassing me"; and "My mother won't allow me to grow up."

Counseling should be aimed at enabling the client to assume the responsibility for behavior, to come to the realization that although other persons and situations make some contribution to the existence of a problem, the resolution of the problem occurs when the client senses that he or she possesses the free will to change personal behavior—to manage one's destiny, to control one's life and behavior—rather than relying upon the comfortable crutch of blaming other persons or situations (deChardin, 1959; Frankl, 1970; Tillich, 1952; Van Kaam, 1966).

The client must arrive at this realization on his or her own terms. The counselor can't convince the client that the client possesses personal freedom. The client comes to this realization by existing in a counseling relationship that contributes to the realization that one does possess free will. Persons intellectually realize personal freedom by affectively experiencing the emergence and functioning of their free will within the affective context of counseling.

The client possesses an individual conscience and sense of morality that guides personal behavior. Some counselors insist on guiding the client because the client might falter, make inappropriate personal decisions, and generally increase the severity of a problem. Some counselors have a basic distrust of the client's sense of conscience and morality. Such counselors tend to prod their clients toward responsible behavior. They point out the inappropriateness of certain behavior, indicate the consequences of norm-violating behavior, or even dictate to the client the size and shape of one's conscience and sense of morality. What the counselor is saying to the client, explicitly or implicitly, is, "I don't trust your conscience to bring you to a truly moral decision."

The counselor creates a relationship with the client in which the client may explore a personal conscience and sense of morality (Mowrer, 1964). If the client is encouraged to encounter the self, to communicate openly about the rationale that undergirds personal behavior, the client can begin to sense the existence of a personal conscience and the degree to which it affects the morality of the client's behavior. Morality is the relation of behavior to one's values. We see human nature as essentially tending toward being loving and cooperative. We see moral values as values that flow from this nature and guide behavior—behavior that facilitates and enhances human development. If the client exists in a consciousness expanding relationship with a counselor, the client will move toward more selfless, and hence more moral, behavior. A moral person is moral simply because the person has transcended neurotic selfish needs and reflects this tendency by being selfless in behavior. Clients can become more selfless, more loving and cooperative, and hence more moral, in proportion to the degree to which the counselor is selfless, loving, and facilitating (Branden, 1971).

The client enhances the self by fulfilling obligations to the self and to others. Personal integrity, in relationship to self and others, is not easily attained. There are always easier ways of doing things that will not place a heavy responsibility upon the self. The client often finds it easier to avoid doing something about a personal problem since an active involvement in its resolution would mean that the client would have to change. The counselor finds it easier to tell the client what to do since such behavior seems more expedient than assisting the client to grapple with the time-consuming and burdensome elements of self-responsibility.

Both clients and counselors often find it easier to avoid the self rather than confront the self. Such an avoidance often leads to an erosion of a sense of personal integrity and responsibility. Both the client and counselor, in their relationships both inside and outside of counseling, can avoid a sense of obligation to self and to other persons, but it is this type of attitude that leads the client and counselor toward behavior that is neither personally sustaining nor objectively helpful.

The counselor fulfills the obligation to love and assist others by the very quality of the counseling relationship. The counselor's personal obligation is to make a difference in the life of the client, to transform a caring attitude into behaviors and responses that will enable the client to feel accepted, understood, and valued as a person. When existing in a qualitative counseling relationship, the client begins to assume an ever-increasing responsibility for personal behavior and the impact of that behavior upon persons in his or her life (Rogers, 1970).

Counseling relationships are not unselfish events—they are encounters that enhance the self of the giver, the self of the receiver, and the quality of the environment in which the giver and receiver live. In counseling, the selfish and unselfish fuse. The person helping another is helping the self.

The client evolves toward others in a sense of personal responsibility and ethical behavior. When the person, as either a client or as a counselor, is ego-centric we can expect a no-growth relationship for both the client and the counselor. In effective counseling, the client moves away from values that center exclusively on the self and moves toward values that include the self in relationship with others (May, 1969). Instead of merely saying, "This is good for me," the client begins to say, "This is good for me in my relationship with other people—there is a balance between what I want and what others want." The client who is beginning to resolve personal problems will begin to see the consequences of personal behavior beyond the self; he or she moves from behavioral needs that merely enhance the self toward behavioral needs that enhance both the self and others.

The counselor's sense of responsibility evolves in much the same manner. Instead of engaging in counseling behavior that merely makes the counselor feel comfortable in counseling, the counselor moves toward counseling behavior that will be therapeutically helpful to the client. Such a counselor possesses a sense of responsibility that goes beyond idiosyncratic needs. The counselor exists for the emergence of the client and translates this attitude into a relationship that is beneficial for the client, rather than just satisfying the counselor's needs. The counselor who exists for the client will more easily resolve issues of personal responsibility and ethical behavior.

Responsible personal action occurs within the context of a respect for the dignity and worth of others. When the client begins to respect the dignity and worth of others, the client moves toward interpersonal behavior that enhances and expands the self. When the mother expresses her respect for the dignity and worth of her adolescent daughter, it is within the context of such respect that the mother moves toward responsible personal action in her relationship with her daughter. When the adolescent daughter expresses her respect for the dignity and worth of her mother, she too becomes engaged in personally responsible behavior toward her mother. When either the mother or daughter loses a sense of the dignity and worth of the other, then a gap in their relationship becomes a chasm.

Counselors can also become so hardened to dealing with persons who possess problems that they lose their sense of respect for their dignity and worth as persons. Clients, instead of being treated as honorable persons, become objects, and when a client becomes, consciously or unconsciously, an object, the counselor's sense of responsibility to that client is diminished. When this sense of responsibility is diminished, then there is a decrease in the effectiveness of the counseling relationship. Counselors who possess respect for the dignity and worth of persons translate that respect into counseling relationships in which the client feels fully prized, accepted, and understood. The client experiences nonpossessive love, which prompts the client to value the self and move toward more appropriate behavior (Frankl, 1963).

Love and peace are basic strivings and must be advanced during one's lifetime. Love and peace are abstract terms that are given lip service by various segments of our culture and this, in itself, is to be valued since we are at least beginning to talk about the meaning and behavioral translation of such terms. The client who has experienced a successful counseling relationship is essentially a more loving person who attempts to bring to personal behavior, and the relationships with others, an increase in the personal expression of peace and love. This person senses the degree to which love is proportionately related to a personal and psychological well being and attempts to be more loving and acceptant in relationships with others (Fromm, 1956; Hammarskjold, 1969).

For the counselor, these same strivings are expressed in the quality of his or her relationships with clients. The counselor's counseling should be a representation of how people should behave toward other people. The counselor's attitude toward clients should be the embodiment of the characteristics of a person of love and peace. The counselor should conceive counseling as a contribution to the human evolvement. Humanity's journey toward the values of love and peace is a long one but the counselor must possess a sense of urgency in helping persons move closer to these values during the counselor's lifetime.

The client transcends the self by moving toward a good beyond the self. The person realizes the *raison d'etre* of life when the person moves from self-centered values and behaviors toward those that enrich the lives of others. The psychologically incapacitated person thinks and lives just in terms of the self; the psychologically whole person generates personal behavior toward the well being and emergence of others. The good beyond the self can be an abstract concept, but the very existence of other people enables the person to translate an abstraction into concrete behavior that contributes to the well being of others.

For the client the good beyond the self may be relatively simple, but the awareness of a good beyond the self is the energizing force that begins to move that client from selfish to more selfless behavior. To be aware of others, to be sensitive to their needs and interests, to be compassionate, to be willing to relate affectively, and to empathize with the human condition; all of these serve as evidences that the person deflates one's ego needs and moves toward a good, an attitude, that embraces others. If we look life squarely in the eye, we don't just see ourselves. We see ourselves in relationships with others; we see our lives linked to the lives of others; we see our behavior as it affects others.

The client who transcends the self moves toward a good, a goal, in which the self enriches and expands the lives of others. The counselor who transcends the self moves toward the very same good. The person will engage in more psychologically mature behavior when there is a greater convergence among the goals of currently divergent people. At this moment in history, the person's *selfless* caring for others may be appropriate not only for clients and counselors, but for all of humanity.

The client is not determined by forces external to the self—at all times the client possesses the capacity to choose freely. Counseling is an open relationship in which the client is free to move in any direction. This demands enormous faith and consistency on the part of the counselor—faith in the client's capacity to choose and consistency in holding to that faith regardless of the choices made by the client. The counselor conveys this faith in the client not only by what the counselor says but through the counselor's attitudes, which indicate to the client "you are the determiner of your destiny," "the directions for your life come from you," and "you can become more independent and self-sustaining." Through such attitudes the counselor communicates that the client *can be* more, rather than the feeling that the client *must be* more. Even though the potential for change exists, the client does not feel a compulsion to change. The client can choose to change or not to change, can choose to speak or not to speak, can choose to be defensive or not to be defensive, and can choose to be independent or dependent (Kostenbaum, 1974).

In this kind of relationship the client begins to trust the self and becomes aware that personally satisfying values and behaviors emerge from within the client. There is a world of external reality but it cannot be interpreted as being real apart from the client's definition of reality. Reality lies in each person's experience and perception of events and forces. In counseling the client learns that instead of reacting to reality he or she can influence reality in ways that enhance the self and others. The clients who made the following statements chose a new inner reality, although their environmental influences remained unchanged:

> Now I'm not nervous . . . I used to be afraid . . . I thought everyone would laugh at me or make fun of me . . . now I'm not scared.

> I'm learning things about myself I never knew before . . . it's funny . . . I don't want to sound conceited . . . but I'm not as bad as I thought . . . you know the more I talk . . . ah . . . the more good I see in me.

> If I fight with my brother, well, I consider that natural . . . well, now, I say to myself if Ma and Dad fight that's natural . . . it's not the fight but the way you look at it . . . I think . . . ah grown-ups are people, too . . . in other words . . . there must be times when they get mad . . . but the next time there's a fight at home . . . it won't bother me as much because I won't be the same . . . the way I think won't be the same.

As these client statements suggest, the capacity to choose is freely implemented in a counseling atmosphere that promotes and facilitates the individual's discovery of the personal meaning of experiences and events. This means that the counselor, rather than directing or manipulating people, creates an opportunity in which people are freely able to express their needs and values. In such a situation the client has the feeling that personal ideas, feelings, and perspectives have value and significance; consequently, the client develops an awareness that choice and change are not a function of external forces but more a matter of individual perception and creation.

The client can evolve toward the good.   Counseling relationships reflect humanity's basic thrust to love, to grow, to share, and to nourish others psychologically. Although the wear and tear of life does blunt, and often pushes down, the tendency of the person to cooperate and love, this caring motivation is rooted so deeply in human nature that it emerges as nourishing, enhancing behavior in the most pedestrian activities of living as well as counseling.

Without each other, we cannot love, we cannot care, and we cannot be compassionate, empathic, accepting, and confronting. Giving and receiving help are nutrients that enable persons to function more fully and richly (Fabry, 1968). The rendering of assistance in counseling reflects the counselor's sense of social responsibility and is therapeutically reciprocal – for both the counselor and the client. Both grow and expand because they resonate to each other in time of trial, they touch each other's inner feelings, they share themselves, and they open themselves to their positive impulses.

In the encounter of the counseling relationship, hypocritical behavior is transcended. People trusting in their natural and intuitive feelings move out from behind their masks and expose their humanness in such ways as to seek "the greater good" for themselves and for others.

The person is a transcending being. Despite the powerful negative forces that operate to counter the natural thrust of the person to love and to cooperate, this tendency is so strong that it is never completely entombed. It emerges in the form of human therapeutic experiences, at many different moments in the life of each person, and is expressed with particular clarity and meaning in the counseling relationship.

Openness to self and others is a requisite for developing the self. The counselor's role as a counselor and the client's role as a client are transcended by their humanness. The humanness of the counseling relationship implies that counselor and client must be prepared to reveal themselves – their strengths, liabilities, joys, sorrows, feelings, and values. Client openness and honesty is facilitated by counselor openness and honesty (Bugental, 1978).

A number of counselors find it extremely difficult to live the flow of experience they feel while counseling another person. Society teaches us to put on a facade, to pretend to be that which we are not. But counseling has no room for facades. People do not disclose themselves to people who play a role (Pietrofesa, Leonard, & Van Hoose, 1971). The counselor facilitates personal revelation and growth in the client when the counselor is openly *being* the feelings and attitudes that are flowing within.

It requires courage to be real. Self-disclosure involves risk but so does personal growth. For the counselor who is willing to make the psychological investment necessary to close the gap between the role self and the real self, the risk of sacrificing the depersonalized professional mask is more than compensated for by the richness and fulfillment that comes with the liberation of the "essential" self.

The transparent self of the counselor facilitates the client's unfolding of self and encourages the client to discover the meaning of personal experiences and existence. By becoming more human and transcending a role, the counselor nurtures openness and enables the client to recognize and use personal human potentialities, to become more aware of idiosyncratic human qualities and the uniqueness of personal existence. Disclosing one's self to others provides a therapeutic release, enables one to develop strong affiliations with others, and affirms the uniqueness and the fusion of our existences.

In an atmosphere that encourages openness of self the client's processes of learning and discovery are enhanced. The client becomes more open to personal feelings, more open to the data of personal experiencing, more open to the stimuli of environment, more open to the points of view expressed by others, and more open to what is going on *now* internally. With openness to self and others, one's perceptual field expands, allowing new, varied, and rich data to come to light. Such openness and new data are necessary if one is to develop and change the self.

Periodically doubting one's basic beliefs can lead toward developing the self. Counseling, implicitly and explicitly, is an experience that expresses values. The data an individual chooses to internalize are functions of that person's values. The data an individual chooses to share and exchange are reflections of what that person deeply cares about. The questions the person seeks to answer, the skills the person desires to acquire, the values the person weighs and ponders over, and the ideas the person develops ultimately emanate from the deeply rooted first concerns inherent in the person's natural transcending tendencies—Who am I? What is my relationship to the world in which I live? These are deeply human questions that lie at the base of growth and change. They are questions that belong to all persons.

A person often must be alone in reflection, in contemplation, and in meditation to consider these questions, to reach into the inner recesses of a personal existence, and to penetrate the personally therapeutic experiences that can lead toward the development of the self. These quiet times enable the person to engage in the struggle of finding the self and to move toward an awareness of the relevancy and meaning of a personal existence and its relationship to others.

Such quiet times can be found within the process of counseling that provides opportunities for the personal and responsible use of freedom to discover and create moral values for living through a critical examination of beliefs, values, and behavior. Moral values that have emerged from an examination of the self provide a coherent framework for interpreting experiences and events and requires reflection, honesty, courage, and a willingness to question and to doubt (Daniels & Horowitz, 1976). These qualities can emerge in a counseling atmosphere that encourages openness, accepts ambiguity, emphasizes the uniquely personal and subjective nature of understanding, promotes and facilitates the client's discovery of the personal meaning of ideas, and encourages the client to trust in the self as well as in external sources of beliefs and ideas. Through counseling, beliefs, values, and behavior can be freely scrutinized and questioned. From client scrutiny and questioning there can evolve a greater degree of

self-knowledge, an expanded sense of self-determination, and an awareness that behavior is tentative and requires continual examination (Moustakas, 1975).

*Death is inevitable—it is the person's preparation for death that indicates the
degree to which the self has been developed.*   The anxiety of fate and death is
basic, universal, and inescapable. Fate and death are the way in which our
ontic self-affirmation is threatened by nonbeing. In anticipating one's own
death, the person experiences existential anxieties when confronting one's
finiteness (Kubler-Ross, 1975; Martin, 1975; Weisman, 1972). In dealing
with this finiteness, the individual can give up and resign the self to being
powerless and impotent, or the person can become neurotically active and
manipulative to hide from the dread of powerlessness.

Some clients who enter counseling express the feeling that they have no
control over their situations and problems. They seem to be helpless in
handling their concerns. Other clients appear to control their anxieties by
aggressively manipulating and exploiting people. In a facilitative counseling relationship the client moves from resignation or neurotic activism to
recognize the needs that each of us has for rootedness, relatedness, affilia-
tion, and faith in our own being as a starting point in dealing with the con-
tingencies of life.

Becoming more aware of a capacity to move from being a creature to
becoming a creator of one's own being, the client discovers that experiences can be created that will nourish and expand the client's life and
the lives of others. The client discovers an increasing pride and confidence
in making personal choices, guiding one's own life. The client tends to
value those objects, experiences, and goals that contribute to a personal
survival and development and for the survival and development of others.
In effective counseling the client moves from valuing power, personal
recognition, and superiority over other people, to a valuing beyond the self
and to the attributes and tendencies that ennoble the person and make
human life the highest form of existence. To value one's life makes the in-
evitability of death acceptable and a natural part of the human process.

Life has direction and meaning, but the answer is not clear.   Choices and
actions emanate from the quest for personal values. The quest for values is
a personal search for an answer to the most human of all questions—What
is the meaning of my life? This is essentially a spiritual question, a question
that humanity has sought to answer for centuries and a question that must
be dealt with by every person (Hammarskjold, 1969). The meaning of life,
from both a personal and universal perspective, has captured the attention,
imagination, and thought of poets, philosophers, dramatists, and novelists.
At the personal level the meaning of one's life is a question that often
permeates the counseling relationship—a question that deeply engages the
counselor and the client.

The world of the client is composed of all things that have meaning for the client. The counselor cannot know beforehand what life means to a client. The counselor cannot find the client's world in a learned textbook, nor can the counselor predict it with accuracy. The only way to discover it is for the counselor to be totally open to what a client will reveal about the client's world, providing the counselor is deeply respectful and understanding. As the client unfolds a personal world, the client opens the self toward creating meaning and direction in his or her personal life.

The client's searching and processing of values in relation to the question—What is the meaning of my life?—is the essence of the client's movement in counseling. The process of counseling essentially involves the client's discovery of self and the meaning of one's existence. As the client searches for the meaning of a personal existence, he or she comes to grips with defining the self. The client's discovery of personal values and the ensuing processing of these values into a hierarchy of importance clarifies personal meanings and influences behavior.

Through this process of self-discovery the client comes to see life as a continuous process of becoming rather than a static state of being. Living becomes an adventure, tentative and risky, with meaning and direction created by, and coming from within, the client.

Every aspect of living presupposes moral and human values. Counseling, as an aspect of living, is an expression of values and attitudes. The counselor expresses unfolding attitudes and values that mirror a continual examination of the self, life, and the unique relationships in which the counselor participates. Values are part of functioning people, and developing a sensitivity to their existence and to their influence on behavior is a necessary investigation for the counselor who desires to bring a greater meaning and awareness to the various aspects of counseling (Macquarrie, 1970). Such an investigation will not only enable the counselor to develop a greater awareness and understanding of clients, but it will also enable the counselor to develop a keener sensitivity to his or her substance as a person and to ways in which his or her personal values can either inhibit or facilitate the personal growth of clients (Upham, 1973).

PROFESSIONAL VALUES

Counselors are under more external pressure than ever before in the history of the profession. Today's counselors are bombarded by demands that come from a variety of sources and these demands have left many counselors wondering if remaining in the counseling profession is worth the effort. The values that counselors internalized in a program of studies do not seem operable in the real world and many counselors have become personally and professionally discouraged. The counselor's culturally different clients demand that the counselor become more sensitive to their individualized needs; others demand that the counselor become more of a social activist and support the causes of certain alienated groups; institutions pressure the counselor to become more accountable by developing evidence attesting to the effectiveness of counseling; career development professionals prod the counselor to become more sensitive to the importance of assisting clients to make more accurate vocational decisions; and computer advocates insist that the counselor make expanded use of data. The pressure from all sources increases and swirls around the counselor, and the counselor becomes professionally confused and sometimes burned out.

All groups that pressure the counselor to do more and to do different things are well intended. They identify certain needs their constituents possess and demand that these needs be met. In the process of demanding that certain needs be met, these groups turn to the counselor and typically insist that the counselor is in the best position to meet these needs. After all, since the counselor is interested in meeting the needs of people, the counselor becomes the logical provider of a certain service identified by a group with particular interests.

Counselors become easily discouraged because of the pressures exerted by these sources. So many human needs are emerging in today's society, and the counselor is being looked upon as the one who can effectively meet these needs. Such demands and pressures not only place a heavy burden on the counselor's time and energy but they create a psychological burden for the counselor which ultimately has a negative effect upon his or her professional functioning. The pressured and harassed counselor becomes easily confused regarding professional identity, mission, and role.

Never before in the history of the counseling profession have so many demanded so much from the counselor. Because of these demands, some counselors have become so psychologically frayed that they have had no recourse but to move into different careers in which the chances for making a personal and professional contribution are much more encouraging. This is unjust, especially in a profession that is publicly committed to the crucial importance of personal and professional identity and self-realization.

Consideration and examination of the following professional value commitments may prevent counselor burnout, help counselors not to be personally and professionally enervated by conflicting and ubiquitous influences, and provide hope and optimism. If the counselor is able to assimilate and identify with the following professional value commitments, then perhaps he or she will improve the quality of the counseling rendered because of the emergence of a personal answer to the question, "Who am I and where and I going?"

A commitment to spend the major portion of the working day in counseling relationships with clients. Many counselors have so many noncounseling responsibilities associated with their roles, they lose a sense of perspective and personal direction. The committed counselor sees counseling as the central activity that sustains the counselor both as a person and as a professional (Corey, 1977). After all, counseling is what the counselor expected to do after expending time, energy, and money in a preparational program.

At the end of a heavy working day, the counseling counselor feels satisfaction that counseling was a concrete contribution to the development and emergence of clients. The counseling counselor possesses an inner satisfaction because, although the working day may have included consultation and coordination, the counselor was still able to devote the major portion of available time and energy to counseling relationships. Such a counselor senses the importance of counseling because of its direct influence upon the behavior of clients; and the counseling counselor has expressed a caring for others by being available to them for counseling.

An important value, then, is to commit oneself to *really be a counselor* rather than become enmeshed in superficial noncounseling activities that erode one's visceral sense of contribution to the lives of others. Effective counselors counsel because they want to counsel. They develop better organized systems to meet their noncounseling obligations because they realize that such improved systems yield more time for counseling. The counselor who identifies counseling as the core of one's professional functioning, and who becomes involved in counseling relationships for the major portion of each working day, has identified a value that enables the counselor to have a basic sense of contribution to the lives of others.

A commitment to know and understand the authentic needs of clients. Institutions, and pressure groups that influence the organizational behavior of institutions, often identify human needs that are not the actual needs of clients within a community. Such institutions and groups often identify needs that are politically expedient, needs that flow into the interests and competencies of staff, needs that are in concert with the interests of funding agencies, needs that have a certain ethical or moral bias, and needs that have become popularized by the mass communication media (Boy & Pine, 1978).

Meanwhile, clients within a given institution or community are not having their real needs met, but the institution or community continues to rumble on, perpetuating itself while remaining ignorant of the authentic client needs that exist and are not being met. If the counselor continues to support inaccurate or inappropriate institutional goals that do not meet the needs of clients, then this is one short-range and inappropriate way of surviving. The counselor can collect a salary and derive a certain contentment in not having rocked the institutional boat. But in the long run, such a counselor is bound to have professional pangs of conscience because the authentic human needs of clients were not being met.

Out of the myriad of human needs that have been identified in all kinds of settings there emerges one paramount and crucial human need: the need of the client to be attended to, and engaged as a person, within the context of the relationship called counseling. Some institutions are so busy doing superficial things for clients that they have forgotten the client's need for sustained and periodic human contact and conversation with this person carrying the title of counselor; but this authentic human need for counseling is not often supported by institutions. After all, counseling takes time and diverts the counselor away from the functions by which an institution is administered. But when the counselor has identified the authentic counseling needs of clients, that counselor is in contact with a value that enables the counselor to invest the self in a profession.

A commitment to careful selection of the work setting. Effective counselors select a work setting that has a sense of mission and that is committed to the emergence of the person. Counselors become frustrated when a work setting is characterized by the coordination of loose ends trivia and there is no clear organizational identification of a bona fide human goal to motivate its existence and professional behavior. Services are rendered in a haphazard manner and the clients receive services only in proportion to the political and environmental pressure being exerted. Today's crisis is not identified and linked to a sense of organizational purpose, and there is no hope that tomorrow's crisis will result in a clearer sense of mission on the part of the organization (Loye, 1977).

When a counselor has a sense that individual efforts are related to a larger and unified organizational effort, he or she pursues work with commitment and vitality because there is a clear understanding that personal effort is congruent with, and a significant contribution to, the organizational effort. Both the counselor and the organization should be involved in a partnership in which there is a reciprocal relationship between the work of the individual counselor and the mission of the organization.

Unfortunately, too many service organizations have become so embroiled in politics, "wheeling and dealing," and the pursuit of funding, that they have lost their organizational sense of purpose and mission. Staff members only half function because of the atmosphere of organizational confusion. The simplicity of the organization's mission and goals has become complicated by a network of questionable motives.

One viable solution for the counselor is to engage in the challenging and necessary process of attempting to change the behavior of the organization. The professionally committed counselor will have a better sense of commitment in an organizational climate that is truly geared toward serving human needs and that encouarges the full use of the counselor's professional talents in meeting those needs.

Identification with colleagues who are committed and concerned. There are still some counselors and members of the helping profession who simply occupy space. They put in their time, drink their coffee, engage in superficial conversations, shuffle a few papers, and go home. They look upon counseling as an intrusion upon their working day. Such persons are a blemish upon the counseling profession, and to avoid confronting them will eventually take its toll (Mueller & Kell, 1972). To assimilate such attitudes can only result in the erosion of the counselor's personal and professional commitments.

The concerned professional counselor confronts such persons directly, and ultimately works toward the exclusion of such persons from the counseling profession. The counselor also avoids being influenced by such attitudes and identifies with colleagues who possess an authentic concern for their work and a visceral commitment to the importance of counseling.

Our society has had a dramatic increase in the number of people who are manipulating organizations for personal gain. We are living in an era in which the stealing of goods and services from organizations has become more commonplace. Another kind of covert and subtle stealing comes from a small group of counselors who don't counsel and whose only commitment is to do as little work as possible. They busy themselves with administrative trivia while remaining uninvolved with clientele who desperately need their services. Such counselors hopefully are being replaced by counselors who are truly committed to assisting clients. An increase in the number of committed colleagues is a professional value that not only benefits the individual counselor but also the organization and clients served by that organization.

A commitment to organizational involvement. The easiest way to become disgruntled about one's work is to engage in a soliloquy of complaints about the organization; complaints that bubble and boil inside or are only expressed to a small circle of trusted colleagues.

Effective counselors become involved with the organization because they know it won't devour them. It may occasionally rattle them, but they survive. They expend the time and energy needed to learn about the organization's inner sanctum and how it influences organizational behavior. Within this inner sanctum they find people, no cogs in a machine. By becoming involved in an organization these counselors learn about the fulcrums of influence and how they can be energized for the well being of clients. If a counselor avoids organizational involvement, then that counselor has little complaint when organizational behavior is not attuned to the needs of clients (Sergiovanni & Starratt, 1971).

Some counselors have remained uninvolved with the organization that employs them because they have been too busy counseling. Organizational involvement for the counselor can be qualitative rather than quantitative. It means developing access to units of organizational power that set the momentum and goals of the organization. Such access requires the counselor to be well organized so that his or her contriubtions and observations can be made without an erosion of the time that is typically devoted to counseling.

The counselor who possesses evidence that an organization is not working in the best interests of clients has a professional responsibility to present that evidence to the organization and to become involved in developing a better method for meeting client needs. But doing this requires that the counselor become involved with the organization; and such involvement translates itself into a personally rewarding value because the counselor's sphere of influence has become expanded in the process of better serving clients.

A reasonable commitment to a theory of counseling. Too many counselors are so theoretically neutral, sterile, and random in their counseling that they never develop a true awareness of which counselor attitudes and behaviors produce results. They do what seems to feel right without having their counseling behavior connected to any identifiable philosophic core.

To be personally and professionally committed to a certain counseling theory gives the counselor a sense of identification with an approach for assisting persons in need; and such an identification does other positive things. It enables the counselor to develop a consistency of procedure that can be identified and improved; it enables the counselor to review research studies done by others employing the same approach and to modify an approach because of the findings of these studies; it enables the counselor to conduct personal research studies that contribute to the effectiveness of the approach; it enables the counselor to have a consistent base from which modifications in an approach can be launched; it enables the counselor to contribute to the advancement of personal and professional knowledge regarding a particular theory; it presents the client with a behavioral consistency that sharpens the accuracy of the client's pattern of responses; and it presents the client with a professionally responsible approach that possesses a philosophy, a set of goals, and for which there is research evidence supporting its effectiveness.

Although adherence to a certain theory of counseling is a necessary value, the effective counselor is also tentative and provisional in that adherence. The effective counselor realizes that no one theory of counseling is absolute; a theory is not dogma, but is malleable in the light of new evidence and experience. It has the flexibility to be refined, modified, reformulated, and serve as an impetus for the generation of new hypotheses. Having a theory of counseling is of the highest priority because it provides the counselor with a framework within which his or her attitudes and behaviors can be clearly identified, monitored, and modified.

A commitment to self-assessment. Some counselors have so deeply involved themselves in the mechanistic dimensions of their work that they have lost any sense of personal identity or professional purpose. They are not unlike the bricklayer who becomes so conditioned to laying brick upon brick that eventually all bricks look alike and become mortared in exactly the same way. Counselors can become so stagnated in their behavior that eventually clients are to the counselor what bricks are to the bricklayer; exactly alike and worked on in the same way.

A counselor without a deep and personalized commitment to clients has no need to engage in self-assessment. Such a counselor functions at a level designed to maintain a personal status quo while implementing superficial organizational goals. This counselor withers on the vine because of a lack of sensitivity to the problems faced by the counselor and by the profession.

If a counselor does not take the time to evaluate professional performance, then it is easy to become complacent; and complacency is the soil from which bitter fruits emerge (Maslow, 1970; May, 1975).

Self-assessment is professionally invigorating for the counselor because it leads to new insights regarding one's professional behavior, and it propels the counselor to develop new perspectives regarding the many challenges currently being faced by the counseling profession. Self-assessment is a value that continually renews the counselor's sensitivity to personal and professional performance.

Self-assessment can be a threat because it requires that the counselor take a nondefensive look at personal attitudes and counseling skills. What is discovered may not be easily assimilated by the counselor's self-concept; but such self-assessment will enable the counselor to sharpen and hone the therapeutic effectiveness of the self, and the ultimate beneficiaries of such a process will be clients. When the counselor deeply penetrates the self, he or she reaches toward a creative inner core which, when unleashed, enables the counselor to perform functions at a higher level of effectiveness. Self-assessment is a value that can periodically reenergize the counselor's personal and professional commitment and performance.

A commitment to periodic evaluation of the counselor's role. Effective counselors resist becoming swallowed by a myriad of noncounseling activities. They see themselves primarily as counseling counselors who also engage in related consultative and coordinative activities so that the well being of clients will be better served.

The evaluation of a counselor's role demands that the counselor examine daily work behavior and sort out and separate the important from the trivial (Boy & Pine, 1968). By doing this, the counselor achieves a clearer sense of which aspects of professional functioning serve clients and which aspects are totally unrelated to the needs of clients. The next step is to simply reinforce and strengthen the performance of the important and to eliminate the performance of the unimportant. Sometimes counselors become so overloaded in performing meaningless functions that these functions eventually occupy the greater part of the counselor's day (Corey, 1977). The professional counselor realizes and resists this tendency and makes a concentrated effort to function truly as a counselor rather than a loose-ends coordinator, administrator, or information dispenser.

When counselors become involved in the process of evaluating their roles, the light at the end of the tunnel is clients. The purpose of evaluating one's role is to develop a functional role concept that enables the counselor to devote more time to working with clients rather than continuing to remain overloaded with tasks that do not contribute to an improvement in the human condition of clients.

An increasing number of counselors have evaluated their roles and converted their professional behavior toward an increase in the amount of time available for the counseling of clients. These counselors have discovered a core value because such counseling has moved them away from superficialities and toward a counseling involvement with clients—the ultimate purpose of a counselor's professional existence.

A commitment to hope. To the pessimist, a half-filled glass of water is half empty. To the optimist, this same glass of water is half full. Each of us has a choice to perceive life, and our professional existence, from either a perspective of pessimism or one of optimism. It would seem that a counselor, dedicated to the process of uplifting and bettering the human condition, would have no recourse but to be, internally and operationally, hopeful and optimistic.

The optimism with which we identify is not a sugary, pollyannish, and unrealistic burying of one's head in the sand. It is a wide-eyed and realistic hope based upon a realization that the real enemy of hope is our own personal and professional pessimism. If we feel that personal and professional events are out of our hands, that our attitudes and behaviors are preconditioned and predetermined by external forces beyond our control, then the easiest thing to do is to sit back and allow these forces to grind us into oblivion. But if we feel in control of the attitudes that generate our behavior, we can influence and move these attitudes in positive directions that benefit ourselves, our clients, and the organizations employing counselors (Kostenbaum, 1974; Vaillot, 1970).

The roots of personal pessimism are within ourselves; conversely, the roots of personal optimism are also within ourselves. We face an existential choice of furthering and developing our pessimistic or optimistic internal inclinations. If we choose to encourage our pessimistic tendencies, we do ourselves, our profession, and our clients a disservice. If we instead choose to encourage our tendencies toward optimism, we have uncorked a value that will enable us to endure, manage, and change the circumstances that surround our personal and professional existence. The choice is ours; historically, it has always been ours and in our future it will always remain ours.

REFERENCES

Allport, G. W. *The person in psychology.* Boston: Beacon, 1968.

Arbuckle, D. S. *Counseling and psychotherapy: An existential-humanistic view.* Boston: Allyn and Bacon, 1975, 392, 93.

Barnes, H. E. Motivation and freedom. *Rehabilitation Counseling Bulletin*, 1962, 5.

Boy, A. V., & Pine, G. J. *The counselor in the schools: A reconceptualization.* Boston: Houghton Mifflin, 1968.

Boy, A. V., & Pine, G. J. Counseling and the quest for values. *Counseling and Values,* 1974, *19,* 44–46.

Boy, A. V., & Pine, G. J. Effective counseling: Some proportional relationships. *Counselor Education and Supervision,* 1978, *18,* 140.

Branden, N. *The disowned self.* Los Angeles: Nash, 1971, 171.

Bugental, J. F. T. *Psychotherapy and process: The fundamentals of an existential humanistic approach.* Reading, Mass.: Addison-Wesley, 1978, 126.

Corey, G. *Theory and practice of counseling and psychotherapy.* Monterey, Calif.: Brooks/Cole, 1977.

Curran, C. A. *Counseling and psychotherapy: The pursuit of values.* Mission, Kans.: Sheed, Andrews, and McNeel, 1976.

Daniels, V., & Horowitz, L. *Being and caring.* Palo Alto, Calif.: Mayfield, 1976, 18.

deChardin, P. T. *The phenomenon of man.* New York: Harper and Row, 1959.

Egan, G. *The skilled helper.* Monterey, Calif.: Brooks/Cole, 1975, 22.

Eysenck, H. J. *Psychology is about people.* New York: Library Press, 1972, 115–116.

Fabry, J. *The pursuit of meaning: Logotherapy applied to life.* Boston: Beacon, 1968, 147.

Frankl, V. *The doctor and the soul.* New York: Knopf, 1963.

Frankl, V. *The will to meaning.* New York: New American Library, 1970, 6–62.

Fromm, E. *The art of loving.* New York: Harper and Row, 1956.

Glasser, W. *Reality therapy.* New York: Harper and Row, 1965.

Glasser, W. *The identity society.* New York: Harper and Row, 1972.

Hammarskjold, D. *Markings.* New York: Knopf, 1969, 205.

Hansen, J. C., Stevic, R. R., & Warner, R. W., Jr. *Counseling: Theory and process.* Boston: Allyn and Bacon, 1977.

Hart, J. T., & Tomlinson, T. M. *New directions in client-centered therapy.* Boston: Houghton Mifflin, 1970, 565.

Kostenbaum, P. *Existential sexuality.* Englewood Cliffs, N.J.: Prentice-Hall, 1974, 13, 67.

Kubler-Ross, E. *Death: The final stage of growth.* Englewood Cliffs, N.J.: Prentice-Hall, 1975.

Loye, D. *The leadership passion.* San Francisco: Jossey-Bass, 1977, 2.

Macquarrie, J. *Three issues in ethics.* New York: Harper and Row, 1970.

Martin, D. An existential approach to death. *Journal of Thanatology,* 1975, *3.*

Maslow, A. *New knowledge in human values.* Chicago: Henry Regnery, 1970, 131.

May, R. *The art of counseling.* Nashville: Abingdon, 1967, 77.

May, R. *Love and will.* New York: Norton, 1969.

May, R. *The courage to create.* New York: Norton, 1975, 127.

Moustakas, C. *Who will listen? Children and parents in therapy.* New York: Ballantine, 1975, 132.

Mowrer, O. H. *The new group therapy.* New York: Van Nostrand, 1964.

Mueller, W. J., & Kell, B. L. *Coping with conflict: Supervising counselors and psychotherapists.* New York: Appleton-Century-Crofts, 1972, 6.

Okun, B. F. *Effective helping: Interviewing and counseling techniques.* Belmont, Calif.: Wadsworth, 1976.

Peterson, J. A. *Counseling and values.* Scranton, Penn.: International Textbook, 1970.

Pietrofesa, J. J., Leonard, G. E., & Van Hoose, W. *The authentic counselor.* Chicago: Rand McNally, 1971, 159.

Rogers, C. R. Toward a modern approach to values: The valuing process in the mature person. *Journal of Abnormal and Social Psychology,* 1964, *68.*

Rogers, C. R. *On encounter groups.* New York: Harper and Row, 1970.

Rogers, C. R., & Stevens, D. *Person to person.* New York: Pocket Books, 1975, 47.

Sergiovanni, T. J., & Starratt, R. J. *Emerging patterns of supervision: Human perspectives.* New York: McGraw-Hill, 1971, 57.

Smith, D., & Peterson, J. Values: A challenge to the profession. *The Personnel and Guidance Journal,* 1977, *55,* 227–331.

Tillich, P. *The courage to be.* New Haven, Conn.: Yale University Press, 1952.

Tolbert, E. L. *Counseling for career development.* Boston: Houghton Mifflin, 1974, 172.

Upham, F. *Ego analysis in the helping professions.* New York: Family Service Association of America, 1973, 78.

Vaillot, M. C. Hope: The restoration of being. *American Journal of Nursing,* 1970, *70.*

Van Kaam, A. *The art of existential counseling.* Wilkes-Barre, Penn.: Dimension, 1966.

Weisman, A. D. *On dying and denying.* New York: Behavioral Publishers, 1972.

Wrenn, C. G. *The world of the contemporary counselor.* Boston: Houghton Mifflin, 1973, 7.

Chapter 5

THE COUNSELOR'S ROLE

In order for a counseling theory to meet the requirements of being legitimately labeled as a theory, it must possess and promulgate a concept of the counselor's role (Stefflre & Grant, 1972, pp. 4–7). Client-centered counseling has described the role of the counselor in terms of in-process counselor behaviors that characterize a client-centered relationship. Client-centered counseling theory, however, has neglected to identify the role of the counselor in terms of the counselor's on-the-job functions, responsibilities, and commitments. In fact, no theory of counseling has done this in *explicit* terms although all theories of counseling, including the client-centered view, contain implicit concepts that can be translated into an on-the-job role description for the practicing counselor. The purpose of this chapter is to develop a functional concept of the client-centered counselor's role, which is a natural extension of the basic philosophic view of the client-centered approach.

Practice emerges from a theoretical foundation that is substantive and has applied credibility. We consider theory by considering the successful implementation of that theory; and when we apply theory we attend to the counselor's role because such a role concept naturally evolves from a theoretical viewpoint. This is the essential difference between professional and nonprofessional viewpoints regarding the counselor's role. A professional viewpoint of the counselor's role is an applied extension of a theory; a nonprofessional viewpoint of the counselor's role is not undergirded by an explanatory theoretical rationale.

We cannot automatically assume that, once a person is called a professional, all that is done is defensible in the name of professionalism. There is more substance to the counselor's role than dispensing information, writing evaluative reports, or administering tests. If the counselor's role revolves exclusively around such activities, we would abandon the idea that counselors should be specially educated in therapeutic counseling. Unfortunately, some counselors who have been prepared to function therapeutically are currently applying only a small fraction of what they have learned because of the diffusion of their roles.

When conceptualizing a counselor's role, one needs to substantiate that role in terms of a counseling theory that serves as the basis for the counselor's specific functions. A concept regarding what a counselor should or should not do is meaningless unless there is a rationale for the role concept. When discussing foreign policy, one often hears someone say, "The United States should . . . ," and what follows is a particular opinionized statement. When considering what the United States should do, one cannot separate such a pronouncement from a democratic theory of government. A pronouncement becomes credible because it is an extension of application of a particular theory of democracy. When someone states that "The United States should . . . ," and then is unable to handle the questions, "Why? What is the rationale for your position? How is your viewpoint consistent with the tenets of democracy?" we then are justified in questioning the relevancy of what that person thinks the United States should do in regard to its foreign policy.

Sometimes there is a tendency to hide behind the word *professional*, the feeling being that as long as we use the word all that we do suddenly becomes purified and acceptable. A degradation occurs when one proceeds to use the term *professional* as a protective adjective to give apparent sanction to *any and all* functions of the counselor.

The counselor's role concept is an extension of a counseling theory, which in turn depends upon the counselor's behavioral definition of the person as expressed through a personality theory. But these influences on the counselor's role emanate from what the counselor is as a person; the counselor's existential totality, life style, human experiences, and inner philosophy. When we begin to look at the counselor as a person, we come to grips with the extent to which the counselor's personhood influences what the counselor does or does not do on the job (Hart & Tomlinson, 1970; Rogers, 1942, 1961). It would be naive to think that all a counselor had to do in order to function professionally would be to read a distributed policy statement regarding the counselor's role. If the attainment of professionalism was this simple, any profession could achieve a functional credibility simply by producing documents that could be fed to members. The problem does not lie in the dissemination of professional standards. It lies in the value system of the counselor—his or her personal needs when responding to the process of role definition.

FACTORS INFLUENCING THE ROLE
OF THE COUNSELOR

The counselor's role is not created in a vacuum. It is conceived and developed as an outgrowth of certain influences that impact upon and affect the counselor. Some of these influences are positive and result in the counselor, or group of counselors, developing a role description truly aimed at meeting the needs of clients. Other influences are negative in that they result in role descriptions that involve the counselor in a potpourri of activities that circumvent the needs of clients. These influences affect how the counselor conceives and executes a role description, and it is the purpose of this section to identify such influences and the degree to which they enhance or diminish the counselor's inclusion of therapeutic counseling as the top priority in a role description.

The degree to which a counselor develops a therapeutically meaningful role is proportionately related to the influence of the following factors. Factors influencing the counselor in a positive manner yield a role description that is therapeutically inclined. Factors negatively influencing the counselor result in a role description that is not therapeutically inclined.

Community Expectations

Some community expectations can have a positive influence upon the role of the counselor. In communities where the counselor is perceived as someone to whom personally troubled persons can turn, the counselor is encouraged to develop a role that emphasizes his or her commitment to therapeutic counseling.

When a community senses the need and importance of therapeutic counseling in the lives of people, it furnishes the counselor with the needed attitudinal support, which prompts the counselor to move toward a role in which therapeutic counseling is the core of a counselor's responsibility.

When the community expectation is that the counselor will counsel, then the counselor feels comfortable in fulfilling community expectations by devoting the major portion of each working day to counseling; and the community's recognition of the importance of therapeutic counseling becomes spelled out in the counselor's role description.

Some other communities expect the counselor to function as a super clerk who pays careful and detailed attention to tabulation. Such a community expectation would prompt the counselor to develop a role in which his or her super clerk capabilities are given prominence. Therapeutic counseling would be given a low level priority in this counselor's role because of the community's expectation.

Institutional Policies

Some institutional policies have a positive influence upon the role of a counselor, especially in those institutions that recognize the need and importance of therapeutic counseling. When the counselor is bolstered by such an institutional policy, the counselor is encouraged to feature the importance of therapeutic counseling in the development of a role description.

When institutional policy is sensitive to the personal and human needs of clients served by that institution, the counselor is prompted to acknowledge this sensitivity by giving therapeutic counseling the highest priority in a role description. The counselor is motivated to engage in therapeutic counseling because institutional policy encourages such an involvement.

Other institutional policies have a negative influence upon the counseling dimensions of a counselor's role. Some institutions desire that the counselor administer institutional policy and therefore cast the counselor into the role of an administrator rather than allowing him or her to engage in therapeutic counseling. Such institutional policies are designed more to preserve the institution as an institution rather than to serve the personal and human needs of clients (Hurst, Moore, Davidshofer, and Delworth, 1976). Faced with the need to administer institutional policies as a primary function, the counselor features such administrative activities in a role description while relegating therapeutic counseling to a secondary level of importance.

Other institutions require that the counselor function as a gatekeeper of institutional policy, making judgments regarding which clients will or will not receive the services and benefits of the institution. When counselors perceive themselves as gatekeepers of institutional policy, therapeutic counseling is given low priority in the counselor's role.

Administrative Behavior

Some administrators can have a positive influence upon the counselor's interest in therapeutic counseling. Such administrators perceive the counselor as a colleague and have no need to prostitute the role of the counselor toward the administrator's needs and interests. They listen to and acknowledge the counselor's judgment that therapeutic counseling will best serve clients, and they give the counselor the administrative and moral support that is necessary for the counselor to emphasize therapeutic counseling as the primary responsibility.

Some administrators desire to facilitate the use of existing skills among staff members, and therefore create an administrative environment that encourages staff utilization of their specialized skills. These administrators further realize that services will be more efficiently delivered to clients by the staff if the administrative atmosphere is supportive and encouraging (Bogue & Saunders, 1976; Boy & Pine, 1971; Flowers & Hughes, 1978). In such a reinforcing administrative environment, the counselor is encouraged to feature therapeutic counseling as the core dimension of his or her role.

Other administrative behavior can deflect the counselor away from primarily engaging in therapeutic counseling. Some administrators desire to make use of the counselor as a loose-ends coordinator or junior executive. They are so overwhelmed by their administrative responsibilities that they seek relief from these responsibilities and enlist the aid of the counselor in the performance of these administrative responsibilities. Once committed to the performance of administrative functions, the counselor has difficulty in finding the time or inclination to engage in therapeutic counseling.

Counselor's Formal Preparation

Some counselors are graduates of programs that emphasize the need and importance of therapeutic counseling. Such counselors have intellectually and attitudinally committed themselves to the importance of furnishing clients with therapeutic counseling and identify such counseling as the primary responsibility within their roles.

Such counselors realize that when all the layers of human problems are peeled away, what is left is the personhood of the client and how that personhood impacts upon and effects the behavior of the client. Such counselors invest themselves in providing clients with therapeutic counseling relationships. They invest themselves essentially because they are products of preparational programs that give primacy to the importance of therapeutic counseling as the core dimension of the counselor's role.

Other counselors are products of preparational programs that have prepared the counselor to do everything but counsel. Such programs have constructed courses and learning experiences in which prospective counselors learn how to assess, count, diagnose, manage, evaluate, measure, administer, and manipulate. Products of such programs do not identify with the importance of therapeutic counseling but instead identify with activities and functions more characteristic of the behavior of psychometricians, researchers, or administrators.

Attitudes of Colleague Counselors

Some colleague counselors furnish the counselor with the peer support necessary to give therapeutic counseling major consideration in the role of the counselor. They are counselors who have seen the depths of human personal turmoil and have come to the conclusion that the only way to alleviate that turmoil is to assist clients through therapeutic counseling. They viscerally understand how the process of therapeutic counseling enriches the lives of clients and leads to behavior change. They construct a role description that identifies and emphasizes the counselor's obligation to therapeutic counseling. Such colleague counselors compose the support system that encourages the counselor to list therapeutic counseling at the top of a list of role priorities.

Other colleague counselors function as obstructionists when a therapeutically inclined counselor attempts to give priority to therapeutic counseling. Such counselors have developed a comfortable work existence for themselves and they do not want that existence disturbed (Sweeney & Witmer, 1977). They identify more with paperwork than the personal needs of clients and always manage to create a mountain of paper behind which they can hide their indifference toward the human condition of clients. They desire to support and maintain the status quo because such an attitude is a better guarantee that they will have a job tomorrow. Looking busy is more important than being busy.

Such counselors resent the therapeutically committed counselor. The resentment is essentially due to a selfish desire not to become involved with the human trials and tribulations of clients. It is much easier for them to shuffle paper than to attend to the more fundamental human needs of clients. The existence of such colleagues makes it difficult, but not impossible, for the therapeutically inclined counselor to give role priority to counseling.

Governmental Priorities

Some governmental priorities can have an indirect influence upon the therapeutic nature of the counselor's role. Title VB of the 1958 National Defense Education Act, enacted by the U.S. Congress, resulted in the spending of millions of dollars for the preparation of new and existing school counselors. The central purpose of this legislation was to produce school counselors who would identify and encourage secondary school students to enter the scientific, technical, and engineering fields so that the United States could keep pace with Russia in the race to harness outer space. In 1968, the U.S. Congress enacted the Education Professions Development Act designed to produce a wider variety of educational specialists, among whom were school counselors. In 1962, President John F. Kennedy gave an executive grant of funds directly to states with the highest percentages of school dropouts so that school counselors could encourage dropouts to return to school. In these three examples, governmental priorities were clear and the implementation of these priorities was ultimately left to practicing school counselors. Many school counselors realized that the students affected by these federal actions would first have to solve and resolve their personal problems before they dealt with career choices or the issue of returning to school. School counselors were given an indirect opportunity to engage in therapeutic counseling and some began to include therapeutic counseling as part of their role description. Therapeutic counseling, so to speak, got in the back door.

Counselors would be more encouraged to include therapeutic counseling as a core dimension of their roles if governmental priorities directly and openly recognized the need for counselors to be involved in therapeutic counseling. It may take some time for this to occur because governmental officials who determine priorities still perceive the counselor as an information dispenser or advisor. But there is a proportionate relationship between the degree to which governmental priorities directly and openly recognize the need for therapeutic counseling and the degree to which counselors are encouraged to include it as part of their role description.

Priorities of Professional Associations

When professional associations for counselors promulgate the importance of therapeutic counseling, counselors are more prone to feature it in a role description. Professional associations have the opportunity to highlight therapeutic counseling in their conferences, journals, newsletters, workshops, documents, and public testimonies. They reach an audience of professional counselors and they can influence such counselors to develop skills, interests, and roles in therapeutic directions. When a professional association for counselors is administered and staffed by persons with credentials in therapeutic counseling, the association has a clear identification with the importance of therapeutic counseling and counselors are prompted to include it as a vital dimension of their roles. When therapeutically inclined counselors have the support of their particular professional association to engage in therapeutic counseling, such counselors expend the time and energy necessary to highlight it in their roles.

Sometimes professional associations for counselors do not aid in the development of the therapeutic dimension of the counselor's role because they themselves are not committed to this aspect of the counselor's role. Such associations often become immersed in issues that tend to primarily perpetuate the association's administrative, political, and public relations functions. Sometimes it appears that they are more interested in preserving and strengthening the association's financial and political base rather than attending to vital professional goals. When a professional association for counselors engages in a wide range of miscellaneous activities (Wubbolding, 1978) without featuring the importance of the counselor's therapeutic commitment, counselors respond by being just as miscellaneous themselves, and the importance of therapeutic counseling becomes lost in a maze of superficialities.

The Counselor's Self-Concept

The counselor's self-concept often influences the degree to which the counselor includes therapeutic counseling in a role description. The counselor who conceives the self to be a giving self, a person-centered self, a self that desires to be of service to clients in the improvement of behavior, gives high priority to therapeutic counseling. Such a counselor realizes that the more willing the counselor is to affectively extend and expand the self toward the client, the more positive will be the outcomes of counseling (Hulnick, 1977). The giving aspect of the counselor's self-concept will directly influence the counselor's featuring of therapeutic counseling in a role description. The selfless counselor, the giving counselor, the counselor who exists for the client's existential and behavioral improvement, desires to translate such a self-concept into counseling relationships. The existence of such a self-concept becomes concretized when the counselor develops a role that emphasizes the importance of therapeutic counseling.

Other counselors possess self-concepts that are inclined to see the self of the counselor as dominant, more knowledgeable, and better able to provide answers to problems than clients themselves. Such counselors perceive the self more in terms of doing things to and for clients rather than furnishing clients with opportunities to engage in self-conceived and self-motivated decisions. Action for these counselors centers around themselves and the best action evolves from the counselor's ability to analyze a problem and plan the client's behavior for dealing with the problem. Such counselors would give low priority to the counselor's time-consuming involvement in therapeutic counseling.

The Counselor's Theoretical Inclinations

A counselor's theory of counseling is essentially an expression of the counselor's self-concept. The counselor who knows the self and recognizes certain personal needs that must be met, will be inclined toward a theory of counseling that fulfills the self and those needs. Certain theories of counseling are focused on the personal needs of the client and feature the importance of therapeutic counseling. Client-centered counseling is explicitly one of these theories. Such theories accommodate the counselor as a counselor, rather than conceiving the counselor as an information dispenser, psychometrist, advisor, or human behavior engineer. Therapeutic counseling is central to such theories and those counselors who identify with such theories are inclined to emphasize therapeutic counseling in their role descriptions. They see therapeutic counseling as the primary mode for assisting clients, and they express this commitment in their role descriptions.

The Counselor's Career Goals

Some counselors, see themselves as counselors for the lifetime of their careers. In their early professional development, they make an intellectual and visceral commitment to serving human needs through the process of therapeutic counseling. They stay with that commitment throughout their professional careers because they realize that counseling affords them with a unique opportunity to significantly help the human condition to improve. They are internally motivated toward clients whom they wish to serve and assist through the process of therapeutic counseling. They are professionally fulfilled because they are truly making a contribution to the improvement of the human condition. They desire to serve clients and they express that desire through the therapeutic dimension of the counselor's role. They never waver in their commitment to function as professional counselors. They see counseling as a noble, person-centered, and continuing professional commitment.

The Needs of Clients

Counselors who engage in therapeutic counseling do so because the needs of their clients are best met through this process. They intellectually and viscerally realize that as organizations and agencies do many things in an attempt to render assistance to clients, there must be a therapeutically inclined counselor who has the time, energy, skills, and inclination to attend to the personhood and behavioral development of the client. They further realize that behavioral change will take place within a client only when the client is exposed to a series of steady, sustained, and continual counseling sessions with a therapeutic counselor. A client basically needs to be attended to as a person; to be in an association with a counselor who possesses and expresses attitudes of caring, understanding, empathy, acceptance, positive regard, authenticity, and concreteness. It is this kind of relationship that best meets the needs of the client and induces behavioral change. A client exposed to such counselor attitudes is able to move toward behavioral change. Such a counselor will feature therapeutic counseling as a priority in a role description because it best meets the human and behavioral needs of clients.

Other counselors conceive client needs in a far more superficial way and are therefore not inclined to give therapeutic counseling a high priority when developing a role description. Such counselors appear to want to isolate themselves from legitimate and therapeutic client needs. Since such counselors perceive client needs superficially, they perceive the role of the counselor superficially.

Many current counselors are much like Shakespeare's *Hamlet*. They have reached a point where they must decide whether they are "To be . . . or not to be" when considering the issue of giving top emphasis to therapeutic counseling in their role descriptions. But unlike the procrastinating Hamlet, counselors cannot mull over the question for too long. If they do procrastinate, they will find that pervasive and negative influences have gained in strength and the future of the counseling profession will be a shell of what it might have been.

AN APPROACH FOR DEFINING
THE COUNSELOR'S ROLE

For many years, the counselor's proper role has been hotly debated on a national, state, and local level. A few years ago, the following observation was made regarding the hesitancy of counselors to move toward a more professional role (Stefflre, 1964, p. 657). Among some counselors, this observation still applies today:

During the period of change in an occupation some members will become more experimental and open-minded in regard to functions while others will become more worried and apprehensive. We might all examine our own reactions to the controversy regarding professionalism. Do we see this period of change as an opportunity to develop approaches which we previously could not try, or do we see it as a threat to the familiar and comfortable?

Today the issue regarding the counselor's proper role, although somewhat better clarified, is still an issue of concern for the counselor at the local level.

Many counselors still feel that if an insightful and acceptable local role description could be developed then there would be a corresponding increase in the clarity of the counselor's role. Such a well developed role description would move the counselor away from the clerical and administrative role requirements and move the counselor toward a more therapeutic set of functions.

Various committees and organizations that have attempted to operationally define the role of the counselor have been well intended. Their documents have possessed clarity, depth, and a reasonable sense of the counselor's proper mission, but far too many counselors still see such role descriptions as being abstract and having little effect upon their actual role in a local setting and their relationship with a particular administrator.

Local realities can often have a suffocating effect upon the role of the counselor. On the local scene, political maneuvering, economic constraints, administrative barriers, and idiosyncratic personalities and behaviors often deflect the role of the counselor in nonprofessional directions. The local realities are often totally unrelated to the role descriptions conceived and hatched by well intended national groups.

We see the counselor's role as being a continuing critical issue that our profession has yet to adequately clarify. There have been some reasonable national, state, and local statements regarding the proper role of the counselor but the unfortunate fact is that far too many of these statements have fallen on deaf ears. The vast majority of counselors still find themselves immersed in a wide variety of activities that are administrative, managerial, and clerical in nature. Far too many counselors still find themselves professionally unfulfilled.

Rather than proposing a newly inspired role description for the counselor that will look good, sound good, but never be realistically implemented at the local level, we instead propose a workable approach whereby the counselor will have a reasonable opportunity of developing a more professional role relationship with an administrator with whom the counselor has to deal on a continuing basis. Our approach to role definition will not deflect the efforts of others to more adequately define the role of the counselor. Such efforts must continue if counseling is to maintain its unified sense of mission as a profession. Further, our approach for role definition can draw upon those role description statements the counseling profession has already produced. The ideas contained in these statements are often sound; the only problem has been translating them into practice within the realities of a local setting.

Our recommended approach essentially revolves around the concept of behavioral contracting. Many adherents of behavioral counseling have used behavioral contracts with clients as a vehicle for establishing the parameters of the counseling relationship as well as the behavioral goals of that relationship. Krumboltz and Thoresen (1969) have offered a clear and simple definition of a behavior contract: "A behavior contract is an agreement between two or more persons specifying what each person will do for a stated period of time. I'll do _____ for you in exchange for your doing _____ for me."

We suggest that many local problems regarding the proper role of the counselor can be solved if the counselor and administrator enter into a behavioral contract with each other; a behavioral contract in which each other's roles are clearly defined to each other in simple declarative sentences (Hurst et al., 1976). By doing this, the counselor will be able to work out a clear and uncomplicated role relationship with an administrator, and the administrator's role will be clearly understood and absorbed by the counselor. We suggest that the administrator be the first person with whom the counselor develops a mutually agreeable behavioral contract since most current problems of role clarification still largely revolve around administrators who do not have a clear perception of the counselor's proper therapeutic role.

The process of negotiating a behavioral contract should be an enriching experience for both the counselor and administrator. Each will have to develop preliminary drafts of the behavioral contract, each will have to develop a greater appreciation of each other's role, and each will have to engage in substantive and insightful dialogues in order to clarify and negotiate the final form of the behavioral contract. The contract will give meaning and direction to their mutual functions and relationship and it can be renegotiated by either party whenever it begins to lose its clarity or usefulness.

Such a locally conceived behavioral contract will certainly be far more workable than one developed by an outside group that is insensitive to the realities of being a counselor in a local organization, institution, or agency. Externally conceived roles can still serve as desirable models from which the local counselor can extract salient concepts that can be locally implemented. Both the external and local conceptualizations of the counselor's proper role can coexist and each can expand and enrich the other.

THE COUNSELOR AS A PROFESSIONAL

In recent years professionalism has been under attack. One reason for this antiprofessional posture has been the disappointment of many with the aloof, impersonal, and money-centered attitudes of some members of the various professions. Another reason is the public realization that many service functions that have been performed by professionals can be performed by persons who possess far less training. In the field of counseling, lay counselors have been able to provide therapeutically effective relationships for clients (Carkhuff & Truax, 1965; Goodman, 1970; Vriend, 1969).

From our view, the field of counseling is in need of *both* professionals and nonprofessionals if the counseling needs of people are to be adequately met. We support the concept of the professional counselor, while respecting the counseling contributions of nonprofessional counselors. In the long run, however, if counseling is to be maintained, developed, and accepted by the general public, institutions, governmental credentialing agencies, funding sources, and members of allied professions, it must possess credibility as a profession. In order to develop the necessary professional credibility, counselors must involve themselves in activities that go beyond, but reinforce, the counseling relationship, for example: (1) participating in investigations and research that further the therapeutic effectiveness of counseling, (2) clarifying the roles of the professional and nonprofessional counselors, (3) examining how the counseling process can be introduced to groups and organizations that are currently ignorant regarding its potential, (4) preserving and expanding the body of knowledge upon which counseling is based, (5) documenting the history and contributions of counseling in improving the human condition, (6) furthering the awareness of therapeutic counseling as a priority in the role of the professional counselor, and (7) examining how other professions can make use of counseling skills to better serve human needs.

Counseling has a rich heritage and an enormous potential for serving humanity as our world becomes more technological and impersonal. But counseling's past, present, and future contributions can be lost unless its professionalism is preserved. Without a sense of mission and a unity of purpose that professionalism can contribute, counseling can become lost in a sea of pervasive influences.

If counseling is to maintain and develop its credibility as a profession, then it must meet the criteria that make it a profession. These criteria, which give an occupation the credibility of being a profession, were first introduced shortly after the beginning of this century (Flexner, 1915), have been clarified and reinforced in more recent years (Gibson, 1965; Liberman, 1956), and may be summarized as follows:

1. The performance of a service to the public
2. The possession of a specialized body of knowledge and skill
3. The requirement of formal preparation
4. The regulation of admission to practice
5. The organization into professional groups
6. Professional autonomy balanced with public accountability
7. Adherence to a code of ethics.

Carl Rogers (Warren, 1972) is decidedly against one of the preceding criteria; the certifying of licensing of members of the helping professions: clinical psychologists, group leaders, marriage counselors, psychiatrists, and psychoanalysts on the basis that "There are as many certified charlatans and exploiters of people as there are uncertified." We agree with Rogers' observations but we would not want to throw the baby out with the bath water. Obviously, the solution will be the development of more intelligent and human certification and licensing standards that serve clients rather than serving the ego, territorial, manipulative, or monetary needs of those who are certified or licensed. Through the development of more rational and human standards *plus* the establishment of what Rogers calls a Consumer Protective Service that would enable the public to report ineffective or unethical behavior, "the public would be served and protected and the professional's qualifications, responsibilities, and behavior would be clearly identified and monitored."

CONSULTATION

The client-centered view has been represented in the thought and action of consultation but the involvement has been marginal when compared to the total effort of other viewpoints regarding the rationale and process of consultation. The major client-centered contributions have come from Gordon (1955) in his book, *Group-Centered Leadership,* especially Chapter 6, "The Plan of the Workshop Experiment;" Chapter 11, "Some Outcomes of an Experience in a Self-Directing Group;" and Chapter 13, "An Evaluation of an Industrial Leader." Rogers (1969) addresses the issue of consultation in Chapter 15 of his book, *Freedom to Learn,* which is entitled "A Plan for Self-Directed Change in an Educational System" and in the Epilogue to the book, "Self-Directed Educational Change in Action." In his book about the basic encounter group process, Rogers (1970) presents his concept of consultation in Chapter 8, "Areas of Application" and in Chapter 9, "Building Facilitative Skills." Pierce and Drasgow (1969), Vitalo (1971), and Orlando (1974) have used the process dimensions of client-centered counseling in psychiatric settings to teach patients facilitative interpersonal functioning that they could use with others. On balance, however, the interest of client-centered counselors has been more in the areas of therapeutic individual and group counseling rather than in consultation.

Our experience and observations indicate that client-centered counselors have not generally emphasized consultation for the following reasons:

1. Human problems are essentially interpersonal and intrapersonal rather than environmental.
2. The phenomenological influence has prompted client-centered counselors to concentrate more on the perceptions of clients rather than to examine those institutions and situations that contribute to these perceptions.
3. The existential influence promulgates that the individual can insulate the self against the negative influences of institutions, or situa-

tions; and further, if the individual is psychologically strong enough, the individual can influence the environment to change or transcend the environment.

4. There is a lack of sensitivity to the fact that changes can occur within an organization as a result of structural changes or work role changes as well as changes in attitudes and interpersonal communications patterns among members.

5. The process of consultation has been perceived as having manipulative connotations.

6. Client populations of the past have been generally middle class and their institutions and environments were either supportive or neutral regarding a client's behavioral movement toward authentic confrontation. Today's clients come from a wider range of classes, especially lower-middle and lower, and their institutions are generally neither neutral nor supportive but are instead threatened and defensive when clients behave in authentic confrontations. These institutions often contribute to the development of problems among clients.

7. The client-centered theory has been generally interpreted as being a reactive process rather than as a proactive process.

The importance of consultation as part of the counselor's role emerges from the writings of Schein (1969), Caplan (1970), Havelock (1973), Dinkmeyer and Carlson (1973), Dwyer (1974), and Kurpius and Brubaker (1976). Lewin (1951) pioneered the interest in his landmark contribution that called attention to the process of improving the human condition through consultation.

The counselor's role as a consultant has engendered so much professional interest that both the February and March 1978 issues of *The Personnel and Guidance Journal* were devoted to the topic of consultation. The two issues presented 21 articles concerning consultation in: elementary schools (Aubrey, 1978), secondary schools (Carrington, Cleveland, & Ketterman, 1978), university environments (Westbrook, Leonard, Johnson, Boyd, Hunt, & McDermott, 1978), community mental health (Werner, 1978), career development and sex role stereotyping (Hansen & Keierleber, 1978), interpersonal conflict management (Roark, 1978), organizational development (Huse, 1978), learning environments (Wigtil & Kelsey, 1978), community agencies (Heller, 1978), college faculty groups (Parker & Lawson, 1978), and with groups planning for the future (Brubaker, 1978). As part of the concept of consultation, there has also been a growing interest in the counselor functioning as a teacher. That is, the counselor becomes involved in teaching facilitative skills to others so that they can use these skills for personal behavioral management and in improving the behavior of institutions toward people. This teaching approach to consultation has been evidenced in the work of Carkhuff (1971), Guerney, Stollak, and

Guerney (1971), Alschuler and Ivey (1973), Ivey (1974), and Authier, Gustafson, Guerney, and Kasdorf (1975).

During our nation's cultural revolution of the 1960s and 1970s minority group members did not see themselves as problems that needed to be adjusted in order to meet the needs of institutions. They instead saw institutions as the problem and individually and collectively protested that these institutions should reverse their behavior and instead meet the needs of people. People moved away from being placid about the behavior of institutions to becoming more assertive and insisting that these institutions serve human needs. During this period some counselors became sensitized to this attitudinal and behavioral change among people and began to become involved in a proactive role by serving as intermediaries and advocates for those clients whose needs were not being met by institutions. Counselors realized that these institutions needed to change their attitudes and behaviors toward people, they needed to become more person-centered, and engaged the issue through the process of consultation. Consultation began to take form as a legitimate and necessary part of the counselor's role.

Rationale for Consultation

Gunnings (1971) indicates that the counselor must be willing to confront systems that have dehumanized the person and oppressed minorities. Osipow (1971) states that counselors are obligated to foster institutional changes so that these institutions will more accurately meet human needs. Morrill and Hurst (1971) show that counselors can best meet human needs by becoming involved in preventive and developmental outreach programs. Ivey (1973) indicates that unless the counselor gives greater priority to consultation, the human condition for all persons will never be significantly improved. While counselors counsel, organizations are grinding on and engaging in behaviors that tend to produce negative psychological consequences for persons.

Lewis and Lewis (1977, pp. 156–157) emphasize that social action should be part of *every* counselor's role because:

1. Negative aspects of the community environment may be detrimental to the growth and development of individuals.
2. Positive aspects of the community environment can support individual growth and development.
3. Counselors are helpless in their attempts to serve individuals if environmental factors do not change to keep pace with individual change.
4. Self-determination itself is not only a political goal, but a mental health goal.
5. Counselors, working alone, and individual citizens, working alone, are both powerless to make the community responsive to the needs of community members.

Aubrey (1978) states that the counselor must deliver consultative services in the following areas in order to fully meet institutional needs: as a resources obtainer, a system negotiator, a teacher collaborator, and a developmental educator.

Brubaker (1978, p. 431) writes about providing consultation for organizations interested in designing desirable futures rather than responding to momentary needs in a haphazard manner. He indicates that the future's consulting process is: ". . . a consultation for involving individuals, groups, or organizations in the creation of their own future. The purpose of this process is not to predict what the future will be, but rather to explore various future images that remain open to change, as a result of our individual or collective actions, and are accessible to human decision making."

In presenting an organizational development model of consultation, Huse (1978, p. 403) says that the process is based upon the following assumptions:

1. Most people desire and need opportunities for growth and self-realization.
2. When basic needs have been satisfied, most individuals will respond to opportunities for challenge, responsibility, and interesting work.
3. Organizational efficiency and effectiveness are increased when work is organized to meet individual needs for challenge, growth, and responsibility.
4. Shifting the emphasis of conflict resolution from "smoothing" or "edicting" to open "confrontation" facilitates both personal growth and the accomplishment of organizational goals.
5. Organizational structure and the design of jobs can be changed and modified to meet more effectively the needs of the organization, the group, and the individual.
6. Many "personality clashes" in organizations are the direct result of improper organizational design.

Kurpius (1978b, p. 335) points out the following in presenting a rationale for consultation:

Persons functioning as consultants do not model authority and control. Rather, their newly developing image and related functions are quite the opposite—they model helping behaviors that are nonjudgmental and noncompetitive. Such behaviors reinforce openness and collaboration that create mutually beneficial work situations and work outcomes. These persons are being recognized as the long needed "new professional" in the work force.

Some consulting comes from counselors who are already employed within an institutional setting. Walz and Benjamin (1978, p. 331) indicate that being an "insider" has an inherent advantage:

Counselors usually have freedom of movement: They can move around, see people and interact with them. Counselors usually know and are known by the system; they speak the language, know the norms, and can relate to the system's needs and interests. In many ways, counselors are in an excellent position to assess the impact of the system on its members: what the system does to people in its efforts to do something for people, what is going well, and what may be causing unhappiness or dissatisfaction.

Price (1972, p. 365) develops a community perspective in evaluating psychological dysfunction and focuses on understanding the stressful and hostile social and environmental influences that contribute to the development of personal problems among individuals:

> Wholesale use of traditional psychotherapy is inappropriate in that not everyone experiencing some emotional discomfort requires the intensive intervention of individual or even group psychotherapy. For many, educational experiences in stress management, relaxation techniques, career planning, or interpersonal communications among many others may be of the most benefit and a wiser use of our limited professional resources.

Werner (1978, p. 368) emphasizes a preventive rationale for consultation when he states that the process of consultation: ". . . kindled our imaginations to the possibilities of preventing emotional and behavioral problems."

In describing a team-building concept of consultation, Wigtil and Kelsey (1978, pp. 412–413) first define team building and then present its rationale by indicating its purposes. Team building is:

> . . . planned events with a group of individuals who have or may have common organizational goals or relationships that focus on the improvement of the manner in which work is accomplished by them. The main purposes of team building are to: (a) facilitate problem solving; (b) maximize the utilization of skills, competencies, interests, and resources toward organizational goals; (c) improve the planning and decision making process; and (d) provide the natural forum for conflict resolution.

In terms of consulting in a school setting, Wigtil and Kelsey (1978, p. 416) go on to state that: "No longer is it appropriate or even ethical to only adjust the students to the system, it is also important that counselors influence the adjusting of the learning environment to the students."

Regarding the choice faced by counselors to affect behavioral changes within individuals or institutions, Heller (1978, p. 420) indicates that:

> Ultimately, of course, we need a balanced view; both social change and personal change are important. Environments influence behavior, but persons also have the capacity to shape environments. What this means is that psychological professionals should recognize the need for both individual and social change skills and should understand the conditions under which each approach might be optimal.

The Process of Consultation

Carrington et al. (1978, p. 356) have outlined the conditions for effectively utilizing what they call "collaborative" consultation:

1. Obtaining group ownership of the problem under consideration
2. Keeping the group on task
3. Encouraging concreteness and specificity from the group
4. Gaining consensus from the group regarding solutions.

They go on to indicate that the collaborative consultant takes a group of consultees through the following stages:

1. Problem identification
2. Agreement on a concise statement of the problem
3. Converting the problem statement into a goal statement
4. Brainstorming solutions to the problem that will enable goal attainment
5. Evaluating solutions
6. Ranking solutions
7. Reaching consensus on a solution
8. Stating objectives
9. Arranging for process evaluation.

Kurpius (1978b, pp. 337–338) presents the following steps in his concept of an effective process of consultation:

1. Preentry
2. Entry
3. Gathering information
4. Defining the problem
5. Determination of the problem situation
6. Stating objectives
7. Implementation of the plan
8. Evaluation.

Schein (1978, p. 342) states that the process of consultation begins with the ability of the consultant to: ". . . observe interpersonal conflicts, leadership struggles, communications breakdowns, emotional outbursts, and other interpersonal process events."

Parker and Lawson (1978, p. 427) indicates that the process of effective consultation is highly dependent upon the attitude and process flexibility of the consultant: "Perhaps the most crucial observation that we can make about consultation from this experience is the importance of the openness, flexibility, and adaptability of the consultant."

Roark (1978, p. 402) presents five functions that must be provided in constructive conflict management:

1. The intensity of the conflict must be reduced or kept low enough for constructive interaction.
2. The issues must be narrowed to one or two that can be used as a starting point.
3. Norms, rules, and structure must be available for nondestructive solutions to be adopted.

4. The real issues in the conflict must be uncovered and understood by all parties to the conflict.
5. Nonrealistic conflicts must be converted to realistic (issues or resources) conflicts so that objective goals can be agreed on and lose-lose situations avoided.

The following is a summary of what Havelock (1973) considers to be the important dimensions of the process of consultation:

1. Energize the system to change by confronting the system to do something about its problems.
2. Counselors must have insight regarding required changes and be able to offer solutions.
3. Systems typically do not have the informational resources to make changes, and the counselor can serve as the link to these resources.
4. By attitude and experience, the counselor is well credentialed and in the best position to serve as a consultant.

Walz and Benjamin (1978, p. 334) state that, "Counselors need not be casual observers or passive recipients of change but can be active leaders in the process. Change will occur. The fundamental question is whether counselors are willing to acquire new skills and use a systematic strategy for planned change." The systematic strategy Walz and Benjamin (1978, pp. 332–333) recommend is based upon the following steps in the consultative process:

1. Establish the need
2. Build interactive relationships
3. Assess
4. Generate options
5. Decide
6. Facilitate adoption and implementation
7. Refine and renew.

The role of the counselor as an advocate for clients and an agent for institutional change has been clearly articulated by Lipsman (1969), Ciavarella and Doolittle (1970), Simon (1970), Szasz (1970), Loughary (1971), Baker and Cramer (1972), Cook (1972), Banks and Martens (1973), Kincaid (1973), and Warnath (1973). The following guidelines have been developed by Boy and Pine (1976, pp. 112–118) for counselors functioning as advocates for clients and as agents for institutional change:

1. In presenting a case to an institution, base that case on concrete evidence.
2. Present the evidence in a clear, concise, and well organized manner.
3. Document the evidence.
4. Devote a significant portion of the working day in counseling relationships in order to develop the evidence.
5. Select the proper audience for the presentation of the evidence.

6. Develop credibility as a person; the counselor's credibility will determine the degree to which evidence is accepted, and acted upon, by an institution.

For the client-centered counselor, the counselor's consultative contributions are essentially an extension of the human attitudes that characterize the relationship and process dimensions of client-centered counseling. That is, the client-centered counselor perceives the consultative aspect of the counselor's role as a reflection of the fundamental attitudes and processes of client-centered counseling rather than being an embodiment of mechanical procedures.

Client-centered counselors have traditionally emphasized the primacy of therapeutic counseling as the most essential and effective contribution toward improving the human condition of clients. Counseling has been seen as the one and, sometimes, only activity in which the client-centered counselor should be involved. We support the critical importance of the counselor functioning as a therapeutic counselor but we also recognize that the theory and practice of client-centered counseling has been generally remiss in failing to more explicitly conceive the counselor as also being a consultant, social activist, advocate, and change agent. It is logical that the counselor's role also emphasizes the importance of the counselor engaging in consultative activities that serve to improve not only the human condition of individual clients but the humanness of organizations established to serve those clients. As Kurpius (1978a, p. 320) has noted: "Consultation is one process for synthesizing environmental and human adjustments, and although consultation is not a panacea for all ills, it does provide an alternate form for influencing change."

The client-centered counselor's role more accurately serves human needs when it gives priority to both therapeutic counseling and consultation. The impact of the client-centered counselor's role becomes enlarged when it includes both therapeutic counseling and consultation.

REFERENCES

Alschuler, A., & Ivey, A. Getting into psychological education. *The Personnel and Guidance Journal,* 1973, *51,* 682–691.

Aubrey, R. F. Consultation, school interventions, and the elementary counselor. *The Personnel and Guidance Journal,* 1978, *56,* 351–354.

Authier, J., Gustafson, K., Guerney, B., & Kasdorf, B. The psychological practitioner: A theoretical-historical and practical view. *The Counseling Psychologist,* 1975, *5,* 31–50.

Baker, S. B., & Cramer, S. H. Counselor or change agent: Support from the profession. *The Personnel and Guidance Journal,* 1972, *50,* 661–665.

Banks, N., & Martens, K. Counseling: The reactionary profession. *The Personnel and Guidance Journal,* 1973, *51,* 457–462.

Bogue, E. G., & Saunders, R. L. *The educational manager: Artist and practitioner.* New York: Worthington Jones, 1976, 4–5.

Boy A. V., & Pine, G. J. *Expanding the self: Personal growth for teachers.* Dubuque Iowa: W. C. Brown, 1971, 45–46.

Boy, A. V., & Pine, G. J. The process of counselor advocacy. *Counseling and Values,* 1976, *20,* 112–118.

Brubaker, J. C. Futures consultation: Designing desirable futures. *The Personnel and Guidance Journal,* 1978, *56,* 428–431.

Caplan, G. *The theory and practice of mental health consultation.* New York: Basic Books, 1970.

Carkhuff, R. Training as a mode of treatment. *Journal of Counseling Psychology,* 1971, *18,* 123–131.

Carkhuff, R. R., & Truax, C. B. Lay mental health counseling; The effects of lay group counseling. *Journal of Consulting Psychology,* 1965, *29,* 426–431.

Carrington, D., Cleveland, A., & Ketterman, C. Collaborative consultation in the secondary schools. *The Personnel and Guidance Journal,* 1978, *56,* 355–358.

Ciavarella, M. & Doolittle, L. W. The ombudsman: Relevant role model for the counselor. *The School Counselor,* 1970, *17,* 331–336.

Cook, D. R. The change agent counselor: A conceptual context. *The School Counselor,* 1972, *20,* 9–15.

Dinkmeyer, D., & Carlson, J. *Consulting: Facilitating human potential and change processes.* Columbus, Ohio: Charles E. Merrill, 1973.

Dwyer, C. E. Training for change agents: A guide to design of training programs in education and other fields. *Industrial and Labor Relations Review,* 1974, *27,* 658–659.

Flexner, A. Is social work a profession? *Proceedings,* National Conference of Charities and Corrections, Chicago, 1915.

Flowers, V. S., & Hughes, C. L. Choosing a leadership style. *Personnel,* 1978, *55,* 51–59.

Gibson, D. N. *Social perspectives on education,* New York: John Wiley, 1965.

Goodman, G. Companionship as therapy: The use of nonprofessional talent. In J. T. Hart, & T. M. Tomlinson (Eds.), *New directions in client-centered therapy.* Boston: Houghton Mifflin, 1970, 348–371.

Gordon, T. *Group-centered leadership.* Boston: Houghton Mifflin, 1955.

Guerney, B., Jr., Stollak, G., & Guerney, L. The practicing psychologist as educator—An alternative to the medical practitioner model. *Professional Psychology,* 1971, *2,* 271–282.

Gunnings, T. S. Preparing the new counselor. *The Counseling Psychologist,* 1971, *2.*

Hansen, L. S., & Keierleber, D. L. Born free: A collaborative consultation model for career development and sex-role stereotyping. *The Personnel and Guidance Journal,* 1978, *56,* 395–399.

Hart, J. T., & Tomlinson, T. M. *New directions in client-centered therapy.* Boston: Houghton Mifflin, 1970, *74,* 120.

Havelock, R. G. *The change agent's guide to innovation in education.* Englewood Cliffs, N.J.: Educational Technology, 1973.

Heller, K. Facilitative conditions for consultation with community agencies. *The Personnel and Guidance Journal,* 1978, *56,* 419–423.

Hicks, L. H., & Aspy, D. N. The counselor's role in helping teachers with career education within an HRD system. *Counselor Education and Supervision,* 1977, *16,* 178–184.

Hoyt, K. B. Career education and counselor education. *Counselor Education and Supervision,* 1975, *15,* 6–11.

Hulnick, H. R. Counselor: Know thyself. *Counselor Education and Supervision,* 1977, *17,* 69–72.

Humes, C. W., II. Implications of PL 94-142 for training and supervision. *Counselor Education and Supervision,* 1978, *18,* 126–129.

Hurst, J. C., Moore, M., Davidshofer, C., & Delworth, U. Agency directionality and staff individuality. *The Personnel and Guidance Journal,* 1976, *54,* 313–317.

Huse, E. F. Organizational Development. *The Personnel and Guidance Journal,* 1978, *56,* 403–406.

Ivey, A. E. Counseling–Innocent profession or fiddling while Rome burns? *The Counseling Psychologist,* 1973, *4,* 111–115.

Ivey, A. E. The clinician as a teacher of interpersonal skills: Let's give away what we've got. *The Clinical Psychologist,* 1974, *27,* 6–9.

Ivey, A. E. An invited response: The counselor as a teacher. *The Personnel and Guidance Journal,* 1976, *54,* 431–434.

Kincaid, J. The challenge of change and dissent. *The School Counselor,* 1973, *20,* 169–175.

Krumboltz, J. D., & Thoresen, C. *Behavioral counseling: Cases and techniques.* New York: Holt, Rinehart and Winston, 1969, 87.

Kurpius, D. Introduction to the special issue. *The Personnel and Guidance Journal,* 1978, *56,* 320. (a)

Kurpius, D. Consultation theory and process: An integrated model. *The Personnel and Guidance Journal,* 1978, *56,* 335–338. (b)

Kurpius, D. J., & Brubaker, J. C. *Psychoeducational consultation: Definition, functions, preparation.* Bloomington: Indiana University, 1976.

Lewin, K. *Field theory in social science.* New York: Harper, 1951.

Lewis, M. & Lewis, J. *Community counseling: A human services approach.* New York: Wiley, 1977, 156–157.

Lieberman, M. *Education as a profession.* Englewood Cliffs, N.J.: Prentice-Hall, 1956.

Lipsman, C. K. Revolution and prophecy: Community involvement for counselors. *The Personnel and Guidance Journal,* 1969, *48,* 97–100.

Loughary, J. W. To grow or not to grow. *The School Counselor,* 1971, *18,* 332, 333.

Morrill, W. H., & Hurst, J. C. A preventive and developmental role for the college counselor. *The Counseling Psychologist, 2,* 1971.

Orlando, N. The mental patient as therapeutic agent: Self change, power and caring. *Psychotherapy: Theory, Research and Practice,* 1974, *11,* 58–62.

Osipow, S. H. Challenges to counseling psychology for the 1970s and 80s. *The Counseling Psychologist,* 1971, *2.*

Parker, C. A., & Lawson, J. From theory to practice to theory: Consulting with college faculty. *The Personnel and Guidance Journal,* 1978, *56,* 424–427.

Pierce, R., & Drasgow, J. Teaching facilitative interpersonal functioning to psychiatric patients. *Journal of Counseling Psychology,* 1969, *16,* 295–298.

Pietrofesa, J. J. The school counselor in sex education. *The Personnel and Guidance Journal,* 1976, *54*, 358–361.

Pines, A., & Maslach, C. Characteristics of staff burnout in mental health settings. *Hospital and Community Psychiatry,* 1978, *29*, 233–237.

Price, R. H. *Abnormal psychology: Perspectives in conflict.* New York: Holt, Rinehart and Winston, 1972.

Roark, A. E. Interpersonal conflict management. *The Personnel and Guidance Journal,* 1978, *56*, 400–402.

Rogers, C. R. *Counseling and psychotherapy.* Boston: Houghton Mifflin, 1942, 11, 29.

Rogers, C. R. *On becoming a person.* Boston: Houghton Mifflin, 1961, 55.

Rogers, C. R. *Freedom to learn.* Columbus: Merrill, 1969.

Rogers, C. R. *Carl Rogers on encounter groups.* New York: Harper and Row, 1970.

Schein, E. H. *Process consultation.* Reading, Mass.: Addison-Wesley, 1969.

Schein, E. H. The role of the consultant: Content expert or process facilitator. *The Personnel and Guidance Journal,* 1978, *56*, 339–343.

Simon, L. J. The political unconsciousness of psychology: Clinical psychology and social change. *Professional Psychology,* 1970, *1*, 331–341.

Sperry, L. A study of planned attitude change in an integrated school. *Elementary School Guidance and Counseling,* 1972, *2*, 162–165.

Sproles, H. A., Panther, E. E., & Lanier, J. E. PL 94-142 and its impact on the counselor's role. *The Personnel and Guidance Journal,* 1978, *57*, 210–212.

Stefflre, B. What price professionalism? *The Personnel and Guidance Journal,* 1964, *42*, 657.

Stefflre, B., & Grant, W. *Theories of counseling* (2nd ed.). New York: McGraw-Hill, 1972.

Sweeney, T. J., & Witmer, J. M. Who says you're a counselor? *The Personnel and Guidance Journal,* 1977, *55*, 594.

Szasz, T. S. *The manufacturing of madness.* New York: Dell, 1970.

Vitalo, R. Teaching improved interpersonal functioning as a preferred mode of treatment. *Journal of Counseling and Clinical Psychology,* 1971, *35*, 166–171.

Vriend, T. J. High performing innercity adolescents assist low performing peers in counseling. *The Personnel and Guidance Journal,* 1969, *47*, 897–904.

Walz, G., & Benjamin, L. A change agent strategy for counselors functioning as consultants. *The Personnel and Guidance Journal,* 1978, *56*, 331–334.

Warnath, C. F. The school counselor as institutional agent. *The School Counselor,* 1973, *20*, 202–208.

Warnath, C., & Shelton, J. The ultimate disappointment: The burned-out counselor. *The Personnel and Guidance Journal,* 1976, *55*, 172–195.

Warren, J. Rogers challenges psychologist to become future oriented. *APA Monitor,* 1972, *3*, 1, 7, 14.

Werner, J. L. Community mental health consultation with agencies. *The Personnel and Guidance Journal,* 1978, *56*, 364–368.

Westbrook, F. D., Leonard, M. M., Johnson, F., Boyd, V. S., Hunt, S. M., & McDermott, M. T. University campus consultation through the formation of collaborative dyads. *The Personnel and Guidance Journal,* 1978, *56*, 359–363.

Wigtil, J. V., & Kelsey, R. C. Team building as a consulting intervention for influencing learning environments. *The Personnel and Guidance Journal*, 1978, *56*, 412–416.

Wubbolding, R. E. The counselor educator and local professional associations. *Counselor Education and Supervision*, 1978, *18*.

Chapter 6 ‖‖

THE COUNSELING RELATIONSHIP ‖‖

The following sections of this chapter will identify what we consider to be the basic characteristics of an effective client-centered counseling relationship.* We view these characteristics as being applicable to both Phase One and Two of our refinement of client-centered counseling.

An effective client-centered counseling relationship is characterized as being:

A face-to-face relationship

A person-in-person relationship

A human relationship

A relationship of reciprocity and commitment

A relationship in which the client is voluntarily involved

A relationship possessing mutual respect

A relationship possessing effective communication

A relationship possessing genuine acceptance of the client by the counselor

A relationship in which the counselor empathically focuses on the needs and feelings of the client

A relationship that is liberating

An open-ended relationship in which outcomes essentially emerge from the client, not from the counselor

A relationship in which the client's desire for confidentiality is respected

A professional service that calls for acquired attitudes and skills on the part of the counselor

A professional service based upon a substantive rationale reflecting

---

*Sections of this chapter have been adapted with permission, from A. V. Boy and G. J. Pine, *The Counselor in the Schools: A Reconceptualization* (Boston: Houghton Mifflin, 1968), Chapter 7.

philosophical and psychological principles emanating from theoretical and empirical considerations of the person, human behavior, and society

A relationship in which the counselor possesses a concept of the person

A relationship in which being precedes becoming.

FACE-TO-FACE

In a world that is becoming more technological, some are encouraging counselors to make more use of technology in their counseling (Stewart, Winborn, Johnson, Burks, & Engelkes, 1978). From our viewpoint, the necessary face-to-face dimension of counseling precludes the notion of counseling conducted via telephone, television, letters of correspondence, and other nonpersonal modes of communication. In the past, some writers have indicated that counseling can occur between two individuals through the mails, for example (Jones, 1963, p. 216). Although one could consider some letters as highly personal and emotionally evocative, a telephone conversation as cathartic and helpful in immediate crisis situations such as the threat of suicide, and television and computers as vehicles of communication that have the potential for accommodating some of the numerous and varied needs of humans, counseling, according to our definition, includes the idea of a face-to-face relationship. The physical presence of two people, counselor and client, provides an emotional contiguity that does not exist in a person-thing-person medium of communication. It is difficult to imagine a troubled client feeling free to cry to a computer or to an image on a picture tube. A telephone call cannot accommodate the nuances and subtleties of communication represented in body language, facial expression, physical gesture, and the messages of the eyes. A visual image on a picture tube cannot open a door, embrace, or project the emotional warmth of a fully dimensioned person. Counseling is a human relationship involving the physical presence of persons who freely share themselves in an emotional and cognitive togetherness not found in a face-to-image or face-to-voice communication. In counseling, the client's world is being elucidated by the counselor's *being there* in an atmosphere of *openness*. Counseling takes place in the light of *dasein*–the "being there" of two persons in an existential encounter.

PERSON-IN-PERSON

The word *encounter* is used by some existentialists to convey the idea of a special kind of relationship that can exist between two persons. Counseling is an encounter in which the client is not just flesh and bones but becomes a "thou." The client becomes a special being in the eyes of the counselor who enters into the client's world of reality and effectively participates in that world. Counseling is a special relationship in which the counselor does not focus on problems and solutions, but on communion. The client is not viewed as an object to be dissected according to theoretical requirements, but a person whose phenomenological world is experienced by another person—the counselor. For the counselor, *knowing* the client as a person becomes more important than *knowing about* the client. It means counselor movement from an external, objective perspective to an internal, subjective, and personal experience of the client (Kemp, 1971; Leaman, 1973; and Rogers, 1975). It seems appropriate to describe counseling as a person-in-person relationship.

Counseling asks the counselor to see, feel, and experience as the client sees, feels, and experiences and, in a sense, almost to become the client. Some professionals would not agree with the person-in-person concept, since they hold the psychological distance must be maintained between the counselor and the client, and that it is nonproductive to become emotionally involved. The client-centered counselor, however, does not hesitate to allow the counselor's self to enter into the person of the client emotionally and cognitively. The world of the client is unique, and entrance into that world is gained by an emotional commitment—the kind of commitment in which the counselor is willing to involve the self, as a person. It is when the counselor is freely and fully invested in the relationship that the counselor can begin to experience the counselee as a unique individual.

HUMANNESS

Counseling is a human experience characterized by a human understanding of human existence (Patterson, 1969). It is subject to the frailties and limitations of the finiteness of being human. However, because counseling is a human relationship, it is also remarkably resilient. Mistakes and errors can be made, and yet the human transaction can and usually does continue. The relationship is destructible but also reparable; client and counselor can break down communication and they can revitalize it. Resiliency and reparation reflect the humanness of counseling.

The humanness of the counseling relationship implies that counselor and client must be prepared to reveal themselves—their strengths, liabilities, joys, sorrows, feelings, and values. The counselor who attempts to conceal the self, who strives to view the client objectively and dispassionately, will ultimately see the client as an object. The reciprocity of the counseling relationship would seem to indicate that the client who is perceived as an object will in turn view the counselor as an object. Human interaction, as it takes place in counseling, is primarily subjective. This does not exclude a reasonable degree of objectivity.

The counselor and client must respond to each other with humanness. For the counselor, this means first accepting and respecting the self before another can be accepted and respected. The counselor who does not accept and respect one's own self will find it difficult to accept and respect others; the counselor who is threatened by inner feelings may not be able to handle the feelings of clients. The warm and secure counselor exposes this warmth and security, and the counselor who values persons cannot help but communicate this value to the client. Being a counselor requires an honesty with oneself and with others. Being a counselor entails the ability to become aware of one's strengths and shortcomings and the effect they have on others.

The counselor must be willing to involve the self in the process of introspection so that the counselor can become more aware of the influencing aspects of his or her personal philosophy and how it affects personal counseling values, attitudes, and behaviors. The counselor's self must be known and cannot be denied.

The counselor must be human and real. A number of counselors find it is difficult to live the flow of experience they feel while counseling another person. They have difficulty being human and real. Society conditions us to put on a facade, to pretend to be that which we are not. We are compelled in daily living to be human despite a nagging toothache, financial troubles, mood, and worries. We cultivate what we consider to be the ideal personality. We learn to pretend interest when we feel disinterested. But counseling has no room for facades. Clients do not reveal themselves to counselors who pretend, who operate from behind a front. The humanness of the counselor facilitates personal revelation and growth in the client when the counselor is openly *being* the feelings and attitudes that are flowing within. Rogers (1964, pp. 160–161) uses the terms "congruence" and "incongruence" as a nomenclature to describe the presence or absence of this condition of being what one is experiencing and feeling.

The transparent self of the counselor facilitates the client's discovery of self. It requires courage to look at one's self honestly, to remove the mask that conceals the real being. Such courage is necessary for the counselor to be congruent and genuine and for the client to discover the meaning of personal experiences and existence. The barriers that inhibit congruence and genuineness reside in the counselor. By becoming more human, the counselor nurtures the humanness of the counseling relationship that enables the client to recognize and utilize his or her own human potentialities.

RECIPROCITY AND COMMITMENT

To understand and know what a counseling relationship is, we need to focus beyond counselor and client behavior to the reciprocal and complex interplay of counselor and client. A relationship exists when there is mutual interaction of persons and a reciprocal human exchange. Two subjects, counselor and client, form the essence of a third subject—the relationship—that is, the totality of what goes on concurrently *in* the counselor and the client and *between* the counselor and the client. Client behavior has a reciprocal impact on counselor behavior, which in turn has a reciprocal impact on client behavior; that is, counselor and client each have a stimulus and response value. A counseling relationship represents a circular flow of experience; it is a continuous unbroken stream of counselor and client behavior merging one into the other in such ways as to be at one moment cause and at the next moment effect.

The interrelationship of content and affect begins with the opening of the initial counseling session. Emerging from the first-expression of communication by the client or counselor and from the consequent response of the client or counselor is a tentative movement toward interpersonal commitment. To be sure, some kind of commitment must exist for counseling to begin at all, but this represents a generalized kind of commitment to a process. All counselors would probably say they are committed to assisting clients. Clients would say they commit themselves to a counselor and a process because they deeply feel the need for help or the need to communicate. Such involvement leads to interpersonal commitment.

When sharing affect and content, the counselor and client begin to know each other and become aware of their feelings regarding the evolving interaction. As the flow of experience and behavior becomes more intense and expanded, counselor and client invest themselves more deeply to the process and to each other. In turn, the increased psychic investment accelerates and intensifies the commitment to experiential and behavioral reciprocity.

VOLUNTARY INVOLVEMENT

The counseling process begins when the client becomes voluntarily involved (Patterson, 1969; Rogers, 1970). In seeking help the client takes an independent and responsible step of much significance. The client has arrived at the point where life has become discomforting enough to prompt the client to do something about resolving the discomfort.

Client-initiated counseling has a more human foundation than one into which the client has been forced. It is very doubtful that the counselor can develop any kind of acceptable human image among clients who are required to see a counselor.

Unfortunately, in all too many situations, counselors are directed by administrative fiat to see certain clients. Some counselors try to work around this by saying to clients that they are not being required to engage in counseling, they are being invited. But counselors are only deluding themselves to think that clients perceive a required association with a counselor as anything but a compelled relationship.

Client initiation of counseling is an essential ingredient for a meaningful relationship from our point of view. Beck (1965, p. 1) has pointed this out to counselors in discussing the implications of the view of existential philosopher, Sartre:

... it must be remembered that the whole act of counseling is voluntary because of the twin ideals of freedom and dignity assigned to the individual. The last thing an existentialist counselor would want to do is to give a person a chance to evade his own responsibility for choice and action, a chance to hide behind "authority" or the "collective demands of society." This would be a negation of what existentialism stands for. In that one structures the counseling situation toward a counselor's choice, to that degree does he infringe upon the freedom and commitment of the client.

Clients will not typically utilize counseling on their own if the counselor makes no attempt to motivate them to seek help. Well developed orientation procedures delineating the role of the counselor, the purposes of counseling, and the counseling experience are necessary for developing a positive image of the counselor and the counseling process.

Of course, the most valuable way of helping persons to freely choose counseling for themselves is through qualitative counseling relationships. The counselor who can assist clients can expect them to return for further counseling assistance; those clients who have a reasonably good reaction to counseling will transmit this feeling to their peers within an institution and within a community.

The number of client requests for counseling provides a good measure of the quality of a counseling service. If counseling is not meaningful and not characterized by warmth, trust, and acceptance, the number of voluntary client requests for counseling will be small, indicating the poor quality of the program.

In the case of referred clients, we feel that if the counselor indicates the source of referral and the reason why the referral was made, and clarifies the relationship by indicating what the client may expect from counseling, then the client may decide if counseling is to occur. The client will usually react by relating to the counselor and freely choosing to enter the relationship. The concept of human rights necessitates that the counselor respect the client's freedom of choice regarding whether or not to enter a counseling relationship.

Clients need to see counseling more in terms of the relationship than as a problem-centered process. Counseling then would not only emanate from a client's need for help but could also be based on a need to communicate. Such a notion would question the commonly held idea that counseling begins only when the client experiences a degree of anxiety or discomfort. But does ontological communion with other humans need to be based on the existence of a problem? Counselors can encourage clients who have had exciting or pleasant experiences to share these in the counseling. Sharing pleasant experiences with a counselor can be a rewarding and enriching experience for a client. Learning to express and deal with positive emotions is a developmental experience deserving of the counselor's attention and worthy of being accommodated in a counseling service. Positive relationships built upon pleasant experiences should be available to clients. Although it is true that clients may be able to find other persons in a community with whom they can communicate, the counselor, more often than not, can offer the time, the privacy, and the atmosphere for feelings of happiness to be deeply felt, experienced, understood, communicated, and appreciated. People like to be listened to and understood, and they like to share their periods of elation with others. Counselors need to accentuate the positive motivations for counseling as well as the problem-centered reasons. By emphasizing the possibility of the positive in the orientation process, the counselor helps clients to see counseling as an opportunity to relate with a counselor in an atmosphere of understanding in which a satisfying dimension of the self can be revealed and explored. Such contacts with a counselor will enable clients to feel more free to renew the relationship should a problem emerge in the future, and will motivate voluntary associations because the counseling service is seen as being person-centered rather than problem-centered.

MUTUAL RESPECT

One of the common factors that seems to appear in all approaches to counseling is the attitude of mutual respect and confidence. Effective counseling derives from a philosophy in which respect for the individual is uppermost (Kemp, 1971, p. 19). This means respecting the client's individuality, complexity, uniqueness, capacity for making choices, humanness, right to self-management, and potential. Respect for the person is based upon the counselor's recognition of the dignity and worth of the client. When we behave in recognition of the dignity and worth of the individual we represent that each person has value—value that is not determined by what the person has done or said, the clothes worn, where one lives, how one looks and speaks, one's job, how one relates to other people, and so forth. The value of each person is not a product of such superficialities.

The counselor who believes in the client's dignity and worth will epitomize respect for the individual by actions. It might be said that a belief one is not willing to translate into action is not a belief at all. It is one matter to verbalize a belief; it is another to put it into action. For example, how will the counselor who has a religious perspective behave with the hostile delinquent who sees God and religion as "phony"? Will the counselor see the delinquent as someone created in the image and likeness of God? Will the counselor behave in such ways as to facilitate the delinquent's use of free will even if it means the client's moving in the direction of values opposite to those of the counselor? Counseling, from a client-centered viewpoint, challenges the counselor to fully implement a belief in the dignity of the person and a deep respect for the individual. Respect for others can be implemented only as far as that respect is an integral component of the counselor's values. The counselor who is moving in the direction of feeling deep respect for the dignity and worth of other persons is more easily able to assimilate the essence of client-centered counseling than one who verbalizes respect that is not reflected operationally in the counselor's attitude toward clients. Talk of respect for others is easy. Action based on the recognition of the intrinsic value of each person speaks louder than words.

To value others, the counselor must first value the self. The person who does not have self-esteem and dignity cannot view others with esteem and dignity. Erich Fromm (1956, p. 49) has stated this with insight:

> . . . the logical fallacy in the notion that love for others and love for onself are mutually exclusive should be stressed. If it is a virtue to love my neighbor as a human being, it must be a virtue – and not a vice – to love myself, since I am a human being too. There is no concept of man in which I myself am not included. A doctrine which proclaims such an exclusion proves itself to be intrinsically contradictory. The idea expressed in the Biblical "Love thy neighbor as thyself" implies that respect for one's own integrity and uniqueness, love for and understanding of one's own self, cannot be separated from respect and love and understanding for another individual. The love for my own self is inseparably connected with the love for any other being.

Mutuality of respect will occur at the beginning of the first session if the counselor attitudinally conveys that the counselor has confidence and faith in the client's capacity to make decisions, that the client is free to develop, and that the client is a person of value. The counselor cannot communicate such respect through words. It is communicated through the counselor's attitude. The client develops faith in the self when the client *experiences* that it can be done. The client feels valuable when the client *experiences* being valued. In counseling, the client is and become what is experienced, not from being told this by the counselor. Confidence in and respect for the counselor are important ingredients in the development of positive and effective client-centered counseling relationships. However, initial confidence and respect can be lost unless the counselor behaves in ways that enable the client to feel and experience that the client is appreciated and valued as a person.

EFFECTIVE COMMUNICATION

Communication between counselor and client is expressed via affective, cognitive, verbal, and nonverbal modes. Effective counseling requires open modes of communication, and is encouraged and facilitated by a nonthreatening atmosphere. Effective communication occurs when the counselor receives what the client wants to communicate and the client receives what the counselor wants to communicate.

In order to respond to a client, the counselor must be reasonably free from the influence of personal needs and anxieties, which distort perception. The counselor needs to develop an affective sensitivity that is keenly attuned to the nonverbal and subtle cues conveyed through *tone* of voice, posture, bodily movement, a way of breathing, physical mannerisms, expression of the eyes—in other words, the subterranean signals that constitute the subliminal "language" of counseling. Counselor sensitivity to the complementary combination of verbal and nonverbal, cognitive and affective codifications opens up possibilities of communication that otherwise would be closed. Such awareness and sensitivity enable the counselor to directly experience the client, to receive and transmit intuitively. Although productive communication does demand that the counselor be sensitive to what the client says and how it is said, it further asks the counselor *to experience what the client is and what the client experiences.*

The client-centered counselor is maximally open to experience. The counselor's perceptual field is capable of change and adjustment, and it is not necessary for the counselor to distort perceptions to fit a previously formed concept. Openness to experience is contingent upon the counselor's freedom from threat, which in turn is an expression of the counselor's positive feelings about the self. The more positive the self of the counselor, the more positively he or she relates to clients. The more acceptant the counselor is of the self, the more acceptant he or she is of others. The client who is accepted and who experiences a relationship in which openness is prized becomes more open to personal experiences. The client's perceptual field widens.

To hear the client, the counselor must immerse the self in the client's flow of experience. Hearing the client means being in complete cognitive and emotional contact with the individual. It is a process requiring the counselor to be selfless so that personal expectations are not allowed to interfere.

When the client experiences deep listening there is a recognition that the counselor is attentive, cares, and is interested. Deep listening encourages self-revelation and facilitates the development of empathy, another critically important element in effective client-centered counseling. Empathy and sensitive listening are entwined. Empathy is the placing of one human spirit within another so that there is emotional congruence between counselor and client. The counselor empathizes when he or she assimilates the internal frame of reference of the client, perceives the world as the client perceives it, lays aside all perceptions from the external frame of reference, and communicates this assimilation to the client; but in order to be empathic the counselor first needs to listen and hear.

The empathic counselor is able to experience the client's reality even though that reality may not be congruent with "objective" reality. This is difficult to do, since most of us have learned to look at others according to external and objective criteria. But looking at another person according to external and objective criteria is one of the most inhibiting barriers to effective communication. Productive communication cannot occur unless the counselor first assimilates the personalized perceptions of the client. Viewing the client from an external frame of reference may help the counselor to *know about* the client but this does not mean the counselor *knows* the client. Empathy enables the counselor to know and understand the client.

GENUINE ACCEPTANCE

When a person is not required to defend the self, when that person can be what he or she is, there is an opportunity for behavior to change. The client who is free to be unique, to be different, and to hold values, is also free to look at the self. Acceptance of the client means giving the client the opportunity of holding and expressing personal meanings without ridicule, attack, or moralization; the right to see things in the client's own way (Glendlin, 1970; Patterson, 1969, p. 17).

When the client experiences acceptance of the self as the self currently is, the individual also feels safe to explore personal meanings. The client feels accepted only when he or she experiences genuine acceptance by the counselor. If the client does not feel that "it's all right to be myself here," or if difference is not valued, the client becomes defensive. The defensive client feels compelled to defend perceptions and consequently narrows these perceptions because of the threat represented in a counselor moralization, condemnation, or attack. A constricted view of the self by the client results in the constriction of communication with the counselor and a closing of the self to the counselor. On the other hand, the client who is accepted, who feels that "it's all right to be me, I can say what I like, I can be negative, I can be positive, I can be confused, I can talk, I can be silent, no one is going to judge me or preach to me, I can be what I feel," will freely and openly relate to the counselor.

Acceptance means that there are no reservations, conditions, evaluations, and judgments of the client's feelings, but rather a total positive regard for the client as a person of value. The client is valued and accepted as a person regardless of the negative feelings expressed. Genuine acceptance is unaffected by any differences in the client. It is not acceptance up to this or that point and no further, but acceptance even though the client possesses values, attitudes, and feelings different from those of the counselor. Acceptance of the client is not dependent upon the client's meeting certain moral or ethical criteria. It is complete and unconditional.

FOCUS

The more the counselor empathically focuses on the needs and feelings of the client, the more the counselor emphasizes the existential character of client-centered counseling. This means attitudinally communicating to the counselee that his or her feelings and experiences are of value and relevance. It means giving to the client the feeling that he or she can trust the self and draw from within the self in order to discover new meanings.

Empathically focusing on the client's needs and feelings enables the client to become more aware of internal strengths. The counselor who centers on the needs and feelings of the client, freely and without reservation, says, in effect, "You are the more important person in this relationship." In this kind of atmosphere the client begins to feel that the most meaningful learning is the learning that comes from within; that out of the client's values, attitudes, feelings, and experiences emerge the best possible answers and guidelines for personal behavior. When the client experiences the full empathic understanding of the counselor, the client begins to realize that those inner meanings can lead to more personally satisfying, appropriate, and self-enhancing behavior (Aspy, 1975; Patterson, 1969, p. 16; Rogers, 1975).

The counselor who concentrates on the client's problem is not necessarily concentrating on the client. Too many counselors work with problems and not with people. A problem is an abstraction. It can be analyzed and dissected; it can be explored and discussed; it can be written up in a case study; and it can be worked on coldly and scientifically. But to focus on a problem is to attend to a fragment. Counseling, from a client-centered viewpoint, should not be concerned with fragments. Needs and feelings must be considered in terms of the total person, the client as a being. Too much attention to a problem usually means too much attention to superficials. The client can confront the personal meaning of behavior and move in the direction of becoming more fully functioning only when he or she feels the counselor's primary commitment is an empathic concern with the client as a person and not with the client's problem. The central person in a counseling relationship must be the client. Counseling exists for the client, and counselor empathy for the needs and feelings of the client constitutes a central dimension of client-centered counseling.

LIBERATING ELEMENT

Each parent-child, husband-wife, teacher-student, and counselor-client relationship has unique qualities which, taken together, define a singular kind of human encounter. There are also qualities common to all relationships, and what makes for an effective counselor-client relationship perhaps also makes for an effective teacher-student or parent-child relationship. Yet there are some significant differences: (1) the degree and quality of emotional involvement of the participants; (2) the expectations and social, psychological, and educational preparation needed to assume the appropriate roles; (3) the social and psychological structure of the relationship; and (4) the implied purposes and goals of the relationship.

Client-centered counseling is a unique relationship that emerges from a flow and synthesis of experiences characterized by authenticity, humanness, empathy, congruence, genuineness, openness, acceptance, respect, understanding, direct experiencing, effective communication, concreteness, and complete focus on the emerging, becoming client (Boy & Pine, 1972). The uniqueness of the relationship also stems from what counseling is not. Unlike most human relationships, it is not characterized by sympathy, advice-giving, moralization, evaluation, explicit direction and control, questioning, probing, diagnosis, analytical interpretation, and authoritativeness. The absence in counseling of these elements, some or all of which are found in other human relationships, and the presence there of the unifying flow of existential qualities, delineate a human encounter singular and unique, a transaction differing in substance and quality from other human relationships.

One of the most distinctive and salient aspects of client-centered counseling is its liberating quality. Being liberated means the freedom to have ideas, beliefs, values, and permission to be oneself and to pursue interests and curiosity in search for meaning in life. Client liberation is a result of a counseling relationship characterized by acceptance, empathy, respect, and understanding for the client.

To be a liberating counselor requires emotional security and self-acceptance on the part of the counselor. If a client begins to express bitter invectives against a group, an institution, or an ideal with which the counselor strongly identifies, it requires an emotionally secure counselor to accept such expressions and feelings without moralizing and condemning. The counselor's beliefs and values will be constantly tested by clients who hold different views. But if the counselor truly believes that counseling exists for the liberation of the client, the counselor will not feel compelled to defend personal beliefs and values whenever they come under attack. If the client is to grow and understand the inner meanings of certain experiences, the client must feel free enough to be able to reveal the internal self without fear of contradiction or interference from the counselor. Most clients who enter counseling have been conditioned by society to hide their real selves. They have been taught to conceal their more authentic inner feelings in their relationships with others. The emergence of the authentic self, the evolvement of self-understanding, and the exploration of the internal world of the client come about when the client feels free to hold certain values, to accept them, to change them, or to reject them; and when the client experiences a freedom to remove the protective layers that cover inner feelings.

OUTCOMES EMERGE FROM THE CLIENT

A person often defines the self from the choices and actions taken. Although a person lives in a physically determined world governed by physical laws, the individual still has the awesome power of choosing a life to live. An existential dimension of client-centered counseling is the recognition of the client's capacity to make choices and to take action on the basis of these choices (Kemp, 1971, pp. 20, 28). Counseling is a process and relationship in which the individual is free to become more free. It is *a relationship that facilitates growth and change in the client, which enables the client to become more freely and fully functioning.*

Clients must possess the freedom and right to make choices and decisions. This demands enormous faith and consistency on the part of the counselor – faith in the client's capacity to choose, and consistency in holding to that faith regardless of the choices the client makes. No client is incapable of making choices, although some may feel that they can't. Often individuals have been directed and controlled to such an extent that they feel others should make choices for them. They fear becoming involved in self-determination since it is often an untried behavior. The counselor who is empathic and accepting of this attitude and enables the individual *to be* will facilitate the client's becoming more open to personal experience and perceiving the self with more confidence. The client who has been accepted and understood, and who experiences the deep faith of the counselor, will begin to see that if decisions are to be meaningful, they must be personally conceived and owned.

By transmitting positive attitudes to the client, the counselor communicates the feeling that the client *can be* more rather than the feeling that the client *must be* more. Even though the potential for change exists, the client does not feel compelled to change. The client can choose to change or not change, to speak or not speak, to be defensive or not defensive, or can choose to be independent or dependent. Faith is a two-way street. In the reciprocity of the counseling relationship, it not only flows from the counselor to the client but also from the client to the counselor, indicating that the client feels comfortable about the counselor's attitude and can deeply relate to this person who believes in the client's ability for self-direction.

The client who feels free to choose and move in any direction "discovers an increasing pride and confidence in making his own choices, guiding his own life – he tends to value those objects, experiences, and goals which make for his own survival, growth, and development and for the survival and development of others" (Rogers, 1964, pp. 160–161).

The movement toward free and full functioning is facilitated in an enabling relationship characterized by complete acceptance of the client and a deep belief in the client's strength and potentiality for growth. The more the counselor relies on the potentiality of the client and the client's capacity for choosing, the more the client discovers that potentiality and that capacity. Rogers (1951) emphasizes the significance of having complete faith in the client when he wrote that only as the therapist is completely willing that *any* outcome, *any* direction may be chosen, will the therapist then realize the capacity and the potentiality of the individual for constructive action.

Client-centered counselors believe that the client is responsible for the self and must retain that responsibility. There is no escape from the client's responsibility for choices. The client chooses or does not choose to enter counseling, chooses or does not choose to see a particular counselor, chooses or does not choose to continue the relationship, chooses or does not choose to terminate counseling, and chooses or does not choose to follow the flow of the counseling relationship. That the responsibility for choice must rest with the client has traditionally been indicated by existential thinkers: ". . . man is condemned to be free. Condemned, because he did not create himself, yet in other respects he is free; because once thrown into the world, he is responsible for everything he does" (Satre, 1947, p. 47); and by Vasudeva, who existentially speaks with Siddhartha:

> Could his father's piety, his teachers' exhortations, his knowledge, his own seeking protect him? Which father, which teacher, could prevent him from living his own life, from loading himself with sin, from swallowing the bitter drink himself, from finding his own path? Do you think, my dear friend, that anybody is spared this path? Perhaps your little son, because you would like to see him spared sorrow and pain and disillusionment? But if you were to die ten times for him, you would not alter his destiny in the slightest. (Hesse, 1951, p. 144)

The counselor facilitates client self-evaluation and self-determination, by recognizing, reflecting, and clarifying client values, attitudes, and feelings that surround a choice. As the counselor does this, the client tends to accept personal values, attitudes, and feelings. Since the client perceives values, attitudes, and feelings as coming from within, he or she begins to isolate the significant personal values, attitudes, and feelings that must be further explored. Self-awareness signals the emergence of self-determination. To the degree that the counselor focuses on the client and enables the client to become a self-determining, freely and fully functioning individual—to that degree does the counselor ennoble humanity.

Client-centered counseling is an open relationship, but it does have some structure. The counselor structures the relationship by defining the helping situation. The counselor indicates to the client that the counselor does not have *the answers* but will assist the client to work out self-developed answers through the relationship. Counseling is also structured in terms of time. By adhering to a stated time limit, the counselor contributes to the stability of the encounter. Dependency often occurs in counseling when there is an absence of structure. The client who enters counseling expecting that the counselor has solutions for problems and can tell the client exactly what should be done will find it extremely difficult to assume the responsibility of self-direction. Some counselors, in order to fulfill their own needs, are very happy to take over and try to control the behavior of the client. Other counselors find themselves unwittingly locked in a dependency relationship because they have not delineated the limits of counseling. Many of the problems the beginning counselor encounters exist because the relationship has not been defined in the first session or in a general orientation to counseling. Many problems of dependency can be prevented if the counselor carefully orients clients regarding what to expect from counseling. A well planned and continuous orientation, which spells out the role of the counselor and describes the nature of the relationship, will go a long way in preventing dependency relationships from developing.

CONFIDENTIALITY

Effective counseling cannot occur unless the confidentiality of the relationship is assured. If a client cannot feel secure in revealing the self to the counselor, it is highly doubtful that counseling will be helpful and facilitating. Self-revelation and exploration take place only in an atmosphere of trust (Pietrofesa, Hoffman, Splete, & Pinto, 1978; Pietrofesa, Leonard, & Van Hoose, 1978).

The client enters the counseling relationship more openly when it is known that the counselor will hold in confidence what is said. It is essential that the client feel completely secure about the confidential nature of the relationship; otherwise, he or she is uncomfortable and conceals the self.

Too many clients have bared their souls to counselors in what appeared to be a confidential relationship only to find out later that what they revealed in a "moment of trust" was communicated to others. In some institutions the counselor is perceived as the last person to be trusted.

Maintaining client confidences is not always easy. The ethics of counseling provide that in those situations where information received in confidence indicates that the client may do serious harm to the self or to others, intervention by the counselor may be necessary. If the counselor feels that a confidence must be broken, the counselor should certainly do some soul-searching to find out if the break is necessary, and if it is being done for the good of some organization or group or because of the counselor's insecurity, ignorance, and ineptitude.

No universal standard regarding the maintenance of client confidences can be clearly determined. Each counselor must translate general standards into a personal standard. The secure and competent counselor, who has been able to translate the philosophical foundations of counseling into the practicality of daily work, is aware not only of the depth of the obligation to the client in matters of confidence but of the many uncomfortable moments that will be experienced in maintaining this ethical standard.

ACQUIRED ATTITUDES AND SKILLS

Counseling is a professional service offered in public and private mental health agencies, schools, universities and colleges, rehabilitation centers, state employment service agencies, VA hospitals, and many other institutions and agencies. In our complex and continually changing world, the demand for qualitatively prepared counselors is rapidly increasing.

In the past, the counselor was essentially a dispenser of advice and information who in many cases was insensitive to the larger dimensions of the counseling role and function. Today's counselor must be highly knowledgeable in both the art and science of counseling. Today's counselor can no longer be a mechanic. Regardless of the setting in which counselors work, they must be more sensitive to the potential of their counseling to humanity; their functioning must be based on a broader perspective of the person and the counseling process. They must become involved in contributing to an improvement in the human condition by becoming more knowledgeable regarding the counseling relationship and its potential for assisting persons in the process of becoming self-directing and self-actualizing individuals.

Associations concerned with the professionalism of counseling emphatically support and affirm the concept of a quality educational program as the *beginning* level of preparation for a counselor. This means that there is a specific body of knowledge that the counselor must have; knowledge that must continually be expanded, refined, and modified.

To conclude: (1) the emerging counselor is a professional and belongs to a well established and active professional association; (2) the counselor's behavior is guided by a well thought-out code of ethics; (3) the counselor's role and functioning have been better clarified; (4) the counselor's need for specialized education and preparation have been delineated; and (5) the counselor is employed and screened for employment according to higher standards.

PHILOSOPHICAL AND PSYCHOLOGICAL PRINCIPLES

Professionalism is composed of process competence, ethical behavior, and an attitude that reflects one's philosophical, theoretical, and empirical views of the person, human behavior, and the counselor's society (Bergin, 1970). Counseling as a psychological relationship is a process expressing the counselor's philosophy of life. This means that each counselor must think out certain basic questions regarding the nature of the self and the client before effective counseling can occur.

The counselor cannot be a professional unless he or she has formulated a well thought-out rationale that undergirds professional behavior. Lister (1967) points out that the policy statements of the counseling profession leave no doubt about the need for a firm theoretical and philosophical foundation for counseling. A counselor cannot select appropriate functions without considering such assumptions about the nature of society and the individual's relation to it, the aims of a culture, and the nature of human behavior and the most effective counseling process for dealing with it. The counselor cannot achieve the status of a professional apart from a sound theoretical orientation.

Beck (1965, p. 1) believes it is imperative for counselors to consider the philosophy on which they base their functioning: "No field of endeavor which touches human lives can afford to leave its philosophical presuppositions unexamined."

One of the primary responsibilities of the professional is to examine and understand the basic purposes of professional activity. Arbuckle (1975) sees counseling as an expression of human values and human attitudes, a process in which the counselor gives a clear picture of a personal philosophical concept of the person, human nature, and the purpose of existence. For Arbuckle, the first question that should be examined by the counselor is the question of why we do what we do, rather than how we do it.

The professional counselor has a philosophical and theoretical rationale that gives insight to the what and how of counseling. Out of a rationale for counseling emerges a consistent identity and functioning. Philosopher Nietzche has said, "He who has a *why* to live can bear with almost any *how*." The counselor who has a "why" for counseling can assimilate the "whats" and "hows." The professional counselor does not have to search for methods of facing unusual situations, new experiences, and behaviorally different people. The professional counselor's "why" for counseling serves to clarify the "how" and "what" of counseling. A counselor who does not begin to examine the "why" of personal and professional behavior will perhaps never attain an integrated approach to people, life, and the counseling process.

A CONCEPT OF THE PERSON

We view the person as being free. The person may act or refuse to act, change or not change; as a free existent, the individual is nothing definite or finished, but is constantly coming to be. *Becoming* is more characteristic of the person than mere *being*. As a free existent, the person is responsible for personal human acts, which attach themselves to the self and are owned in a highly personal way (Patterson, 1969, pp. 3, 5, 13).

The person may be described as a responsible being, capable of self-direction, self-regulation, and self-understanding, and a being in the process of becoming. The person is a very complex being in whom many complicated elements fuse to form a unitary constantly interacting whole. Because the person is unique among all creatures and infinitely complex in derivations and being, the person perhaps can never be *fully* understood by the self and certainly not by anyone else. This uniqueness and complexity preclude any final definition of human needs and problems by others, no matter how expert.

Therefore, the counselor assists the client to solve *freely* the client's own problems through the client's own resources and to develop a human relationship in which the client is able to encounter the self in the process.

The goals of counseling are to help the person to become more mature and self-actuated, to move forward in a positive and constructive way, to preserve and nourish personal uniqueness; to release within the person the positive forces for growth that the person possesses; and to facilitate self-clarification and self-understanding so that the client may discover the meaning of a unique and personal existence.

This can be accomplished if the counselor can create a relationship in which the counselor is understanding, acceptant, empathic, permissive, concrete, and genuine, and if the counselor can consistently demonstrate a respect for personhood. This is the essence of good counseling regardless of the organization, institution, or agency in which it occurs.

BEING PRECEDES BECOMING

Before the client can *become*, the client must have the right to *be*. A client moves toward more personally satisfying behavior only when current behavior is examined and judged to be restrictive or inadequate. A certain behavior is rejected only after it has been allowed to exist and only after it has been perceived as being unfulfilling to the self (Combs, 1971; Kemp, 1971, p. 6). A client is motivated to change behavior because of the emergence of an inner awareness and motivation that enable the client to reject an inadequate self in favor of behaviors that enhance the self.

For the self of the client to be freed for growth it must be accepted as it presently exists. Acceptance of the client by the counselor means an acceptance of the client's values and attitudes as an integral part of the client's behavior. The counselor does not have to accept the client's values and attitudes as the counselor's own, but he or she must be willing for the counselee to hold different values and attitudes—for an individual is only free to change personal values and attitudes when there is freedom to hold them. The client is not forced to defend values and attitudes when the client is free to hold them; and when the client feels that personal values and attitudes are not condemned, judged, or labeled as "bad," the client can then allow them to be explored and evaluated. Behavioral change emerges from such an exploration when new supporting values and attitudes are developed.

The freedom to have ideas, values, attitudes, and beliefs—the permission to be oneself—exists in a counseling climate that is marked by a deep respect for the individuality and uniqueness of the client. The client's discovery of self, the unlocking of one's inner core, is a deeply personal matter. In the final analysis each individual must discover one's unique being in a highly personal way. In an atmosphere where uniqueness and difference are respected, the client is able to perceive the self as possessing dignity and worth. This counseling atmosphere that engenders positive self-discovery also provides protection from threatening experiences such as active attempts to change the behavior of the so-called "maladjusted." When, through the use of devices external to the person, we attempt to change the "maladjusted" person, what we do in effect is to reject that person. We say, "I will accept you, but I'll accept you with some reservation, on some conditions. I cannot accept you as you are; you must change!" In the zeal to change persons, there is often a very real danger that we communicate to the client that he or she is never acceptable as is. If the client has defined himself as a poor husband, if he sees himself as sexually inadequate, then the idea that someone wants to change him—that someone cannot accept him as he is—is highly threatening and will reinforce the client's desire to remain defensive.

The inner positive motivation that is built into each person is uncovered in the client when the counseling relationship encourages self-revelation rather than self-defense. In the relationship, the client is given the feeling that it is "all right to be me; my ideas and feelings can be looked at." Threat to the self dissolves so that personal feelings, values, attitudes, ideas, doubts, fears, and anxieties may be openly brought out and examined. The counselee begins to trust the self. This is important, for without some trust in one's self, the self cannot be motivated to change. When the client receives the external stimulus that what one is is not enough, the client responds by closing up the self. By giving the client the feeling that being oneself is acceptable—without fear or embarrassment, without the anxiety of being judged, or the diminution of the self in the process—the counselor creates an atmosphere in which the self can be honestly explored.

The sensitive counselor accepts differences among clients because he or she knows that where differences cannot be accepted, individuals cannot be. The counselor promotes the existential, ongoing character of human growth by creating an atmosphere that gives the client the feeling that the client's worth is held in high regard. As a result, the client feels a right of ownership regarding personal meanings, values, attitudes, feelings, and ideas. The counselee begins to respond to the acceptant counselor because the client has no need to defend the self. This is the impetus that enables a client to move toward more personally satisfying attitudes and behavior.

If the client is to move toward behavioral change, the counseling relationship must encourage the client to take a view from within. The client's emergence as a person is encouraged by the counselor creating an atmosphere in which the client is able to honestly explore personal values and behavior. Once again, if the client is to move toward improved behavior the client must first have the freedom to be; the client must exist in an acceptant counseling atmosphere. A person cannot move toward more personally satisfying attitudes and behaviors unless one has the opportunity to explore those which are currently held. But too many counselors inhibit such movement by presenting their own ideologies and values to the client. Instead of responding to and accepting the counselor's values and ideologies, the client retreats into a defense of his or her values, attitudes, and behaviors. When the client is confronted with a counselor who is attempting to break down the client's values and attitudes, the client's natural reaction is to reinforce the rationale upon which these values and attitudes are based. The client builds a defensive wall around the self which defies penetration by the counselor, and the counseling relationship becomes more of a debate than a stimulant for self-discovery.

Clients do not attitudinally move toward positive behavior because the counselor was victorious in a struggle of values. Clients move toward more adequate behavior because their existing values, attitudes, and behavior were not negatively judged by the counselor. They possessed the right to be before they could involve themselves in the process of becoming. The client's right to be must be deeply regarded by the counselor if the counselor expects the client to become involved in the process of changing behavior. A client's movement toward more personally satisfying behavior can only be achieved when he or she is given the opportunity to own current behavior nondefensively. The client moves toward more self-enhancing behavior when the individual is able to take a long, hard look at the self, reject those values and attitudes that inhibit functioning, and move toward values and attitudes that are personally more satisfying and influence more personally enhancing behavior.

REFERENCES

Arbuckle, D. S. *Counseling and psychotherapy: An existential-humanistic view.* Boston: Allyn and Bacon, 1975.

Aspy, D. N. Empathy: Let's get the hell on with it. *The Counseling Psychologist,* 1975, *5,* 10–14.

Beck, C. E. *Philosophical foundations of guidance.* Englewood Cliffs, N.J.: Prentice-Hall, 1965.

Berdie, R. F. Interdependency is freedom. *National Catholic Guidance Conference Journal,* 1971, *15,* 85–89.

Bergin, A. E. Psychology as a science of inner experience. In J. T. Hart & T. M. Tomlinson (Eds.), *New directions in client-centered therapy.* Boston: Houghton Mifflin, 1970, 61–69.

Boy, A. V., & Pine, G. J. *The counselor in the schools: A reconceptualization.* Boston: Houghton Mifflin, 1968.

Boy, A. V., & Pine, G. J. Values in the counseling relationship. *Counseling and Values,* 1972, *16,* 191–201.

Combs, C. The treatise on existential counseling by C. G. Kemp. *The Counseling Psychologist,* 1971, *2,* 43.

Fromm, E. *The art of loving.* New York: Harper, 1956.

Gendlin, E. T. Existentialism and experiential psychotherapy. In J. T. Hart & T. M. Tomlinson (Eds.), *New directions in client-centered therapy.* Boston: Houghton Mifflin, 1970, 73.

Hesse, H. *Siddhartha.* New York: New Directions, 1951.

Jones, A. J. *Principles of guidance.* (5th ed.). New York: McGraw-Hill, 1963.

Kemp, C. G. Existential counseling. *The Counseling Psychologist,* 1971, *2,* 2–30.

Leaman, D. The counselor's use of existential sharing in a synergistic relationship. *Counseling and Values,* 1973, *18,* 40–44.

Lister, J. L. Theory aversion in counselor education. *Counselor Education and Supervision,* 1967, *6,* 92.

Patterson, C. H. A current view of client-centered or relationship therapy. *The Counseling Psychologist,* 1969, *1,* 2–24.

Pietrofesa, J. J., Hoffman, A., Splete, H. H., & Pinto, D. V. *Counseling: Theory, research and practice.* Chicago: Rand McNally, 1978, 374–375, 427–428.

Pietrofesa, J. J., Leonard, G. E., & Van Hoose, W. *The authentic counselor* (2nd ed.). Chicago: Rand McNally, 1978, 177–178.

Rogers, C. R. *Client-centered therapy.* Boston: Houghton Mifflin, 1951 (renewed 1979), 48–49, 101.

Rogers, C. R. Toward a modern approach to values. *Journal of Abnormal and Social Psychology,* 1964, *68.*

Rogers, C. R. A conversation with Carl Rogers. In J. T. Hart & T.M. Tomlinson (Eds.), *New directions in client-centered therapy.* Boston: Houghton Mifflin, 1970, 532.

Rogers, C. R. Empathic: An unappreciated way of being. *The Counseling Psychologist,* 1975, *5,* 2–10.

Satre, J. P. *Existentialism.* New York: Philosophical Library, 1947.

Stewart, N. R., Winborn, B. B., Johnson, R. G., Burks, H. M., & Engelkes, J. R. *Systematic counseling.* Englewood Cliffs, N.J.: Prentice-Hall, 1978, 43–44.

Chapter 7

EDWARD: A CLIENT
IN THE PROCESS
OF BECOMING

INTRODUCTION

We wish to thank Elaine L. Cole for the transcription of the counselor-client dialogue contained in this chapter. The transcription was developed from a series of audio tape recordings that Cole made of her counseling with Edward, the client, and with his permission.

Elaine Cole received her Master's Degree in Counseling from the Graduate Program in Counseling at the University of New Hampshire. She is currently a counselor in private practice in Amherst, New Hampshire.

The purpose of this chapter is to provide an example of the application of our concept of client-centered counseling presented in Chapter 1. Cole begins her relationship with Edward by applying Phase One of the approach. She essentially responds to Edward by reflecting his feelings. By applying this reflective approach, she develops the necessary foundation for the second phase of her counseling. Through her reflections, Cole (1) establishes the relationship with Edward, providing him with the feeling that he is accepted, understood, and that the counselor perceives him and his feelings, from *his* internal frame of reference; and (2) assimilates a full picture of Edward: his attitudes, behaviors, life style, feelings, and the causal factors that influence each. Cole's attention to the importance of Phase One sets the stage for her movement toward Phase Two.

Before beginning the second phase of her counseling with Edward, Cole makes the transitional judgment that Edward needs encouragement from the counselor. In Phase Two, Cole begins to integrate the encouragement elements of an Adlerian counseling model with her reflections of feelings. She is supportive of Edward and Edward senses this support and responds to it.

Our concept of client-centered counseling is individualized in that whatever occurs in Phase Two is tailored to the individualized needs of a particular client. This philosophical and applied concept of individuality enables the model of client-centered counseling we have described to be flexible in meeting the identified Phase Two needs of individual clients rather than always applying one process model to all clients, regardless of their unique and individualized therapeutic needs.

THE CLIENT

Edward is a 58-year-old man involved in a cardiac rehabilitation program. He suffered a major coronary two years prior to the beginning of his counseling with Elaine Cole.

In the beginning, Edward, although talkative, was depressed and out of touch with many of his feelings regarding his heart attack. At the conclusion of his counseling, Edward is finally able to recognize and experience his anger, fears, depression, and guilt, as well as many other emotions that he repressed, which interfered with his recovery. Instead of feeling that his life's work is over, Edward terminates counseling with a new zest for experiencing life and with newly recognized personal goals and aspirations.

His relationship with his wife and six sons becomes markedly improved as Edward becomes more honest with himself and more open with his family. His feelings of self-pity and resistance are replaced by a deep sense of contentment as he recognizes and responds to the devotion and pride his children feel for him. His physical and psychic condition progresses from being weak to being strong and active. Counseling provided Edward with the *courage* to reach forward and *emerge* as a freer, more spontaneous, more authentic person who could deal with himself, others, and the various dimensions of his coronary.

COUNSELING SESSION FOUR

Counselor-Client Dialogue

Co: How are things going?

Cl: It can't get any better. It's as good as can be expected. Life goes on with its little "ups and downs."

Co: Tell me a little bit about the "downs."

Cl: Down is when I feel I should be able to do more than I'm doing. When I say to myself, "Ed, you can do more than that." I don't feel I'm doing what my body should be doing at its full capacity. But if I try—then I notice—well—I get tired but I don't know where to draw the line. Then I think possibly I get discouraged a bit—to a point. To a point where I say to myself, "How come you can go just this far?"

Co: Uh, huh.

Cl: There is so much to do. If I can't finish a job, I smile at it and say, "I tried."

Co: So, I've improved but I'm also a little bit disappointed that when I think I can do more and I find I really can't.

Cl: Umm. (now *experiencing* the feeling of discouragement and disappointment that he was not fully aware of in beginning of session) Down deep I think – there's a little jealousy in me about the human race. That is – I've got to come down and face facts and look at it that way. I've had a heart attack. I look at the other person. If I'm trying to walk and carry something – that's really difficult. If you ask me to pick up this chair and carry it across the hall – that's a strain. I know it and I see people with packages in their hands and they walk and walk. I'm a little envious of that. I used to do it. I've lost all this. To me it's natural to feel the way I do. I had this strength and now it's gone.

Co: uh, huh.

Cl: Well – my down days – I do get them. It's so odd because I question myself – how come you're down? I try to blame it on other things like the weather.

Co: Sounds to me like you realize you feel a lot of anger, disappointment, and jealousy about the fact that this had to happen to you.

Cl: Well, this is what I think "down days" are really about.

Co: Why me?

Cl: Yeah, why me, Lord? But I also look around and know a lot of people who haven't made it. So there's a bright side and a low side and sometimes I'm thankful.

Co: So, I can look at my heart attack and say – there are people who aren't as well off as I am, but still, there is always that feeling there are a lot of people better off physically than I am – they can carry bags and lift chairs and damn, I wish I were one of them again.

Cl: Yes – Yes! If people only know how valuable life is – how valuable that "ticker" is they wouldn't waste life!

Co: It makes me so angry when I see people not appreciating life.

Cl: Yes – if they could only learn to appreciate. I never appreciated life as I do now.

Cl: Yeah – to live life fully. I don't want to be just forgotten. When you asked me, "Are you afraid to die?" Possibly this is my answer: I am afraid to die before I leave my mark. I'm afraid to live – but, yes, I'm also afraid to die. So what is there to be contented with?

Co: It's good to hear you say that you are afraid to die. When we started our sessions four or five weeks ago you repeated quite often, "I'm not afraid to die, Elaine. I've almost been there and it's not scary. It's just that I don't want to leave what's here."

Cl: I ask myself, have I given enough to this life? I've got too much to share. I want to share it with people.

Co: I deeply want to leave something of myself to people.

Cl: If I keep everything to myself – this is not love and I love people. If you love people you want to give them something. I've got knowledge.

Co: And I want to share it. That means a lot to me – *that* will make my life worthwhile – give it meaning. I can't work at my old job any more, but if I can share part of *me* with other human beings – that will make the rest of my days really meaningful.

Cl: This may be the goal I'm after. Of course you may think I'm an odd ball.

Co: I think you are just a beautiful person, Edward, and I get such wisdom from you. You're right – you have a great deal to give people.

Cl: I've just taken a leadership course in church and I love it. I put a discussion group together; but, how many are ready to receive me? Sometimes, only two people show up. I don't go home smiling. I ask myself where did I go wrong?

Co: I've got so much to give but I can't find the people to give to – and – it's frustrating.

Cl: Yes, like I had this friend who was having headaches, no one could help. Well, I knew a man who was having the same headaches so I arranged for them to talk to each other. Well, it worked great and he feels better and he calls me every day to thank me. It was the communication.

Co: You brought them together and you let it happen between the two of them and you feel good about doing this.

Cl: He feels that he's a different man.

Co: And I feel responsible and really good about it. I feel like a missionary. Look what I did for this guy.

Cl: Yes! Here was a guy who didn't want to come out of his house but I encouraged him and he got so much out of it.

Co: And that's the kind of thing I want to do with people. I want to use my time now to help people.

Cl: This is my idea of beauty. This is my idea of worthwhile living.

Co: I have to have some meaning to my life and this really adds meaning to life.

Cl: I have to tell you something else. Since I started talking with you I've begun to go back over my life and I wondered what happened that made me think differently than I do now about people. It goes back to my rejection from the Army because of shortness of breath.

Co: Uh, huh.

Cl: *Now* I know I took that very hard.

Co: It made me feel weak and rejected.

Cl: Yes. I never had anything wrong before. I never talked about it before, but I think I've spent my whole life trying to get over this rejection.

Co: And I feel the heart attack has been a little bit of that, too. It's been more rejection. The same slap in the face.

Cl: Yeah, the same slap again.

Co: A weakness.

Cl: Yes – weakness – you know, I went back and asked for another checkup when the Army rejected me because I didn't want to believe it. And now I realize I didn't want to believe my heart attack.

Co: Because the heart attack stirs up all those old feelings of weakness and rejection in me all over again. It made me feel like a weak man. Physical strength is important to me.

Cl: I'm tying all this together now, and when you say, "Ed, are you afraid to die?" I'm tying all this in—and possibly I have a reason to say that. From then on (time of rejection from Army) I *realize now* that I overworked my body.

Co: I was so *angry* about being rejected I overworked my body to show people, "See, I'm not weak."

Cl: Yes, yes.

Co: I'm just as good a man as anyone else.

Cl: I think now this is exactly what I was doing.

Co: I was trying to prove to myself and the whole world that I was strong.

Cl: Umm—that gave me the spirit of fighting back.

Co: I was angry.

Cl: Rage! More than anger!

Co: Real rage!

Cl: Right—that's when I went out and learned to be a teacher of mechanics. My wife said, "Why are you working so hard?" I said, "Because I want to"—but I can see now it was not because I wanted it. I can see *that now*. I didn't then, but now I know I did it to prove, "No one's going to knock me down! I've got pride!"

Co: I'll prove to everyone I'm strong!

Cl: Yep—I've done just that—but today I'm paying for it. Then I thought I'd like to go into plumbing. I was 41 and someone said to me, "At your age you'll never be a plumber." Well, I *did* become a plumber.

Co: And a good one! I've showed them I can do it!

Cl: Uh, huh. I showed them I can do it. There is nothing that can't be done if you set your mind to it.

Co: And, that's the fight, Edward, and that's the drive that makes you push. You want to show people here, and everywhere, you can recover from this heart problem.

Cl: This is what I think this is all about. That's why I'm telling you all this—to see if this is what I'm doing now. I've got enough logic in myself now to say, "Hey, Ed, are you going to do that again? If you are—are you going to get hurt by it?" Before, I didn't look at this—I didn't know what was going on. I can say now: "Are you going to fight this heart attack or are you going to accept it? Are you going to challenge everything in life?" It was like coming to see you. I was coming in to challenge *you*, I think, but I've learned in here—instead of challenging—to be open. I know now, if I've got something to say, it has to come out. If it doesn't and I hold it inside

I'll be back to what I was like when I was drafted – keeping it all to myself.

Co: That's right, Edward.

Cl: And, I'm not going back to that stage! So if I talk quietly at times, or repeat myself at times, it is because those feelings are still inside me and until they come out I don't think I'm free.

Co: And that's what we want to work with. That's how I see our counseling relationship – *we together* you and me – will both help you to work through some of these feelings. I can't do it for you, and it's hard for you to do alone, so maybe *together* we can work it through.

Cl: We can work it through (nodding). The point is how – being open – I don't think I ever accepted my heart problem.

Co: That's right, Edward. It was hard for you to accept it.

Cl: I know everything about it – I know I've had one – but *have I* accepted it? This is my question.

Co: I know I've had a heart attack – I could write a book about heart attacks – but *inside*, I still don't want it to have happened to me.

Cl: Uh, huh – yes. Now I ask myself, "If I leave this earth today, did I help another person?" Then, I wouldn't die in vain. These are my goals now.

Co: Because I realize that a lot of the things I did in life, I did to get revenge and to prove myself – they were *selfish reasons*.

Cl: Yeah, did I live a life of revenge. Possibly I'm at the point of saying – enough revenge – start sharing what you've learned with somebody else.

Co: If I've spent most of my life being angry with my fellow human beings, now I've got to put that away and start giving love – and anything else I can give.

Cl: Yes – if I can gain one step forward, I haven't worked in vain. I'm now talking the way I feel.

Co: I don't want to leave life feeling most of my life has been revengeful.

Cl: Yes, I'd like to leave some kind of mark. I've fought to overcome this heart attack – now I've got to do something meaningful. The Lord has given me another chance.

Co: Uh, huh.

Cl: I feel pretty good about coming here.

Co: I'm glad you do because I certainly gained a lot from our times together.

Cl: I'm glad because I don't believe that when I'm over here and you're in that chair, that I have to put you up on a pedestal.

Co: I hope you don't!

Cl: This is what I'm learning – I've got something to give, too.

Co: I don't feel inferior to people anymore because I'm valuable in my own way.

Cl: Yes, I'm valuable and it's good to feel that way.

Co: Good for you! Sounds like it's going well. Looks like our time is up for today—but you're working through a lot, Edward, and I want to encourage that, because you are getting in touch with your feelings and sharing them, and that's such a good thing. It's great! You're putting a lot of pieces of the puzzle together.

Cl: Yes—I really think that.

Co: See you next time. I look forward to our getting together again.

COUNSELING SESSION SIX

Counselor-Client Dialogue

Co: Hi, Edward, how are things?

Cl: O.K.

Co: You know that Wednesday you and I won't meet because we are going to have our first group counseling session (with other heart patients).

Cl: Yes.

Co: I'm really counting on you to help carry the ball because I know you are really interested. For a lot of new group members this will be a strange experience.

Cl: I hope they can open up. I hope there will be a good outcome from the sharing in the group—may be relaxation physically and mentally. If you talk about it, it's not so bad as if you hold it inside.

Co: You feel better now talking about your feelings.

Cl: Yes—really. Sometimes I feel uncomfortable talking to people about my heart attack because it seems like I'm crying on their shoulder. I don't know whether they feel that way—.

Co: But that's how it makes *me* feel.

Cl: Maybe it's my imagination but it seems after I tell someone about my heart attack they seem to protect me more—they take over.

Co: They feel sorry for me and I don't want pity.

Cl: Right! I guess that's it. I don't like to tell people because I don't want pity—yeah. I lowered myself when I got my heart attack.

Co: I'm not clear on what you mean, Edward.

Cl: I mean I blamed myself for my heart attack. I think I still do. I didn't know enough about heart attacks and what to look for.

Co: Maybe if I knew more about heart attacks I could have prevented mine. This makes me feel regretful and upset.

Cl: Yeah. I had the feeling I overworked myself when it was not necessary.

Co: Maybe if I hadn't been a slave to my work I wouldn't have abused my body so much.

Cl: Yes, like when I was on a job with a jackhammer, breaking concrete, and I found myself out of breath and tight in the chest. Now if I had been more educated I'd have known these were symptoms. But no.

Co: I wish I could have done something to prevent it.

Cl: Yes, but since I've been talking to you I've gained an awful lot. Even *with* my heart attack I didn't lose anything—in fact, I believe I've gained. Now I'm looking at what is here today. I realize I can really help people.

Co: So you really feel now—

Cl: Instead of helping with plumbing I'm helping *people* now. This is the switch I've made because I'm leading church groups now. Maybe I kind of knew it in the past—but I never put it into practice before!

Co: I have a chance now to work and share with people. I have a new way of living and I really love it.

Cl: Yes. Now I go and meet people. I used to feel odd because there were a lot of words I don't pronounce right, but now I can say, "Hey, I'm me, I don't pronounce this word right—so what!"

Co: So what! I'm me!

Cl: So, I've overcome this.

Co: I've developed a lot of self-confidence.

Cl: Very much so. And I want to share the beauty I'm getting now. I can't keep it to myself.

Co: The meaning I'm getting out of life . . . what I hear you saying is you're so full of love for people you really want to share it.

Cl: Yes. I have to go on their home ground though. I see so much beauty in life and people overlook it.

Co: And I want them to appreciate life as I do now. I want to help.

Cl: Before, I didn't have time to appreciate what's around.

Co: Life was going so fast because I kept so busy.

Cl: Yes, I was so busy I couldn't keep up and my body couldn't take it. Now, there is so much beauty and I want to share it. So many people reject the beauty around them.

Co: Uh, huh.

Cl: I'm living now in a different world. I have a different approach to everything.

Co: This is what you want to share.

Cl: Yes, I'm enjoying myself. I'm enjoying life.

Co: And I'm so glad and grateful I've had this second chance. I'd have missed *so* much.

Cl: Yes, when you asked me once, "How do you feel about dying?" Well, I'm just starting to live.

Co: I know that. I can feel that in you.

Cl: I'm just starting to appreciate life. I want to give a lot. I don't have any money to give—but I've got much more important things to give.

Co: You do have a wealth to give.
Cl: Because if I see someone who needs help –
Co: Edward, did you just hear what I said to you?
Cl: Yes. You said I've got wealth.
Co: Do you believe that?
Cl: Yes, there are a lot of things I can share with others.
Co: I think you have a whole treasure box of things you can give.
Cl: Yes, and I'm not going to die until I can give those things in my treasure box away and someone can multiply them. In this way, I'm not ready to die. This is when I get scared to die. I don't want to run out of time. I think the future looks brighter, the family is much closer. They don't nag me as much to be careful.
Co: Um, hum.
Cl: I feel pretty lucky.
Co: Things at home are better. I'm not being treated like a sick person . . . the way that they used to treat me.
Cl: Right. It was so aggravating and it used to depress me. I resented it and I'd want to fight it like we've talked about.
Co: But now that I've talked about my feelings with my family, instead of holding them inside, things really do seem to be much better and we are all happier together.
Cl: Amen to that!
Co: I'm happy you are feeling good about the changes that are going on inside of you, Edward. It's really exciting for me to be experiencing your growth.
Cl: O.K., Elaine – I look forward to seeing you next week!

COUNSELING SESSION EIGHT
(Last Session)

Counselor-Client Dialogue

Co: It's good to see you – you look good!
Cl: I feel good. I think I'm at my best.
Co: Stronger.
Cl: I feel stronger – uh – I'm doing more exercise – I feel better – stronger and more like – well, achieving things.
Co: More energy?
Cl: More energy – yep!
Co: That's great.
Cl: I've been doing a little mechanical work on cars.
Co: You feel good about being able to work.
Cl: Yes, but now when I feel tired I quit and it doesn't make me angry anymore. I don't feel nervous about quitting.
Co: Um, hum.
Cl: I've taken on a different attitude and I think I'm really happy. I

haven't been as interested in writing lately but I've been more active. I'm doing more manual work again.

Co: And it really feels good to have energy again and be able to do some of the things I've missed.

Cl: Yes. I'm getting stronger. I really am more of a manual man. And now that I can do more manual things, my writing and work with my church group doesn't seem as important. I'd like to be interested in both the church group and manual things but I realize that I can't do everything.

Co: And my first love is still the manual and creative field and now that I can get back to that, the other thing isn't as important to me.

Cl: Yes, this is where – this is what I'm trying to come out with . . . some kind of balance for myself . . . but I still want to have time for the people at church.

Co: Um, hum.

Cl: Counseling has shown me a lot – done almost everything it possibly can. It's done everything for me . . . much more than I expected.

Co: But you now wonder – if I do keep getting stronger and into more manual things, am I going to let these people down who were counting on me in the church group?

Cl: I don't think I could ever get to the point of forgetting – where I wouldn't work with people at all. Before, the reason I wouldn't do it was that I was making up excuses – I don't pronounce words right or my grammar isn't good enough. But I worked it out.

Co: Yes, you did.

Cl: I talk into a microphone now – all my life I've been afraid to do that, but now I said, "Hey, you've got to do it."

Co: That's really wonderful!

Cl: I've come a long way in being able to work with and help people but I'm still a manual man.

Co: And I still love that.

Cl: I still love that. Like in plumbing, I take nothing, and I create. I go for that. I'm in love with my work . . . but at this point in my life I have to be careful not to overdo it. I've put a lot of time and energy and a lot of love in my work.

Co: Um, hum.

Cl: That's the way I am. I feel a lot of pride in it and in myself.

Co: And now I'm happy to be getting into it again, but I have to be careful not to go overboard and overdo it. I'm excited, too.

Cl: Yes, I am excited and you're right – a little scared because I don't want to go overboard.

Co: Yes.

Cl: I've got more self-control now than before. I can say "no" now.

Co: You're planning more now on how to use your time at manual things and not to overdo it.

Cl: Yes, I save more of my body strength – I've made a tray of tools and use it to save steps.

Co: That sounds like it's going really well for you.

Cl: I feel much stronger.

Co: And I think that's partially because you're exercising more but also because you've got your mentality and emotions "up" now. You've got something to look forward to now and that gives you greater energy.

Cl: Right, I'm getting more strength and I can see it and feel it. Up until now I've been healing, but it hasn't been showing—the inside physical healing of my heart. But now my healing is taking place on the outside of me and it's showing!

Co: That's right, Edward. Finally there is really proof that I am getting better and that's so good to feel it happening!

Cl: So—there's not much more I can say—the best is happening to me!

Co: The best is right! It looks good, doesn't it?

Cl: It looks good, I feel good. Talking with you too—there was some stuff that was in the past I think, that possibly affected me now. But talking about it—made me realize that it's gone.

Co: I've been able to look at that "stuff" and get rid of it.

Cl: It's gone. It came up to the surface after a lot of years and now it's gone.

Co: I'm really glad to hear you say that.

Cl: I've got a different attitude . . . a different approach to life.

Co: That's great! Well, that's what I was thinking—as far as I'm concerned the time we need to spend together is about over. I see you as really strong physically, emotionally, and mentally and I think things are going to go well for you from here on.

Cl: I feel it will! I'm looking forward to my vacation this year. The kids are planning to come with us this year and that's great.

Co: Isn't that nice for you!

Cl: So no matter how I say it, I keep saying, everything is finally good for me!

Co: I can see that, in just the way you look—you know—you have more energy—I can see your energy and satisfaction.

Cl: Another thing that proves that *I'm the one* who's doing the changing—I noticed at first that my wife is changing—then I noticed that my oldest son is changing—then I noticed that my other son is changing. Then I said to myself, "Wait a minute, they can't *all* be changing. Why don't I switch that around and realize that *I'm* the one who is changing!"

Co: Wow!

Cl: See, I've noticed and accepted that . . . and it's great!

Co: Yes!

Cl: Before, I don't know if I could have accepted that or not . . . *me* changing!

Co: Uh, huh.

Cl: If there were only one person, I could say that they've changed . . . but when there are seven of them that are changing—

Co: That's a good observation – really – a great observation!

Cl: I realized that they weren't changing . . . but that *I* was changing.

Co: I am the one doing the changing.

Cl: This is what's happening!

Co: And you're pleased and happy with your change.

Cl: Yeah – because I can talk to my wife – I can talk to my son. It was hard for me before because I was afraid . . . I'd say to myself, "I'm going to hurt them," and things like that.

Co: Uh, huh.

Cl: And now we are getting along better. I show them by my attitude that I've changed . . . I listen.

Co: And you didn't have time to listen before.

Cl: I didn't take the time.

Co: Now you listen.

Cl: I think prior to this I always had to get my two cents into everything.

Co: Uh, huh.

Cl: I'd feel, "I don't care what *they* say, but I'm going to get *my* point across." I found out if you listen you don't have to put your two cents in – they already have the answer.

Co: And you sound, Edward, like you are more able to accept them – who they are and what they are saying to you – better than you could before.

Cl: Oh, yes. Oh, yes. I'm willing to listen – not only willing – in fact, I enjoy it!

Co: Uh, huh.

Cl: I don't think I was trying to control anyone's life, but maybe somewhere along the way, I did that, subsconsciously. Before I was so busy getting an answer ready for everybody.

Co: I didn't really hear what they were saying.

Cl: That's right.

Co: And now that I am listening better I can accept them better and they respond to that.

Cl: We really have some great conversations now.

Co: That's fabulous!

Cl: It's not big stuff – but the big stuff is not what counts – it's the little things that keep happening between me and my family.

Co: The little connections and the little ways your wife and kids are showing you that they like the way you've changed!

Cl: They sure like it!

Co: Yes – and they show it.

Cl: And they appreciate it and I do, too.

Co: I think they're pretty happy about still having you around.

Cl: Yes, yes – I think they are!

Co: And don't forget, Edward, they've been able to see you cope with, and adjust to, this heart problem. Sure you had your "down times," but you didn't let them wipe you out!

Cl: No—those times weren't going to wipe me out.

Co: And your family respects you for that.

Cl: They have mentioned that a few times—"Daddy didn't give up."

Co: And, it makes me feel good to know I licked it and they are proud of me.

Cl: I think too, at some point, I was really feeling scared.

Co: Sure—

Cl: I didn't want to but—I guess it was natural.

Co: I didn't want to admit that I was scared, but I realize now that I was.

Cl: So now I'm saying, "I've got a second chance in life and I'm going to make the most of it."

Co: I believe that! I think it's going to be a beautiful "rest of your life" too—very full—

Cl: I feel good about it!

Co: Well, for us, I guess the way I want to leave it is that I sense that we are about finished. How do you feel?

Cl: I feel finished. You know me like an open book. I've done enough complaining.

Co: Not complaining, Edward, it's been a beautiful book for me. I've seen you grow and become able to talk about your feelings and that's really important.

Cl: I think in your case I'm a little jealous of what you do. You can see people—you take them from being down and build them to a strength where they can stand on their own two feet.

Co: And you'd like to do more of that helping.

Cl: Yes, that's really my goal for my future—I know that now—to share myself more with people.

Co: And I believe you can and will do that and how lucky for those people! (Counselor and client embrace.) Edward, I want you to feel free to get together with me in the future . . . if you feel the need to talk things over. You know where I can be reached.

Cl: I'll do that—if I need to—but for right now, I feel fine. God bless you.

Co: And you also—good-bye, Edward.

Chapter 8

GROUP-CENTERED COUNSELING

Group counseling appears to have reached a period of stability in being accepted as a facilitative human experience that can influence participants to become more psychologically whole. This more recent acceptance is in marked contrast to the controversies that surrounded the group experience in the 1960s and early 1970s. During this controversial period, various groups competed with each other for "ownership" of the group experience and seriously damaged its credibility. This was a confused and turbulent period for group counseling but it should be reviewed in order to understand the influences that existed and how the repercussions of these influences can be still felt today.

During this confused and turbulent period, group counseling was at the crossroads of acceptance and some influential groups were attempting to determine its eventual direction; these influences ranged from blind support to outright rejection but there is no doubt that the credibility of group counseling, and its various forms, hung in the balance.

The purposes of the following section are: (1) to indicate the dimensions of the influence that was exerted; (2) to indicate that the advancement and professionalism of group procedures in counseling was hampered, in various ways, by the commercial communications media, reactionaries, euphoric colleagues, and gimmick-centered colleagues; (3) to indicate that the status of group procedures in counseling was, and will be, sustained only in proportion to our ability to separate sense from nonsense; and (4) to provide the historical and attitudinal context within which our own experiences have been processed and from which our views on group-centered counseling have emanated.

INFLUENCES ON GROUP COUNSELING

Commercial Communications Media

In the 1960s and early 1970s interest in group procedures mounted rapidly on a national scale. Increasing numbers of Americans were being directly or vicariously exposed to the group experience. The catalysts for this interest were the National Training Laboratories, which introduced T Group work; Esalen Institute, which introduced sensitivity training; and the Center for Studies of the Person, which introduced the basic encounter group process.

Whenever a sufficient number of Americans develop an interest in anything (hot tubs, astrology, jogging, health foods, the occult), we have a corresponding interest emerging from those whose prime motive is economic. Because of the public's fascination with the group experience, former rent-a-car magnate Warren Avis assumed ownership of Detroit's Behavioral Science Training Laboratories, while Atlanta's Human Development Institute, which grossed 1.5 million dollars a year, became a subsidiary of the Bell and Howell Corporation ("The Group: Joy on Thursday," 1969).

The media took advantage of this peak period of interest in group work. The consuming public was exposed to the following by the commercial communications media: *Life* magazine published a sensational article entitled, "Inhibitions Thrown to the Gentle Winds" (Howard, 1968); The *New Yorker* gave a bizarre account of the group experience in "The Thursday Group" (Adler, 1967); the *New York Times Magazine* made its contribution with "The Year of the Group: Eavesdropping on Some Highly Intelligent Neurotics" (Lamott, 1968); a novel entitled, *The Lemon Eaters* depicted the participants in the group experience as various kinds of deviates (Sohl, 1967); *Time* magazine produced an article about nude group therapy ("Psychotherapy: Stripping Body and Mind," 1968); the *Boston Sunday Globe* carried the naturalistic, "T-Groups: A New Technique for Preserving Identity Amid Mass Pressures" (Dietz, 1968); the *Star Weekly* magazine produced an article that possessed a soap opera aura, "The Thousand Year Week, a Gripping – and True – Account of the Unique Kind of Group Therapy that is Bringing New Insights into Many of the Hangups of North American Life" (Frazer, 1968); *Look* magazine mingled the experiences of natural childbirth and group therapy in "The Man and Woman Thing" (Leonard, 1968); the Associated Press wire service indicated that apartments for single persons need never be empty if the owner provides "Encounter Groups: Attracting the Singles Market" (1969); *Playboy* magazine provided its insights into the group experience with "Alternatives to Analysis" (Havemann, 1969); and the National Broadcasting Company produced a television melodrama, "Companions in Nightmare," in which murder and intrigue were depicted as part of the group experience (Universal Studios, 1968).

The public responded to these stimulants by being either infatuated or negativistic. Both kinds of response were based upon ignorance since the group experience was neither a miraculous cure nor a psychological lobotomy. Such polarized responses by the public affected the credibility and status of group experiences in professional work settings; and one source for the public's distorted and superficial information was the commercial communications media.

Reactionaries

Because the commercial communications media insisted on sensationalizing the group experience, the response was equally sensational. When certain elements of the commercial communications media equated the group experience with nudity, sexual promiscuity, or drugs, the panic button was firmly pressed by those who possessed diametrically opposed values. The issue became heated and without hope of cooling; the battle became joined.

In an article entitled, "Hate Therapy," which appeared in *American Opinion*, a magazine published by the John Birch Society, Allen (1968) had this to say about sensitivity training:

> The group and self-criticism technique – Sensitivity Training – is used today in every Communist country in the world. Their thought-control people have learned from experience that it is an effective weapon not only for producing "mass man" or "group man," but also for locating "reactionary individualists" who may become opposition leaders.

> . . . there is a sick fascination involved in sensitivity training which brings sadism or masochism. Sensitivity training attracts sadistic personalities and they tend to assume leadership because of their strength and ruthlessness. Verbal voyeurs are attracted by the prospects of vicariously running through everyone else's sex life. The process brings out the worst in everybody.

> This is the essence of Sensitivity Training – substituting the will and judgment of the group for that of the individual. You exchange your personal values, convictions, and morality for those of the group. You subjugate your intellect for their emotions. Group security is substituted by individual security.

The preceding reactionary responses occurred largely because of the misrepresentations of the group experience provided by the commercial communications media which stimulated interest in groups through sensationalism.

Euphoric Colleagues

During this period, there were colleagues who were emotionally committed to group work and who became euphoric about the experience. Such enthusiasm was refreshing, but it was not often tempered with reason and objective evidence. The group experience was, and is, emotionally powerful in terms of the participant's feelings about the self and how it interacts with others. In some cases, the experience was so overwhelming that some were emotionally swept off their feet and became committed to developing a secular theology surrounding the group experience – complete with an affectively based set of beliefs and rituals. Such euphoric colleagues came to be labeled as members of a "touchy-feely" quasi-religious cult whose sole motivation for existence seemed to be, *"sentio ergo sum* – I feel, therefore I am."

During this period, professionals went beyond the label, *sentio ergo sum*, and realized that in regard to group procedures in counseling, yes, there were things to be felt if the person was to emerge; but, at the same time, there were dimensions to be cognitively known if the art and science of group work was to be advanced and preserved as a legitimate professional endeavor. As Franklin Murphy (1968), Chancellor of the University of California at Los Angeles said, in addressing himself to the problems of the larger society: "You cannot build a society on feeling alone. Only a proper blend of reason, action, and feeling will build a better world." What Chancellor Murphy said about the larger society also aptly applied to expanding the professional understanding of the rationale, process, and outcomes of group procedures in counseling.

Gimmick-Centered Colleagues

At this time, there were group counselors, experienced in interacting verbally with clients at an affective level, who were aware of the clinical and empirical evidence that indicated behavioral change occurs as a result of such interactions.

But also on the scene were group leaders who were minimally educated in the process of verbal transactions and, because of this deficiency, they resorted to nonverbal gimmicks as techniques of communicating with group members and helping them to communicate with each other. The less educated and relatively inexperienced group counselor was overwhelmed by the matrix of verbal transactions that occur in group work and was unsophisticated regarding how the counselor should verbally respond. The only quick recourse was to control the group by introducing nonverbal techniques which put the counselor in command of the situation and enabled the process to proceed on the counselor's own terms—nonverbal rather than verbal because the leader was not able to respond verbally at the affective level when group members verbally expressed affect.

The following training exercises were recommended for use by such group leaders: back lift, beating, fantasy game, body positioning, doubling, humming, wordless meetings, bodily feel, no exit dyad, lost person, daydream, new names, break in, milling, pushing, break out, and roll and rock (Schutz, 1967).

The nongimmick counselor, however, had to struggle, in this gimmick-centered atmosphere, to help group members to engage in nonverbal modes of communication *when these modes emerged naturally, instinctively, and spontaneously from group members themselves.* Such a counselor felt no need to manipulate group members toward nonverbal exercises because: (1) the counselor had no psychological need to do so; (2) the counselor was sufficiently transparent in verbal modes of affective communication so that there was no need to rely on nonverbal supports; (3) the counselor respected the right of group members to emerge freely as persons according to their own unique modes which could be verbal, nonverbal, or both; (4) the counselor realized that the most natural and revealing method of expressing the self was through personally open and honest verbal affect; and

(5) the counselor realized that when the affective inner self of a group member emerged within the group at the verbal level, this type of emergence was more easily incorporated into one's behavior outside the group since basic interpersonal communication was verbal. But it was difficult for such a counselor during this period because group participants were influenced to expect games, gimmicks, and exercises.

Credible Colleagues

Fortunately, the counseling profession had creditable colleagues during this period; those who had a balanced and tempered approach when examining the theories, process, and outcomes of group procedures in counseling. They believed in the relevancy of group procedures, but they also had traditionally exhibited intellectual honesty by pointing out its limitations (Corsini, 1957; Dreikurs, 1960; Driver, 1954; Gazda, 1971; Gordon, 1955; Kemp, 1964; Lakin, 1972; Lifton, 1961; Mahler, 1969; Mowrer, 1964; Napier & Gershenfeld, 1973; Ohlsen, 1970; Ohlsen & Proff, 1960; Rogers, 1968; Slavson, 1958).

Any serious and responsible contributor to the professional literature of group procedures in counseling has presented both its strengths and limitations. The professionally responsible person did this because of: (1) the obligation to advance the knowledge regarding group work by looking at its limitations as well as its strengths, (2) the tentativeness of what is known, (3) the realization that today's truth is but a temporary stopover in a movement toward a more enlightened and encompassing truth, and (4) the awareness that no approach to working with people is without flaw, and intellectual honesty compels a professional to let the flaws be known.

During this period, there were professionals who raised some legitimate questions regarding the integrity of group work; they made some pertinent observations and comments. However, those who looked upon group work as a theology generally responded with, "They are persons of little faith." But the criticisms and limitations of the group experience did emerge in the following: "T-Grouping: The White Collar Hippie Movement," in the *Phi Delta Kappan* (Thomas, 1968); "Group Therapy: Let the Buyer Beware," in *Psychology Today* (Shostrum, 1969); "A Little Cube of Sugar Helps the Medicine Go Down," in *Contemporary Psychology* (Hunt, 1968); "Some Ethical Issues in Sensitivity Training," in the *American Psychologist* (Lakin, 1969); "Can Sensitivity Training Be Destructive?" a letter in the *American Psychologist* (Gibbons, 1968); "The Rush to Encounter One's Self," a letter in the *School Counselor* (Rapoport, 1969); and "Encounter Groups—Seance or Sense," a panel program presented at the 1968 Convention of the American Personnel and Guidance Association (Beymer, 1968).

During this turbulent period, professionals made haste in demonstrating that group procedures in counseling were a professionally legitimate approach to working with people. Research evidence supporting the effectiveness of group work appeared in various reviews of the literature

(Anderson, 1969; Shaw & Wursten, 1965). George M. Gazda summarized 107 research studies that indicated the positive outcomes of group procedures in counseling (Gazda, 1968). The professional dimensions of group work were advanced through scholarship that addressed itself to confronting the shibboleths about group work which were rampant at the time.

Progress based upon scholarship was not easy, but it did occur and it enabled group work to continue as a credible process and escape the riptide of pervasive influence. During this period group counseling survived because professionals were intellectually honest, cautious, ethically responsible, and introspective regarding the services they provided. By doing this, professionals were not only able to distinguish superficiality from substance, but were also able to improve the effectiveness of practice, fulfill its public obligation, and preserve the integrity of group counseling so that today it possesses a newly formed foundation of credibility for both professionals and the public whom they serve.

A TRANSITIONAL PERIOD

In the earlier days of Rogerian or group-centered counseling, counselors who worked with groups essentially applied the process of individual counseling to the group setting. As Hobbs (1951, pp. 286–287) indicated in his chapter, "Group-Centered Counseling" which appeared in the book, *Client-Centered Therapy* (Rogers, 1951), there were close similarities between the process of individual and group client-centered counseling in the following areas: (1) the counselor's acceptance of the individual client or group client, (2) the decreased need for client defenses in individual or group counseling, (3) the client's freedom to engage in self examination, (4) the client's responsibility for self management, (5) the client's willingness to make choices, and (6) the client's ability to achieve self realization. Hobbs (1951, p. 308) went on to indicate that reflecting the feelings of group members was the basic process of the group-centered counselor.

When applied to the group setting, however, client-centered counseling began to lose some strength as the counselor relied solely upon reflecting the feelings of group members, even though group-centered counselors were sophisticated enough to also apply the linking function recommended by Gordon (1955, pp. 188–192). That is, the group-centered counselor, while reflecting the feelings of individual group members, attempted to link the feelings expressed to those of other members of the group.

As some group-centered counselors applied the traditional individual process of client-centered counseling to groups, there emerged an uncomfortable feeling of incongruence between the counselor's inner and unexpressed feelings and the process of reflecting the feelings of group members. There were personal issues, feelings, and internal inconsistencies that client-centered counselors were not able to express because of the albatross of having to essentially reflect the feelings of clients.

Although Rogers, from the very beginning of his development of the client-centered viewpoint, had identified counselor genuineness as a significant contributor to the client's progress, too many client-centered counselors were caught between the need to be genuine and the need to stay with reflection of feelings as the primary therapeutic response pattern. Those counselors who dared to be genuine with clients also felt an element of guilt because sometimes that genuineness resulted in the counselor's occasionally moving away from reflecting the client's feelings and toward the counselor's expression of personal meanings and observations.

Another confusing aspect of client-centered counseling during this period was that while the group-centered counselor was utilizing reflections of feelings almost exclusively, clients within counseled groups were instead using a spontaneous, natural, and nonreflective response pattern with peers and were having more therapeutic impact on each other than was the group counselor! This was startling and client-centered counselors began to realize that merely reflecting the feelings of group members was not only inhibiting the counselor's genuineness but other spontaneous, natural, and nonreflective responses by group members possessed more therapeutic effectiveness. In terms of *today's* basic encounter concept of group-centered counseling, Bebout (1974, p. 368) states that: "The style of encounter groups, their technical, innovation and their image bear little relation to standard forms of therapy (even earlier Rogerian therapy)."

Regarding the issue of counselor congruence, Bebout (1974, p. 370) goes on to indicate that deviating from reflecting the feelings of clients was essential if the counselor was to remain congruent as a person and become more of a participant in the group process:

> When therapist congruence was at stake, deviation from this mode or response (reflecting feelings of group members) was theoretically justifiable; and, in this case, focus on the therapist's experiencing allowed his or her emergence as a more initiating and participatory individual.
>
> . . . The therapist becomes free at this point to introduce his own here-and-now feelings, concerns, and perceptions, independent of the sanction of remaining congruent.

Bebout's preceding observations coincide with ours and represent one of the factors that prompted us to move toward a modification of both the individual and group forms of client-centered counseling. Another catalyst for our approach is the issue of consistency. That is, if the counselor can be more therapeutically helpful in groups by introducing personal meanings, perceptions, observations, and feelings, it follows that the counselor should also be able to engage in the same process in individual counseling. We believe that the counselor should be consistent and congruent with both individual clients and group members; and therefore, a refinement of the process of Rogerian counseling will enable this to occur.

This does not mean that the client-centered counselor gives up the process of reflecting the feelings of clients; this is a too powerful and effective process for assisting clients. What it does mean is that the client-centered counselor still utilizes reflection of feelings in Phase One of our model of client-centered counseling but then becomes free to use other responses *as they are related to the needs of clients.*

The client-centered counselor's need to be consistent in responding to clients in both individual and group settings is necessary in order for the counselor to feel congruent as a person and congruent with the process model used to help others. This kind of consistency is not only beneficial for the counselor, it is helpful to clients who see a counselor in both individual and group settings. Further, such a process consistency is important in advancing the appropriateness of client-centered counseling as both an art and a science.

Rogers (1971, p. 275), however, apparently feels comfortable in expressing different behaviors when involved in group and individual experiences: "My behavior is often quite different in a group than my behavior would be in the one-to-one relationship."

A RATIONALE FOR GROUP-CENTERED COUNSELING

In isolation from others, a person possesses a private perceptual world that enables the person to function with apparent clarity and ease. As the individual looks at the self, he or she may indeed see truth; but this truth is often limited because the person's frame of reference is limited to the self. As a private view is taken from within, the person is able to see much, but this private view is often limited because he or she has no external frame of reference to challenge an apparently well-structured self.

When an individual becomes a member of a counseled group, that person cannot continue to rely only upon the self for a view of the self. Through the process of group interaction, the person must come in contact with the group's perception of what he or she is or purports to be. Thus, it is within the context of the group that the person gains a greater self-awareness because of being confronted with the perceptions of the group to add to a subjective perception of the self. The catalytic nature of the group's reaction to an individual brings the person to consider perceptions of the self other than the private.

If a person were to rely only upon a privately gained self-concept, he or she would lose the opportunity to be furnished with the other frames of reference the interactive process of the group can provide. It is only when a person examines these other-than-self perceptions that the individual is able to develop a more comprehensive perception of the self. It is only in the light of this more refined awareness of self provided by group interaction that the person is able to gain a more complete self-awareness, and it is this more enriched concept of the self that enables the person to know the self more fully.

An individual can become so entwined with the self that only selfish perceptions are allowed to exist. One can become so dedicated to preserving and defending the self that the individual loses sensitivity to the necessary balance between what he or she wants for the self and what is good for others. Group counseling affords that individual an opportunity to develop this balance by placing a private concept of existence in relationship to other concepts of existence. If a person were to live as a hermit, relying solely upon an internal frame of reference, it would afford the person with a psychologically comfortable existence since his or her behavioral norm would only be determined by the self, and the person's behavior would have no effect upon other people. But an individual exists in a societal context, and does not live the life of a hermit, and therefore it becomes imperative for the person to synchronize the self with others. This does not mean that one forsakes individuality and becomes a puppet to be manipulated by the desires of a group. It does mean that a person retains individuality while, at the same time, developing a sensitivity to others and their viewpoints. There is a sharp difference between individuality and individualism. Individuality is the ability to be yourself within the context of society. Individualism is the process of rejecting society and building an island unto yourself, being sensitive to only *one* frame of reference — your own.

It is a current myth that one has to give up individuality and conform to the wishes of the group in order to survive. If this were true, none of humanity's progress could have been achieved. The person has progressed beyond the Stone Age, and individuals have been able to exist and make their contributions while maintaining a sensitivity to the world beyond themselves. Personal congruence or self-actualization has never been accomplished in isolation from others; in fact, troubled clients involve themselves in counseling essentially because there is a clash between themselves and those persons, values, or situational factors external to themselves. We could counsel such persons to isolate themselves and pay no heed to things external to themselves, but this would compound their problem. The client who is in a state of disequilibrium with the external world will never become a more adequately functioning person if he or she increases the distance between the self and that world. The client must be able to move toward a behavior pattern that enables the self to be synchronized with that external world. Once again, the individual is not swallowed by that external world, but becomes sensitive to it so that, by understanding it, he or she is able to cope with it and even have an impact upon it. At times the individual may have to do some personal reorganizing in order to survive, but this should be in terms of the client's more adequate functioning, rather than a surrendering of the self to the will of the group.

Group counseling enables the client to move out of an egocentric vacuum, to become increasingly sensitive to how group members perceive the client, and to have the freedom to internalize or reject these external frames of reference in an acceptant counseling atmosphere.

Huxley (1961, pp. 19–20), in his introduction to Teilhard de Chardin's

The Phenomenon of Man, indicates that the human personality, by nature, goes beyond itself in an effort to find meaning:

> A developed human being, as he (Teilhard de Chardin) has pointed out, is not merely a more highly individualized individual. He has crossed the threshold of self-consciousness to a new mode of thought, and as a result has achieved some degree of conscious integration—integration of the self with the other world of man and nature, integration of the separate elements of self with each other. He is a person, an organism which has transcended individualism in personality. This attainment of personality was an essential element in man's past and present evolutionary success; accordingly, its fuller achievement must be an esential aim for his evolutionary future.

> He (de Chardin) realized that the appearance of human personality was the culmination of two major evolutionary trends—the trend towards more extreme individuation, and that towards more extensive interrelation and cooperation; persons are individuals who transcend their merely organic individuality in conscious participation.

CHARACTERISTICS OF
GROUP-CENTERED COUNSELING

Characteristics of group-centered counseling that set it apart from other forms of group work revolve around its emphasis on philosophy, natural goals, definitions, the complexity of the process, the counselor as a person, the mode of communication, confrontation, and voluntarism.

Philosophy

Group-centered counseling finds its philosophic nourishment from those insights made by Carl R. Rogers, and contributing colleagues regarding the nature of the person, how and why the person perceives and behaves and under what circumstances, and the degree to which a person's self-concept influences perceptions and behavior. This is a rich philosophical heritage and the group-centered counselor is not only aware of it but attempts to put it into practice, both professionally and personally.

In translating the basic philosophic constructs of client-centered counseling into the group setting, the Rogerian counselor is still group-centered. This essentially means that the group-centered counselor focuses on the intrapersonal and interpersonal needs of group members and places those group needs above the needs of the group counselor. Although client-centered and group-centered counselors are now generally liberated from the constraint of merely reflecting the feelings of clients, this liberation should not translate itself into an experience in which the counselor's needs to be emotionally open and honest bring about domination of the individual or group experience so that the client's needs are pushed into the background and the counselor's needs are brought to the foreground of the counseling interaction. Our experience indicates that some group-centered counselors have used the group experience to push into the foreground certain personal concerns that the theory prevented them from introducing in the past.

Rogers (1971, p. 278) expresses this concern when he indicates that:

> If I am currently distressed by something in my own life, I am willing to express this in the group. I do have some sort of professional conscience about this, however, because if I am being paid to be a facilitator, and if my problem is severe, I feel that I should work it out in a staff group or with some therapist rather than taking the time of the group.

Kopp (1976, p. 5) clearly illustrates the concern we have that some counselors may use the individual or group process in purely selfish terms: "One of the luxuries of being a psychotherapist is that it helps to keep you honest. It's a bit like remaining in treatment all of your life."

We agree that the counseling profession offers a counselor a vehicle for being personally honest and that a competent and sensitive counselor should be continually examining the personal goals, motives, and values of being a person and a counselor; but this is quite different from the deliberate use of the counseling relationship for selfish reasons. Gendlin (1970, p. 93) presents a balanced view that enables the counselor to be both an experiencing participant in the process of counseling while also being attentive to the needs of clients: "Therapy must be experiential . . . experiencing is a moving directly felt process. Interpersonal relationships carry the experiencing process forward, as the therapist expresses his own actual reactions . . . at the same time gives room, attention, and reference to the client's felt reactions."

If a counselor is philosophically group-centered, then that counselor must give way to the needs of the group when his or her personal needs are in conflict with, or interfere with, the needs of the group.

Natural Goals

The goals of group-centered counseling revolve around the needs of group members, and these goals can never be specifically identified until the counselor has met with a group and goals evolve from within the group through the process of verbal interaction. There are, however, certain goals that characterize group-centered counseling. These goals provide the counselor with a person-centered framework for functioning.

Rogers in Bugental (1967, p. 178) indicates that the group experience is aimed at returning to participants an ownership of self and that the process is naturalistic. That is, participants, by their very nature, will move toward goals that express their humanness and that this movement is a very natural process:

Group members show a natural and spontaneous capacity for dealing in a helpful, facilitative, and therapeutic fashion with the pain and suffering of others.

. . . He (a group member) knew intuitively how to be understanding and acceptant.

. . . This kind of ability (to be understanding and acceptant) shows up so commonly in groups that it has led me to feel that the ability to be healing or therapeutic is far more common in human life than we might suppose.

. . . Psychotherapy is releasing an already existing capacity in a potentially competent individual. (Rogers, 1959, p. 221)

Coulson (1970) reinforces the goal of allowing human nature to take its course in the following statements:

. . . the critical group event is simply the process of time passing and our staying together. (p. 6)

. . . The sole necessary and sufficient condition for an encounter group is that there be an occasion for it. (p. 9)

. . . The encounter will happen if you give people sufficient time together without a distracting task and put someone with them as a leader who will not do traditional leaderly things—who knows enough, that is, not to get people organized, not to tell them how to encounter, or to set an agenda. (p. 11)

Martin (1972, p. 67) has said that if the client is enabled to have the self emerge in a natural way, then the client will: ". . . come as close to the truth that he can stand to come and he will do so repeatedly."

Meador (1975, p. 176) indicates that group-centered counseling is a natural experience for the client that is facilitated by the attitude of the counselor: ". . . the growthful potential of any individual will tend to be released in a relationship in which the helping person is experiencing and communicating realness, caring, and a deeply sensitive nonjudgmental understanding."

Rogers in Bugental (1967, p. 172) further believes that counseling should not only be a natural experience for the client, but that the development of a more enlightened theory of group-centered counseling can be served by naturalistic observation: "I am not aiming at a high level theory of group process but rather at a naturalistic observation out of which, I hope, true theory can be built."

Defining the Process

We prefer to call the application of client-centered counseling to groups "group-centered counseling" because such a titling indicates that the group procedures used flow from a particular and unified theory. Rogers (1970, pp. 4–5) prefers to call the process a basic encounter, although he admits that the process is similar to those encounter processes labeled as "T-groups" and "sensitivity training."

T-group: originally tended to emphasize human relations skills but has become much broader in approach.

Encounter group (or basic encounter group): tends to emphasize personal growth and the development and improvement of interpersonal communication and relationships through an experiential process.

Sensitivity training group: may resemble either T-group or encounter group.

Group-centered counseling is also preferred by us since it gives the process an identity that is separate from those groups with which Rogers (1970, pp. 4–5) does not have a theoretical or process congruence: sensory awareness groups, body awareness groups, body movement groups, creativity workshops, organizational development groups, team-building groups, Gestalt groups, and Synanon or "game" groups.

Rogers (1970, p. 33) defines the basic encounter with an illustration taken from the process:

> A man tells, through his tears, of the tragic loss of his child, a grief which he is experiencing for the first time, not holding back his feelings in any way. Another man says to him, also with tears in his eyes, "I've never before felt a real physical hurt in me from the pain of another, I feel completely with you." This is a basic encounter.

Bebout (1974, p. 372) gives a more formal definition to the basic encounter: "Encounter happens psychologically without physical touching—it is mental contact, lasting or momentary. It requires two or more people being equally and emotionally open, direct, expressive, and personal in communicating with each other."

Although Rogers (1970, p. 5) identifies the basic encounter group as being different from a Gestalt group and indicates the difference by stating that in a Gestalt group the "therapist focuses on one individual at a time, but from a diagnostic and therapeutic point of view," Hansen, Warner, & Smith (1976), in their identification of the different theories of group work, lump both approaches together in a chapter entitled "Self Theory and Gestalt Encounter Groups." On the other hand, Gazda (1975), in his presentation of 11 different theories of group work, retains a traditional labeling of the Rogerian basic encounter group when he calls it "client-centered" group counseling.

Both Rogers and Bebout, in the preceding definitions, indicate that the basic encounter is an event within the process of group interaction. Both definitions imply that groups meet until, at some time, the basic encounter takes place between and among participants. We believe that the basic encounter is a desired and necessary experience within the process of group work but, once again, we prefer to label the process as "group-centered counseling" because such a labeling captures the meaning and range of the entire process of group work rather than a specific event within it.

Coulson (1970) believes that a basic encounter group takes place informally and develops whenever time is available and persons gather in an unstructured way. He goes on to further clarify his definition of the basic encounter group:

> An encounter group is what happens when you have a lot of time to spend with people and no agenda. (p. 6)

> . . . if there is to be room for feelings in our communal lives, as I think there must be if we are to grow, an uncluttered special occasion is necessary. But no more than this is necessary. A basic encounter group is simply such a special occasion. (p. 11)

> Though one hears it so, an encounter group is not really defined as "where one vents his emotions." It is rather where, because there is nothing else to do, one moves eventually toward talking about what is hard to say. (p. 16)

From Coulson's definitions we see that a basic encounter can occur almost anywhere and under any circumstances as long as persons have the time to come together in a group, have no agenda, and are willing to share feelings that are typically difficult to share in other settings.

Both Rogers and Coulson desire to have the basic encounter concept applied in a variety of settings in order to liberate persons from feelings that have typically hampered their existence. In fact, Rogers (1970, pp. 135–148) visualizes the basic encounter concept being applicable in industry, government, race relations, families, educational institutions, a process that can bridge the generation gap, and a process that can contribute to world peace by easing international tensions. By labeling the process as "basic encounter," the implication is that they hope to free it from the formal field of counseling and psychotherapy and make it more available to the average person in a world that is becoming more impersonal and psychologically burdensome. We fully support the intentionality of the basic encounter but we also desire to have professional counselors and psychotherapists exposed to the *gravitas* of the basic encounter concept in an effort to enrich, expand, and make more effective their therapeutic efforts to help people through the group process. Further, by supporting the process identification as being "group-centered counseling" there is a formal attachment to the past and current literature of client-centered counseling. We do not wish to see the philosophy, process, and research of client-centered counseling lost or forgotten. Therefore, we see "group-centered counseling" as a better assurance that this relationship will be preserved. Those who have misinterpreted and misused the basic encounter concept, and Rogers has identified them (1970, p. 158), have partly done so because of an ignorance regarding the undergirding attitudinal and process principles fundamental to the client-centered viewpoint. We wish to keep a spotlight on those principles and feel that this can best be done by the linking label of "group-centered counseling."

Rogers, with every fiber of his being, is committed to the process of basic encounter as a way of saving humanity from interpersonal isolation and oblivion in a world that is rapidly becoming more technological. The deep level of Rogers' commitment is seen in the following statement regarding basic encounter which he made while being interviewed (Evans, 1975, p. 32):

> . . . it's one of the most significant social inventions of this century because it is a way of eliminating alienation and loneliness, of getting people into better communication with one another, of helping them develop fresh insights into themselves, and helping them to get feedback from others so that they perceive how they are being received by others.

Complexity of Process

Group-centered counseling, because of the unstructured nature of the process, presents the counselor with a complexity that is not evident in the more structured and counselor-centered process models of group counseling. In the group-centered process, with its focus on the natural emergence of the self of each of the participants, the counselor is required to be more sensitive, more involved, and generally more attentive to the natural emergence of attitudes and behaviors among group members. In politics, an autocratic leader generally has the process of government under tight control and is less confused regarding what should be done and when it should be done. A democratic leader, in politics, has the process of government under a loose control and governs by consensus and is often more confused regarding what should be done and when it should be done.

Because of the democratic nature of group-centered counseling, its process can become quite complex and can only be made clear by a counselor with the capacity to deeply grasp what is occurring and make sense out of a sometimes confusing current of intrapersonal and interpersonal reactions and exchanges.

If Rollo May's (1967, p. 101) observation regarding what the counselor is required to do in individual counseling were applied in group-centered counseling, we can envision the complexity of the counselor's task when the counselor attempts to absorb all of the following from all members of the group:

> . . . the counselor is sensitive to all the little expressions of character, such as tone of voice, posture, facial expression, even dress and the apparently accidental movements of the body. Nothing, not even the smallest movement or change in expression, is meaningless or accidental and the only question is the counselor's ability to perceive these expressions and sense something in their meaning.

Lakin (1972, p. 61) indicates that when the group counselor is both a participant and observer, the complexity of the process is further compounded. He states that the group counselor must learn: ". . . how to remain rational and intellectually alert while fully immersed in an emotionally involving experience; or put another way, how to be both participant and observer."

Ohlsen (1974, p. 144) observes that the counselor's responsibilities in the process of group counseling are more demanding than in individual counseling:

> The counselor's responsibilities to his clients in individual counseling and group counseling are similar, but his responsibilities are more demanding in the latter. While trying to detect and reflect the speaker's feelings, encouraging him to act, and reinforcing his desired behaviors, the counselor also must note how the speaker's behavior is influencing others and how the behavior of others is influencing the speaker.

Beck (1974, p. 429) confirms the complexity of the process of group-centered counseling by indicating that the counselor's nervous system becomes overloaded: "There is too much going on at one time, in terms of the simultaneous behaviors of the various members, their interactions with each other and the therapist's own reactions, for him to be able to sort out all that is important on the spot. You might say that the nervous system becomes overloaded."

The counselor who utilizes a more structured group counseling process model will find it easier to keep the process under control since such a process is not characterized by the same depth and range of complexity as is the group-centered process. A structured process may, indeed, be good for the well being of the counselor but the more important consideration should be its short- and long-range benefits for participants.

Because the process of group-centered counseling is unstructured and evolves in a spontaneous and natural manner, it is therefore more complex and requires a high level of psychological security and process sensitivity on the part of the counselor.

The Counselor as a Person

A group-centered approach to counseling puts far greater emphasis on the facilitative quality of the counselor as a person rather than emphasizing the counselor's knowledge and use of specific and predesigned procedures. It views the counselor's personhood as the basic catalyst that prompts group participants to make progress or not. Other theories of group counseling emphasize the counselor's use of strategies, gimmicks, and techniques, and assume that the counselor's personhood is therapeutically less important than his or her knowledge of such specific and predesigned procedures. For example, Gross (1977, p. 316) recommends that analytic and evaluative procedures should characterize part of the group counselor's behavior. The use of such techniques, however, would be far removed from the counselor's facilitative role in group-centered counseling. As Rogers (1971, p. 278) has indicated, an effective facilitator avoids such interpretive comments since they can never be anything but high-level guesses. The client-centered view has always emphasized that effective individual or group counseling comes from counselors who possess psychological wholeness and can translate this wholeness into facilitative attitudes that are beneficial to the group.

A group-centered counselor's personhood finds its expression not in leading a group but in the creation of a facilitative climate in which the group can lead itself. Hobbs (1951, p. 292) identified this important quality in the group-centered counselor's role some time ago, and more recently, Bebout (1974, p. 414) emphasized its importance when he stated that the essential difference between Rogerian group counseling and other approaches revolves around the counselor's ability to influence the development of a self-actualizing process for the group. He goes on to indicate that other approaches do not do this. Instead they may: ". . . rely on the leader's charisma or expertise, on methods or exercises, or they may discredit or distrust entirely the value of group self direction."

Upham (1973, p. 78) goes a bit further when he indicates that some practitioners serve their own needs rather than the needs of clients: "The practitioner may also push the client towards change in ways that meet the practitioner's needs and not those of the client."

Corey and Corey (1971, p. 80) and Hansen et al. (1976, p. 300) note the importance of the counselor as a person in group counseling. They indicate that the counselor must be psychologically integrated enough to model behaviors that are facilitative to group members in their intrapersonal and interpersonal exchanges.

Hobbs (1964, p. 158) indicates the tremendous importance of the counselor's personhood when he identifies the following person-centered attitudes that should characterize the group-centered counselor:

> Of primary importance is one's own personal philosophy, one's attitudes toward people. More and more, techniques seem less and less important. Techniques come later; they grow out of and are demanded by one's orientation to human relationships in therapy. To be effective in therapy, it is believed, requires a deep and abiding confidence in the ability of most people to be responsible for their own lives. It requires some humility about how much a person can do for others, aside from making it possible for them to realize themselves. It requires putting aside tendencies to evaluate what is good and right for other people. It requires a respect for their integrity as individuals, for their right to the strength-giving act of making and living by their own choices. And it requires, perhaps above all, a confidence in the tremendous capacities of individuals to make choices that are both maturely satisfying to them and ultimately satisfactory to society.

Kell and Mueller (1966, p. 78) have indicated that the counselor's personhood might be the only *reliable* source for affecting change in clients:

> The counselor, as in any other occupation, has primarily himself to bring to the helping relationship. He may learn of technical aids such as tests; he may learn interviewing techniques; he may read widely and copiously about people; he may search desperately for a philosophy or an orientation; he may even attempt to copy the behaviors of those who are regarded as experts. Yet, ultimately what he brings to his encounters with his clients is himself.

Coulson (1970, p. 10) states that a counselor errs in attempting to manufacture manipulative techniques with a group:

> The leader of an encounter group errs if he tries to *make* the group happen. He errs in missing the opportunity to find out what people *really* are like when they are not being manipulated. He errs in taking away from the members the rare opportunity to be what they want to be, without performance expectations. He errs also because *it simply isn't necessary* to manufacture the events of encounter.

Coulson (1970, p. 13) goes on to indicate that the group counselor's personhood had better be integrated, whole, and real when he identified the process model that the group-centered counselor should utilize if group members are to be brought into contact with their feelings: "If you want people to talk about their feelings, then talk about your feelings."

The group-centered counselor needs to be attitudinally a selfless person in order to engage in the quality of listening identified by Rogers (1970, p. 47):

> I listen carefully, accurately, and sensitively as I am able to each individual who expresses himself, whether the utterance is superficial or significant, I listen. To me the individual who speaks is worthwhile, worth understanding; consequently he is worthwhile for having expressed something. Colleagues say that in this sense I *validate* the person.

Rogers (1971, pp. 276, 277, 279) also calls attention to the importance of the counselor's personhood when identifying elements that should characterize group-centered counseling. These elements are not manufactured techniques; they cannot be contrived. They emerge from the positive attitudinal components of the counselor as a person: acceptance of the group, acceptance of the individual within the group, empathic understanding, and trust in the therapeutic potentiality of the group. A counselor who is less than psychologically whole will have difficulty expressing these attitudes to a group if they are not values contained in the counselor's personhood.

Rogers (1970, pp. 66–67) goes on to identify nonfacilitative attitudes and approaches on the part of a group counselor that will interfere with, and hamper, the process and progress of the group counseling experience for participants:

1. Exploitation
2. Manipulation
3. The counselor who is a dramatist
4. Dogmatism
5. Self centeredness—focusing on the counselor's problems
6. Interpretation
7. Exercises or activities—the counselor who says, 'now we will all . . .'
8. The counselor who withholds himself from emotional participation in the group—holding himself aloof as an expert.

The counselor who is selfish and feels that the group experience exists more for the counselor, or the enhancement of a theory, than for the group, will find it easier to engage in the preceding attitudes and manipulative techniques. It is not easy to be group-centered. It requires the counselor to confront the self and deeply examine attitudes and behaviors and weigh the degree to which they facilitate the group process and the degree to which they are self-serving. Such introspection requires the courage to face one's attitudes, motives, values, and goals before the counselor can move toward selfless behaviors that are truly group-centered.

If the group counselor's personhood is intact, and if the facilitative dimensions of that personhood can be communicated to group members, then Rogers (1970, pp. 15–37) indicates that the counselor will set in motion a series of experiences that will have positive outcomes for group members. They will begin the experience by milling around, resisting personal expression or exploration; they will begin by describing past feelings, expressing negative feelings, and will move toward the expression of immediate interpersonal feelings in the group. A healing capacity will begin to emerge among group members toward each other, self-acceptance will emerge and represent the beginning of change, facades will be cracked. The individual will receive feedback and be confronted, the members will engage in helping relationships with each other outside of the group sessions, the basic encounter will occur, positive feelings and closeness will be expressed, and behavioral changes will occur within the group.

In identifying the goals of the therapist-leader, Beck (1974, pp. 427–430) links these goals to the personhood of the counselor in that these goals are expressions of that personhood and contribute to the establishment of a group-centered climate:

1. The facilitation of individuals (or group members) to take responsibility for themselves in whatever way that is realistically possible at any particular time.
2. Problems and conflicts can be clarified and solved via a process of self understanding and the development of an empathic understanding of others.
3. The recognition of the client as he is, a recognition of his reality as he sees it.
4. Attempts to offer an attitude which is nonjudgmental in order to facilitate exploratory and self reflective behavior in the client.
5. Recognize the significance of maintaining as high a degree as possible of clarity about his own views, feelings, and reactions while he is in the therapeutic relationship.

In a study that investigated the relationship between counselor and client behaviors in the group counseling process, O'Hare (1979, p. 4) found that for behaviors such as: ". . . empathy, congruence, and regard, apparently it is the counselor who has the greater impact on client self-exploration."

The client's self-exploration in a group, according to Meador (1975, p. 176), occurs in proportion to the group-centered counselor's possession and demonstration of three attitudes that flow from the counselor as a person: "A client-centered group is characterized, then, by three attitudes of the therapist. He tries to experience and communicate his own reality, the process of his inner self as that moves and changes in the group; a caring for the persons in the group marked by a respect for their uniqueness; and a deeply sensitive nonjudgmental understanding."

As a person, the group-centered counselor possesses a seriousness of purpose. When group members allow a counselor and other members of the group to enter the internal world of their feelings and meanings, this opportunity carries with it a grave sense of responsibility. Meador (1975, p. 193) puts it aptly when she says:

> . . . underlying the motives of the therapist is a kind of seriousness about what is going on in a group. There is often hilarity, boredom, chit-chat, but the unfolding process of human change has an awesomeness that he cannot take lightly. This seriousness is basic to the client-centered way. When a therapist calls himself into seriousness, realness, caring, and understanding naturally follow.

Whether involved in individual or group counseling, the client-centered view emphasizes the quality of the counselor's personhood as the basic influence for facilitating attitudinal and behavioral changes among clients.

Mode of Communication

In group-centered counseling the mode of communication among group members is essentially verbal but the approach does not exclude other modes of communication when they emerge from group members in a natural and spontaneous way. Other concepts of group counseling identify exercises, gimmicks, and games that the counselor imposes on group members without their consent, or if the consent is given, it is given in an implicit way with a feeling that the counselor knows best. Such manipulative techniques are not only an infringement on the rights of group participants, but they are often used by counselors who are unsure regarding their ability to communicate feelings at the verbal level, don't trust the ability of group members to communicate feelings verbally, and desire to quicken the process.

Some group counselors take it for granted that such manipulative techniques are a part of the group counseling process. Ohlsen (1977, pp. 137-142) identifies the following: magic shop, intimacy exercise, pairing, approach-avoidance exercises, relaxation exercises, fiddler game, self-appraisal exercises, autobiographies, and autobiographies of the future.

Coulson (1970, p. 12), who feels that an effective basic group encounter occurs in a natural and spontaneous process that is free from manipulative techniques, has this to say regarding the issue:

To my mind, there's nothing wrong with exercises, with activities, with structure as such; it is what we do with them that hurts. Better ambiguity than what we are tempted to do with structure, which is to let it substitute for *ourselves.*

. . . They (personal values) can't be "tricked" out any sooner than they will come out, given time and the absence of distracting agendas, tasks, games, and discussion topics. And if the values are tricked out, then they will disappear again very quickly once the trickster is gone.

. . . I walked in on a student encounter group recently just in time to hear one young man say to another, "I wanted to get to know you better, that's why I suggested the backrub." (!) Our culture desperately needs ways you can get to know people like the cop on the street corner. And it won't be through asking him to take his shirt off or offering to pass him around in a circle.

A recent statement by Carl Rogers (1979), included in a brochure describing the 1979 summer basic encounter institute of the La Jolla Program in California, a program in which participants experience the basic encounter process, clarifies his position regarding the issue: "It does not greatly stress the 'exercises' which have become such a large bag of tricks for many group leaders."

Confrontation

Confrontation, within the process of group-centered counseling is used with a sense of responsibility that respects the dignity and integrity of the person being confronted. Confrontation is not the primary emphasis of a group-centered counselor as it is with counselors who use other approaches. Confrontation, for the group-centered counselor, is not a license for the counselor to express a latent hostility toward others or to fulfill ego needs. It is part of the process of group-centered counseling but in no way is it the whole of group-centered counseling. In group-centered counseling it is generally a reactive response rather than a proactive response. Confrontation emerges in a natural and spontaneous manner and it is not preplanned as an expected part of the process of group-centered counseling.

Some (Hansen et al., 1976, p. 144) imply that confrontation has become the major new process dimension of client-centered group counseling and depict Carl Rogers as being more willing to engage in "more active and confrontative interaction with group members." Their observation is linked to an inaccurate past image of the client-centered counselor which depicted the Rogerian counselor as being passive, stoic, and generally sitting on a nondirective backside. Carkhuff and Berenson (1977, p. 75) perpetuated this wooden image when they indicated that the lack of confrontative behavior has been a: ". . . rather precise reflection of a polite middle class, and will function most effectively with persons who share the attitudes, the values, and the potentials of this polite middle class."

In our opinion, client-centered counselors have typically been confrontative. Those who are sensitive to the depth and power of an accurate reflection of the client's feelings realize the confrontative dimension of such a reflection. Those who misunderstand the meaning of a reflection of feeling, and instead interpret it as a repetition of what a client has said rather than a response to the feelings behind the words, will have trouble understanding the confrontative elements that have always been a part of the client-centered process. The essential difference for today's client-centered counselor is an increasing willingness to engage in self-disclosing confrontative statements with clients. That is, today's client-centered counselor has expanded the range of responses beyond reflections of clients' feelings but that does not mean that the counselor has abandoned reflections of feelings as a necessary and effective response mode. The client-centered counselor who is genuine in the counseling relationship, and desires to achieve a congruence between what is being felt inside and what is being said to the client, cannot help but being confrontative when the counselor has persistent feelings of being ingenuine or noncongruent. Client-centered counselors have always had a visceral commitment to being genuine and congruent, and even in its earliest applications we feel that client-centered counselors did engage in confrontation because the attitudes of genuineness and congruence required them to do so. Today's client-centered counselor engages in confrontation both indirectly and directly. Indirect confrontation is engaged in through reflections of feelings that possess a confrontative element:

> You find it difficult to be honest even though you realize that your dishonesty is making you lose respect for yourself.
>
> Being yourself with your family is almost impossible because you fear risking yourself. It takes a lot of courage for you to be you.
>
> You have such a craving for food that you'll almost eat anything, anytime . . . even though you realize that such eating habits are producing disastrous results.

Direct confrontation is engaged in through self-disclosing statements when the client-centered counselor is feeling ingenuine or incongruent:

> I don't feel close to you at all. I feel that you're avoiding being truly honest with me.
>
> I don't feel any sense of commitment on your part. Your words sound reasonable but I don't get any feeling that you're willing to follow through on your words.
>
> I couldn't feel very comfortable doing that. It may make sense to you, but to me it would be an infringement upon the rights of others.

Rogers (1970, p. 52) clearly demonstrates a client-centered attitude toward the issue of confrontation: "I endeavor to voice any *persisting* feelings which I am experiencing toward an individual or toward the group, in any significant or continuing relationship."

In the preceding, Rogers indicates that he is willing to express "any *persisting* feelings." Too many counselors express momentary or fleeting feelings without regard to whether or not these feelings are persistent. They, so to speak, "shoot from the hip" with their confrontations. The client-centered counselor, instead, uses confrontation when *persisting* feelings indicate that the confrontation would be useful for the client, the group, the therapeutic atmosphere of the group, or the counselor's sense of genuineness and congruence.

The client-centered counselor uses confrontation in a professionally responsible manner. Rogers (1970, p. 55) indicates this when he says: "To attack a person's defenses seems to me judgmental. . . . If a person seems distressed by my confrontation of that of others, I am very willing to help him 'get off the hook' if he so desires."

Although Rogers is willing to engage in confrontation, he also indicates that there is a more primary way of communicating with group members (Rogers, 1970, p. 47): ". . . the *meaning* these experiences have for him now and the *feelings* they arouse in him. It is to these meanings and feelings that I try to respond."

Bauer (1966, p. 51) has indicated that with certain clients, confrontation should be avoided: ". . . only the experienced psychotherapist fully appreciates the fact that insight can sometimes be dangerous and a goal in therapy may be to prevent certain insights from ever becoming apparent."

Malouf (1968, p. 393) expressed the same concern when he stated: ". . . one should be extremely cautious in using direct feedback with highly sensitive or disturbed individuals."

Carkhuff and Berenson (1977, p. 29) have indicated that the counselor might fulfill a neurotic need through confrontation: ". . . the necessity of the therapist expressing himself at all times is not supported. Again, genuineness must not be confused with free license for the therapist to do what he will in therapy, especially to express hostility. Therapy is not for the therapist."

O'Hare (1979, p. 7) indicates that the process of confrontation must be well paced and well timed and should not be used indiscriminately: "This study suggests that such confrontation may be inhibitive, perhaps until the later sessions of an ongoing counseling group when sufficient trust and group cohesiveness have developed."

Confrontation does have therapeutic value when used responsibly. It enables the counselor to penetrate meanings and feelings that might not otherwise become exposed. Carkhuff and Berenson (1977, p. 179) had indicated its value when they said: "Confrontation precipitates crisis; but crises are viewed as the fabric of growth in that they challenge us to mobilize our resources and invoke new responses. Growth is a series of endless self-confrontations. The therapist who serves as an authentic model of confrontation offers the client a meaningful example of effective living."

Egan (1973, p. 132) suggests that counselors attempt to develop a balanced and integrated relationship between confrontation and support: "Confrontation without support is disastrous; support without confrontation is anemic."

Moustakas (1972, p. 21) provides insight into the experiencing and process dimensions of confrontation. He indicates that it is:

> . . . the direct challenge of facing a conflict, the willingness to experience fear, anger, sorrow, pain, intensely and deeply, when these feelings are caused by a sense of urgency, loss or disillusionment. The confrontation shakes up the individual, puts him in a turbulent state, and forces him to use new energies and resources to come to terms with his life—to find a way to himself.

Egan (1970) offers guidelines for making confrontation a constructive experience in the group process:

1. Confrontation should be done to demonstrate one's concern for another.
2. Confrontation should be a way of becoming involved with another person.
3. Confrontation should address itself primarily to another's behavior and only tangentially to that person's motivation.
4. Each person should be willing to confront himself or herself honestly in the group.

Voluntarism

A fundamental issue in counseling today is the voluntary use of a counseling service by clients rather than continuing the emphasis on the required counseling of referred clients. If a counseling program is to be respectful of human rights, the determination as to whether to make use of a counseling service should be left to the discretion of the person. If the person feels the need of counseling, he or she should be able to initiate and develop a relationship with a counselor.

To many counselors, allowing the person to decide whether to make use of a counseling service poses a real threat, especially among those counselors whose existence can only continue on the basis of counselor-initiated contacts with clients. The client-centered counselor would not hesitate to allow clients the right to determine whether or not they would make use of a counseling service, since a client-centered counselor would feel that if the counseling were, indeed, qualitative, then persons would voluntarily seek out the service. A counseling program will attract voluntary self-referrals in proportion to the quality of the counseling rendered.

Kneller (1964, p. 100), from an existential viewpoint, had this to say regarding the issue of voluntarism and its relationship to group membership:

> The doctrine of sociality teaches that the individual will lose his loneliness if he is taught the right way to belong to and behave in the group. But even in the group, say the existentialists, the individual does not escape his loneliness. In fact, he may become "homeless," because he has abandoned his real home, which is his own authentic self. The fact of being known under some socially

approved category does not of itself allay anxiety. Not that the existentialist would prevent the individual from joining the group. The opportunity should always be afforded. But acceptance of the opportunity should never result from social pressure; rather, it should spring from one's own uninhibited will. By extension, one should always be afforded the opportunity to be different, even to be eccentric, not for the sake of eccentricity but because all human beings are intrinsically different. A genuine group or society is thus made up of individuals who have made their own decision to join.

In a recent publication, the American Psychological Association established "Guidelines for Psychologists Conducting Growth Groups" (1973). One of the guidelines dealt with the issue of voluntary client participation: "Entering into a growth group experience should be on a voluntary basis; any form of coercion to participate is to be avoided."

McHolland (1976) has indicated that the future credibility of group counseling is highly dependent upon the profession's respect for the individual's right to become voluntarily involved in group counseling. He is alarmed at the tendency among some group counselors to force clients into the group experience.

Hare-Mustin, Maracek, Kaplan, and Liss-Levinson (1979, p. 7), in an article dealing with the rights of clients and the responsibilities of therapists, addressed the issue of voluntarism by stating that: "Ethical principles assert that therapists should inform clients about the purpose and nature of therapy and that clients have freedom of choice about their participation."

Encouraging clients to make voluntary use of a counseling service is not a single act. It is a process in which counselors have developed a public rationale for their existence, have publicly identified their therapeutic roles, have involved themselves in therapeutically qualitative counseling relationships that can be publicly documented, and have provided the public with orientation programs which outline the following: (1) the procedures, goals, and possible side effects of therapy; (2) the qualifications, policies, and practices of the therapist; and (3) the available sources of help other than therapy (Hare-Mustin et al., 1979, p. 5).

The philosophy and goals of client-centered counseling, which ennoble the person by respecting the person's dignity and rights, are expressed in practice by respecting the person's dignity and rights regarding voluntary involvement in counseling.

GROUP-CENTERED COUNSELING:
A PROCESS REFINEMENT

In our concept of group-centered counseling we see a process congruence between our position and the current client-centered view in the following areas: (1) the complexity of the process; (2) the primary importance placed on the personhood of the counselor as the source that enables a group to make progress, make no progress, or regress; (3) avoiding the use of manipulative techniques such as exercises, games, or gimmicks and instead allowing more natural activities to merge from group members as a spontaneous response to their needs; and (4) the importance of clients being voluntarily involved since such voluntary participation has a direct influence on the progress of clients and is respectful of their right to freely choose.

The only process refinement between current client-centered thinking and our refined viewpoint revolves around the issue of confrontation. From our viewpoint, the process of group-centered counseling and individual client-centered counseling is essentially the same. Both have two phases. Phase One is essentially relationship building and enables the counselor to assimilate the needs, interests, attitudes, values, goals, and behaviors of either the individual or group. The counselor does this by basically reflecting the feelings of the individual client, and, in group-centered counseling, does the same with an individual but also links the feelings of the individual, with reflections, with those of the other members of the group. Once the group-centered counselor has established a reasonable communicating relationship among group members the process can move toward Phase Two. In Phase Two, the group-centered counselor can continue to reflect the feelings of group members if such a process is meeting the needs of group members and intrapersonal and interpersonal communication is occurring with depth and clarity and in a natural and spontaneous manner.

In our refined concept of group-centered counseling, when the group has reached Phase Two and is at a standstill and unable to make progress, the counselor can intervene in a group-centered manner and present different alternatives to the group that could enable the group to once again move toward an improvement in intrapersonal or interpersonal communication. These alternatives would not be manipulative techniques but would emerge from the group-centered counselor's natural and spontaneous participation in the process and a sophisticated sense of which alternatives would best meet the needs of a particular group. The group-centered counselor, at this point, would need to be highly flexible in presenting alternatives to the group so that the alternatives would truly meet the needs of a particular group. The group-centered counselor would avoid suggesting a fixed procedure that may meet the needs of the counselor but would be totally inappropriate in meeting the needs of the group.

Gazda (1971, pp. 34–35), in presenting a developmental model of group counseling, indicates that group counseling tends to be ineffective unless it includes an action stage. That is, clients may verbalize about their desire to change their behavior but they must translate that need into action if they are to make behavioral progress.

Carkhuff and Berenson (1977) and Tamminen and Smaby (1978) indicate that successful group counseling is a three-phase process: exploration, understanding, and action. Mowrer (1969, p. 55), in defining what he labels as an *integrity group,* indicates that the following three concepts are emphasized in the process:

1. honesty, especially in regard to self-disclosure,
2. responsibility—keeping one's word, and
3. involvement (which includes learning to be not only factually but emotionally honest with others), coupled with the practice of making commitments regarding change in these areas and using group support and individual effort to bring the change about and sustain it.

At the beginning stages of group counseling, Ohlsen (1977, pp. 10–19) recommends that the counselor use established client-centered responses with group members (reflecting feelings of clients), in the middle stages he or she uses the behavior modification procedure of defining behavioral goals as well as teaching clients necessary interpersonal skills, while toward the end he or she uses action procedures so that clients will be able to implement newly acquired interpersonal skills outside the group setting.

In the preceding examples, the group counselors possessed a wide range of alternatives that could be utilized but all of the examples contained a consistent theme of action. That is, group counseling must not only enable participants to feel better about themselves and others but it must also be a process in which participants can apply these better feelings in relationships with significant persons outside of the counseled group.

In the current basic encounter group literature, the only counselor response that is given any attention is confrontation. And when authors describe the new dimension of client-centered group counseling, it appears that they only identify confrontation. Confrontation is given such focus because it appears to be a radical departure from the way that client-centered counselors have been perceived in the past.

In the second phase of our refined concept of group-centered counseling, we see confrontation as only one of many response patterns available to the group counselor. In addition to these other responses, there are many things the group-centered counselor can *concretely do* with group members without violating the person-centered philosophy of group-centered counseling. If confrontation becomes the only identified response available to the group-centered counselor, then we feel that the outcomes will be limited for participants.

The response and process flexibility we recommend in Phase Two is far removed from the manipulative techniques in which group members are treated as objects rather than persons. From our view, the counselor's flexibility is expressed in natural and spontaneous responses and procedures that flow from the counselor's intuitive judgment. This intrapersonal and interpersonal enrichment provided by group-centered counseling might never be realized if the counselor is locked into only responding through confrontation. Nonmanipulative procedures can be used and can be implemented within a person-centered attitude and group-centered process, provided that these procedures emerge from a natural flow of experiences and fulfill the needs of the group.

VALUES OF GROUP COUNSELING

Gazda (1971, pp. 44–45), in an extensive review of the literature relating to the values of group counseling, listed the following:

1. The client discovers that he is not alone or unique with his problems; that others have similar problems, too.
2. The counselee is encouraged to attack his problems, etc., through the effect of the group acceptance and rewards-support.
3. The group represents a microcosm of social reality (real life) for the members and enables them to test their behavior (interpersonal relations) against social reality.
4. The group provides the counselees a relatively safe place to try out behaviors and experiment with possible changes.
5. The counselee learns to give as well as receive help in the role of co-counselor.
6. The group counselees have the opportunity to learn from each other by observing how others attack and solve problems.
7. The group counseling experience may lead to the counselees seeking further counseling on an individual basis.
8. The counseling group may represent, to some counselees, a family group and thus provide the media through which the counselee can work through family problems.
9. The unique value that group counseling holds for the adolescent who has strong needs to identify with and be accepted by his peer group.
10. Group counseling or therapy sometimes provides a greater economy in the use of the counselor's or therapist's time.

Regarding the values of group-centered counseling or psychotherapy, Hobbs (1951, pp. 289–293) was one of the first to clearly articulate its values. His observations are highly congruent with more contemporary authors who identify the values of group counseling. Hobbs' observations are paraphrased as follows:

1. There is an immediate opportunity for the client to discover new and more satisfying ways of relating to people.
2. The client develops a relatedness to others.
3. The client can give and receive emotional support.
4. It is easier for clients to talk in a group situation.
5. The individual group member may be a giver of help while receiving help.

In describing the values of the group basic encounter process, Rogers (1970, pp. 6–7) lists the following:

1. A facilitator can develop, in a group with meets intensively, a psychological climate of safety in which freedom of expression and reduction of defensiveness gradually occur.
2. In such a psychological climate many of the immediate feeling reactions of each member toward others, and of each member toward himself, tend to be expressed.
3. A climate of mutual trust develops out of this mutual freedom to express real feelings, positive and negative. Each member moves toward greater acceptance of his total being—emotional, intellectual, and physical—as it *is*, including its potential.
4. With individuals less inhibited by defensive rigidity, the possibility of change in personal attitudes and behavior, in professional methods, in administrative procedures and relationships, becomes less threatening.
5. With the reduction of defensive rigidity, individuals can hear each other, can learn from each other, to a greater extent.
6. There is a development of feedback from one person to another, such that each individual learns how he appears to others and what impact he has in interpersonal relationships.
7. With this greater freedom and improved communication, new ideas, new concepts, new directions emerge. Innovation can become a desirable rather than a threatening possibility.
8. These learnings in the group experience tend to carry over, temporarily or more permanently, into the relationships with spouse, children, students, subordinates, peers, and even superiors following the group experience.

It is interesting to note that before identifying the preceding values, Rogers stated that: "The experience often, though not always, includes some cognitive input—some content material which is presented to the group." In our opinion, this statement indicates that the process of the basic encounter or group-centered approach is not diametrically different from other professional approaches to group counseling. Often, the difference is one of emphasis. The group-centered counselor generally functions without an agenda and stimulates a natural and spontaneous development of group interaction. Other approaches typically have an agenda and develop the process of group interaction around that agenda.

Gazda (1971, p. 195) has surveyed 145 research studies in group counseling covering the period from 1938 through 1970. After abstracting and analyzing these studies according to nine criteria, Gazda concludes that group counseling is generally an effective process and the developmental model is most applicable to problem prevention.

The basic encounter or intensive group experience was surveyed by Gibb (1970) who analyzed 106 studies and 24 doctoral dissertations from 13 universities. Following is a summary of his findings:

1. Intensive group training experiences have therapeutic effects.
2. Changes occur in participant's sensitivity, ability to manage feelings,

self-motivation, attitudes toward self, attitudes toward others, and interdependence.

3. There is no basis for making any restrictions as to group membership.
4. Groups without leaders are effective.
5. The group experience must be relevant to the organizational, family, and life environment of the person.
6. Follow-up consultations are at least as important as what occurs in the group experience.
7. The group experience, to be optimally effective, should be uninterrupted and continuous.
8. There is little basis for the concern among lay groups regarding the traumatic effects of the group experience.

Rogers (1970, p. 126) submitted a questionnaire to 481 persons with whom he had participated in basic encounter group experiences. He was able to obtain responses from 82 percent of those surveyed. The results are summarized as follows:

Seventy-five percent stated that their group experience had been positive and helpful.

Thirty percent replied that the group experience had been constructive.

Forty-five percent described it as a deeply meaningful, positive experience.

Nineteen percent stated that the group had been more helpful than unhelpful.

LIMITATIONS OF GROUP COUNSELING

Gazda, Duncan, and Meadows (1967, p. 307) asked contributors to the literature and research of group counseling to identify its limitations. Following are the results of their survey:

1. Inappropriate treatment for certain problem types, e.g., sociopathic or psychopathic children and the severely disturbed
2. Difficult to control confidentiality, depth of involvement, collusion of unhealthy effects, and anxiety level
3. Requires a more skillful counselor, including a greater sensitivity and expertness in group dynamics
4. Is difficult to select appropriate combinations of group members
5. Permits certain participants, e.g., the shy and withdrawn, to refrain from participation
6. Does not provide for adequate individual attention for some counselees
7. Can be difficult, especially in the school setting, to arrange a convenient time for a group meeting

8. Does not represent an economical use of the counselor's time
9. May lead to acceptance of the group milieu which may be artificial
10. Difficult to train adequate practitioners.

Gazda (1971, p. 46) points out the following limitations and calls attention to a philosophic dilemma within group counseling in his first limitation:

1. The group pressures may cause certain members to lose their individuality in their attempt to conform to group codes.
2. Some members may use the group to escape or as a refuge.
3. The threat of group ostracism to some members may be overwhelming.
4. Improper grouping can lead to certain group members being harmed.

Patterson (1972, p. 100) focused on one issue when he identified the following danger inherent in the group experience: "If there is potential danger in groups—and the writer, as well as many others is convinced of this, simply because anything which is powerful for good is also powerful for damage to persons—then there must be some concern for protecting the public."

The limitations of group-centered counseling were first identified by Hobbs (1951, pp. 312–313) and were few in number. This was, perhaps, due largely to the limited knowledge that practitioners had about this new process at that time. Hobbs stated that group-centered counseling was inappropriate for the person who is extremely shy, overly anxious, intensely hostile, or deeply disturbed.

Rogers (1967, p. 263) sounded a clear alarm regarding the negative potential of the basic group encounter for the participant. He stated that he had a: ". . . real concern over the fact that sometimes, and in some way, this experience may do damage to individuals."

Later, Rogers (1970, pp. 37–42) identified limitations that he classified as "failures, disadvantages, risks" for the person involved in the basic encounter or intensive group experience. They are summarized as follows:

1. Frequently, the behavior changes that occur, if any, are not lasting.
2. The individual may become deeply involved in revealing himself and then may be left with problems that are not worked through.
3. It brings into the open marital tensions that have been kept under cover.
4. Close and loving feelings among group members can have a sexual component.

Meador's (1975, pp. 191–192) identification of the limitations of client-centered group therapy are summarized as follows:

1. There is insufficient time for fully effective outcomes.
2. The attentive energies of participants are sometimes drained.
3. Intrapersonal searching is limited because of the focus on interpersonal happenings within group.

4. There is a limited ability among participants to transfer group learn-
    ings to the outside world.

Clearly, group counseling, in whatever form it is practiced, carries with
it a serious and awesome responsibility for the professional. Group
counseling does have an enormous potential for improving the human condition when it is used in a professionally sensitive and responsible manner.

THE FUTURE

Today the furor over the merits of the group experience has diminished
dramatically. As with all things new, people have to have a pro and con
emotional catharsis, and after feelings have been released, there is the
natural tendency to look at the issue with more calm and logic. Today, as
one reviews the output from the commercial communications media and
from professional sources, one will see neither the euphoria nor condemnation of the group experience that was evident in the 1960s and early
1970s. Although not yet *fully* accepted, the group experience has become
more publicly and professionally accepted as a legitimate and effective
model for assisting people with intrapersonal and interpersonal problems
of communication. In the years ahead, this acceptance should grow.

If one places the emergence of the group experience within the context
of that period of time, the suspicious and negative reactions can be better
understood. Our culture was undergoing a revolution that elated some and
offended others. Opinions became polarized on such emotional issues as
homosexuality, bisexuality, pornography, marriage, drugs, alternative life
styles, the rights of minority groups, the structure of education, the limits
of the legal system, the work ethic, protest songs, politics, and religious
values. It was a period that contained both the Vietnam War and the Age of
Aquarius; emotions ran high as some resisted the various dimensions of the
cultural revolution while others protested that the new thinking had not
gone far enough.

Amid the confusion some began to become involved in the group experience as a vehicle for finding themselves and preserving their psychological balance. Others became involved in order to keep themselves open
to the growing edge of the changes that were taking place. Some participated out of a need to overcome feelings of isolation and loneliness.
Others participated because it was something new and their adven-
turesome spirit always prompted them to try something new. Still others
participated because it was becoming an "in" experience and they didn't
want to be embarrassed by having others learn that they had not tried it.
We have always been a nation of trend and fad followers and the group experience became a natural object of this inclination.

Since opinions were so polarized on so many controversial issues, it was
very natural that when the group experience appeared on the horizon it

was seen by some as the sunrise of social awakening in communication and by others as the sunset of individuality. As Charles Dickens noted, in describing an earlier era, "It was the best of times, it was the worst of times."

Carl Rogers, during the past controversial period, still had the professional respect of colleagues because he stayed active in producing articles, books, audio and video tapes, and films that presented the philosophy, process, goals, and outcomes of the group basic encounter experience. He maintained a sense of responsibility toward clarifying the process that had become so controversial. From some quarters, however, he became an easy target for diatribes since he had been so closely identified with the group experience movement. This was nothing new for Rogers since such diatribes had always been leveled at him, even during the earlier stages of his career (Hamrin and Paulsen, 1950; Crow and Crow, 1951; Gustad, 1951; Williamson, 1951; and Marzolf, 1956).

Even today, Rogers is an available target. Using Rogers as a target is much like tracing the evils of Christianity to Martin Luther, the evils of interplanetary travel to Robert Goddard, the evils of rock and roll to Johann Sebastian Bach, the evils of economics to Thomas Malthus, and the evils of the press to the Gutenberg Bible. Recently, Howard Kirschenbaum (1978) wrote a biography on Carl Rogers. DeMott (1979) reviewed the biography in *Psychology Today* and used it as an opportunity to make the following observations: (1) He characterizes the biography as "often silly." (2) He implies that client-centered counseling evolved from Rogers out of a desire to create a "discount-house" or "bargain basement" substitute for Freudian analysis. (3) Rogers had a characterological weakness for tears that prompted him to present himself to the world as "Supersensitive Man." (4) Rogerians come on as caressers, huggers, and "jolly-ups." (5) "For Freud, freedom equals self-understanding; for Rogers, freedom equals self-love—a tranced consent to the repetitive cooing of paid companions whose jobs involve little more than conning folks into feeling well liked" (p. 95). (6) Rogerians have involved themselves in the professionalism of compassion, they laugh all the way to the bank, and are "mercenaries first of all: their bottom line is business" (p. 95).

If one reads the book, *Carl Rogers on Encounter Groups* (Rogers, 1970), one would find no evidence that the group basic encounter approach is radical or outlandish. Instead, it is presented in a cautious and responsible manner. What has happened is that some group leaders have interpreted and translated the group basic encounter movement into a radical and outlandish self-serving process. Hansen et al. (1976, p. 160) touch on this point when they say: "Rogers' basic encounter model served as a beginning point for all other encounter groups. During their evolution, however, encounter groups have, for better or for worse, gone beyond what he originally presented."

Rogers (1970, p. 158) shows his concern for the future of the basic encounter movement in a statement regarding its potential for exploitation:

". . . it may all too easily fall more and more into the hands of the exploiters, those who have come onto the group scene primarily for their own personal benefit, financial or psychological. The faddists, the cultists, the nudists, the manipulators, those whose needs are for power or recognition, may come to dominate the encounter group horizon."

We note that Rogers may have engaged in the following miscalculations, not in the basic theory and process of basic group encounter, but in the process of presenting it:

1. He wanted the process to be usable to the lay group leader rather than preserving it for the professional. This made the basic encounter approach vulnerable to criticism from both lay and professional sources.
2. Although Rogers could not control the time that the basic encounter was presented, it did emerge during a turbulent period in which the nation was undergoing enormous changes in its cultural values. The nation was confused regarding its values and the basic encounter movement became one of many scapegoats for those who were looking for sources of our moral deterioration.
3. In many ways, we exist in an economic democracy. There are those who keep themselves vigilant to consumer interests and are ready to market products that will exploit those interests. The group basic encounter was an idea that was easily exploited by those with financial motivations.

Although we visualize a stable future for the group basic encounter movement, we prefer to adhere to the following in our attempt to contribute to the stability of the group counseling movement, in general. Essentially, we are recommending a return to professionalism—not a professionalism that is cold, aloof, wooden, bureaucratic, distant or exploitative; not a professionalism that would exclude the lay group leader just as lay persons have not been excluded from the medical, dental, legal, technological, and religious professions; but a professionalism that is consumer-centered in all of its behaviors. At this point in time, some control is better than none if the group movement is to continue to have a contributing future. Specifically we recommend that:

1. All group process models be assimilated under the label "group counseling" in order to bring about a unity of description regarding the process we're attempting to understand and present to the public.
2. Professionalism brings with it a better assurance that the process will be publicly and legally understood and accepted.
3. Professionalism enables the body of knowledge surrounding group counseling to be more precisely and clearly understood.
4. Professionalism brings with it the requirement of formal preparation. Such preparation would give better assurance that the practi-

tioner of group counseling knows what to do and how to do it. Such preparation would not exclude lay group leaders; they would be prepared and would function with the sanction and supervision of professional group counselors.

5. Professionalism would regulate the admission into practice of both the professional and lay group counselors and would reduce the possibility of exploitation.

6. Professionalism would be a better assurance that group counselors would form themselves into local, regional, and national associations that could not only monitor the behavior of members but would serve as resources for keeping current with public needs and theoretical developments.

7. Professionalism would produce research evidence that calls attention to ways of improving the delivery of group counseling services to participants. Professionalism brings with it a greater assurance that this research will be conducted.

8. Professionalism would promulgate existing codes of ethics, interpret them to the public and to group counselors, and would make it more difficult for the exploiters to survive.

REFERENCES

Adler, R. The Thursday group. *The New Yorker,* 1967, *43,* 55–146.

Allen, G. Hate therapy. In Robert Welch (Ed.), *American Opinion.* Belmont, Mass.: John Birch Society, January 1968, 73–86.

Anderson, A. R. Group counseling. *Review of Educational Research: Guidance and Counseling,* 1969, *39,* 209–226.

Associated Press Wire Service. Encounter groups: Attracting the singles market. *Boulder Daily Camera,* Boulder, Colo., July 27, 1969, 9.

Bauer, F. C. Guidance and psychiatry. In T. C. Hennessey (Ed.), The interdisciplinary roots of guidance. New York: Fordham University Press, 1966, 51.

Bebout, J. It takes one to know one: Existential-Rogerian concepts in encounter groups. In D. A. Wexler & L. N. Rice (Eds.), *Innovations in client-centered therapy.* New York: John Wiley, 1974, 367–420.

Beck, A. P. Phases in the development of structure in therapy and encounter groups. In D. A. Wexler & L. N. Rice (Eds.), *Innovations in client-centered therapy.* New York: John Wiley, 1974, 421–464.

Beymer, L. Speech made at program entitled, "Encounter Groups – Seance or Sense?" *1968 Convention Program,* Annual Convention of the American Personnel and Guidance Association, Detroit, April 8, 1968.

Carkhuff, R. R., & Berenson, B. G. *Beyond counseling and therapy* (2nd ed.). New York: Holt, Rinehart and Winston, 1977.

Corey, G., & Corey, M. *Groups: Process and practice.* Monterey, Calif.: Brooks/Cole, 1971.

Corsini, R. *Methods of group psychotherapy.* New York: McGraw-Hill, 1957.

Coulson, W. Inside a basic encounter group. *The Counseling Psychologist,* 1970, *2,* 6–22.

Crow, L. D., & Crow, A. *Principles of guidance.* New York: American Book, 1951, 194–195.

DeMott, B. Mr. Rogers' neighborhood. *Psychology Today,* 1979, *12,* 90, 94, 95.

Dietz, Jean. T-groups: A new technique for preserving identity amid mass pressures. *Boston Sunday Globe* (Magazine Section), June 23, 1968, 28–33.

Dreikurs, R. *Group psychotherapy and group approaches.* Chicago: Alfred Adler Institute, 1960.

Driver, H. I. *Mutliple counseling: A small group discussion method for personal growth.* Madison, Wisconsin: Monona Publications, 1954.

Egan, G. *Encounter: Group processes for interpersonal growth.* Belmont, Calif.: Wadsworth, 1970.

Egan, G. *Face to face.* Monterey, Calif.: Brooks/Cole, 1973.

Evans, R. I. *Carl Rogers: The man and his ideas.* New York: Dutton, 1975.

Frazer, S. The thousand year week, a gripping–and true–account of the unique kind of group therapy that is bringing new insights into many of the hangups of North American life. *The Star Weekly Magazine,* Toronto Star Limited, Toronto, Ontario, Canada, September 15–21, 1968, 2–25.

Gazda, G. M. (Ed.). *Journal of educational research and development: Group counseling.* University of Georgia, College of Education, 1968.

Gazda, G. M. (Ed.). *Basic approaches to group psychotherapy and group counseling.* Springfield, Ill.: Charles C. Thomas, 1975.

Gazda, G. M. *Group counseling: A developmental approach.* Boston: Allyn and Bacon, 1971.

Gazda, G. M., Duncan, J. A., & Meadows, M. E. *Survey of group or multiple counseling–Report of findings.* University of Georgia, mimeographed, 1967.

Gendlin, E. T. Existentialism and experiential psychotherapy. In J. T. Hart & T. M. Tomlinson (Eds.), *New directions in client-centered therapy.* Boston: Houghton Mifflin, 1970.

Gibb, J. R. The effects of human relations training. In A. E. Bergin & S. L. Garfield (Eds.), *Handbook of psychotherapy and behavior change.* New York: John Wiley, 1970, 211–276.

Gibbons, C. C. Can sensitivity training be destructive? Letter appearing in *American Psychologist,* 1968, *23,* 288.

Gordon, T. *Group-centered leadership.* Boston: Houghton Mifflin, 1955.

Gross, D. R. *Group counseling in counseling: Theory, process and practice.* Belmont, Calif.: Wadsworth, 1977.

Guidelines for psychologists conducting growth groups. *The American Psychologist,* 1973, *28,* 933.

Gustad, J. W. Test information and learning in the counseling process. *Educational and Psychological Measurement,* 1951, *11,* 788–789.

Hamrin, S. A., & Paulsen, B. *Counseling adolescents,* Chicago: Science Research Associates, 1950, 78.

Hansen, J., Warner, R., & Smith, E. *Group counseling: Theory and process.* Chicago: Rand McNally, 1976.

Hare-Mustin, R., Marecek, J., Kaplan, A. G., & Liss-Levinson, N. Rights of clients, responsibilities of therapists. *The American Psychologist*, 1979, *34*, 3–16.

Hart, J. T., & Tomlinson, T. M. (Eds.). *New directions in client-centered therapy.* Boston: Houghton Mifflin, 1970, 295, 300.

Havemann, E. Alternatives to analysis. *Playboy*, HMH Publishing Company, Chicago: *16*:11, November 1969, 133–134; 142; 214–216; 218; 220.

Hobbs, N. Group-centered psychotherapy. In C. R. Rogers, *Client-centered therapy.* Boston: Houghton Mifflin, 1951.

Hobbs, N. In C. G. Kemp (Ed.), *Perspectives on the group process.* Boston: Houghton Mifflin, 1964.

Howard, J. Inhibitions thrown to the gentle winds. *Life,* Chicago: Time-Life, Inc., July 12, 1968.

Hunt, W. A. A little cube of sugar helps the medicine go down. *Contemporary Psychology*, 1968, *13*, 563.

Huxley, J. *Introduction to Teilhard deChardin: The phenomenon of man.* New York: Harper, 1961, 19–20.

Kell, B. L., & Mueller, W. J. *Impact and change: A study of counseling relationships.* New York: Appleton-Century-Crofts, 1966.

Kemp, C. G. (Ed.). *Perspectives on the group process.* Boston: Houghton Mifflin, 1964, 13.

Kirschenbaum, H. *On becoming Carl Rogers.* New York: Delacorte Press, 1978.

Kneller, G. F. Existentialism and education. New York: Philosphical Library, 1964.

Kopp, S. B. *If you meet the Buddha on the road, kill him.* New York: Bantam, 1976, 5.

Lakin, M. Some ethical issues in sensitivity training. *American Psychologist*, 1969, *24*, 923–928.

Lakin, M. *Interpersonal encounter: Theory and practice in sensitivity training.* New York: McGraw-Hill, 1972, 107.

Lamott, K. The year of the group: Eavesdropping on some highly intelligent neurotics, *The New York Times Magazine*, 1968, 29, 104.

Leonard, G. B. The man and woman thing. *Look*, Des Moines: Cowles Communications, Inc., 1968, *32*, 55–72.

Lifton, W. M. *Working with groups.* New York: John Wiley and Sons, Inc., 1961.

Mahler, C. A. *Group counseling in the schools.* Boston: Houghton Mifflin, 1969.

Malouf, P. J. Direct feedback: Helpful or disruptive in group counseling? *The School Counselor*, 1968, 15.

Martin, D. *Learning-based client-centered therapy.* Monterey, Calif.: Brooks/Cole, 1972.

Marzolf, S. S. *Psychological diagnosis and counseling in the schools,* New York: Henry Holt, 1956, 327–328.

May, R. *The art of counseling.* Nashville: Abingdon, 1967.

McHolland, J. Forced group experiences. *Group News,* Summer, 1976, 6–7.

Meador, B. D. Client-centered group therapy. In G. M. Gazda (Ed.), *Basic approaches to group psychotherapy and group counseling.* Springfield, Ill.: Charles C. Thomas, 1975, 175–195.

Moustakas, C. *Loneliness and love.* Englewood Cliffs, N.J.: Prentice-Hall, 1972.

Mowrer, O. H. *The new group therapy.* New York: Van Nostrand Company, 1964.

Mowrer, O. H. Critique of Patterson's article. *The Counseling Psychologist*, 1969, *1*.

Murphy, F. Quoted in Universities: Of reason and revolution. *Time,* Chicago: Time-Life, Inc., 1968, 42.

Napier, R. W., & Gershenfeld, M. K. *Groups: Theory and experience.* Boston: Houghton Mifflin, 1973.

O'Hare, C. Counseling group process: Relationship between counselor and client behaviors in the helping process. *The Journal for Specialists in Group Work,* 1979.

Ohlsen, M. M. *Group counseling.* New York: Holt, Rinehart and Winston, 1970.

Ohlsen, M. M. *Gudiance services in the modern school.* New York: Harcourt, Brace and Jovanovich, 1974.

Ohlsen, M. M. *Group counseling* (2nd ed.). New York: Holt, Rinehart and Winston, 1977.

Ohlsen, M. M., & Proff, F. C. *The extent to which group counseling improves the academic and personal adjustment of underachieving, gifted adolescents.* Research Project No. 623, College of Education, University of Illinois, Urbana, 1960.

Patterson, C. H. Ethical standards for groups. *The Counseling Psychologist,* 1972, *3.*

Pearson, K. *The chance of death and other studies in evolution.* London: E. Arnold Company, 1897.

Psychotherapy: Stripping body and mind. *Time,* Chicago: Time-Life, Inc., February 1968, 23, 68.

Rapoport, D. The rush to encounter one's self. Letter in *The School Counselor,* 1969, *16,* 228.

Rogers, C. R. *Client-centered therapy.* Boston: Houghton Mifflin, 1951 (renewed 1979).

Rogers, C. R. A theory of therapy, personality, and interpersonal relationships, as developed in the client-centered framework. In S. Koch (Ed.), *Psychology: A study of a science, Vol. III. Formulations of the person and the social context.* New York: McGraw-Hill, 1959.

Rogers, C. R. The process of the basic encounter group. In J. F. T. Bugental (Ed.), *Challenges in humanistic psychology.* New York: McGraw-Hill, 1967, 172, 178, 263.

Rogers, C. R. *The process of the basic encounter group.* La Jolla, Calif.: Western Behavioral Sciences Institute. Unpublished manuscript, 41 pages, 1968.

Rogers, C. R. *Carl Rogers on encounter groups.* New York: Harper and Row, 1970.

Rogers, C. R. Carl Rogers describes his way of facilitating encounter groups. *American Journal of Nursing,* 1971, 71, 275–279.

Rogers, C. R. In R. I. Evans, *Carl Rogers: The man and his ideas.* New York: E. P. Dutton, 1975, 32.

Rogers, C. R. In brochure, *The LaJolla Program.* La Jolla, California: Center for Studies of the Person, 1979.

Schutz, W. C. *Joy: Expanding human awareness.* New York: Grove Press, Inc., 1967.

Shaw, M. C., & Wursten, R. Research on group procedures in schools: A review of the literature. *The Personnel and Guidance Journal,* 1965, *44,* 27–34.

Shostrom, E. L. Let the buyer beware. *Psychology Today,* Del Mar, Calif.: Communications/Research/Machines, Inc., 1969, *2,* 36–40.

Slavson, S. R. *The fields of group psychotherapy.* New York: International Universities Press, 1958.

Sohl, J. *The lemon eaters.* New York: Simon-Schuster, Inc., 1967.

Tamminen, H. W., & Smaby, M. H. You can be a skilled group helper. *The Personnel and Guidance Journal,* 1978, *56,* 501–505.

The Group: Joy on Thursday. *Newsweek,* New York: Newsweek, Inc., May 12, 1969, 104–106D.

Thomas, D. T-grouping: The white-collar hippie movement. *Phi Delta Kappan,* 1968, *44,* 458–460.

Upham, F. *Ego analysis in the helping professions.* New York: Family Service Association of America, 1973.

Universal Studios (Producer). *Companions in Nightmare.* Hollywood, Calif., presented on NBC Television, November 23, 1968, 9:00-11:00 P.M., EST.

Williamson, E. G. Directive vs. nondirective counseling. *Education Digest,* 1951, *16,* 35.

Chapter 9

ACCOUNTABILITY AND EVALUATION

The age of accountability is upon us (Pine, 1976). Governmental agencies are increasing the pressure to demonstrate concrete and tangible results for funds spent to support counseling services. Human engineering, performance contracting, systems analysis, cost effectiveness, behavioral objectives, behavioral audits, and technological systems characterize the efforts to establish accountability in counseling. Accountability has been included in union contracts and has been part of legislation in a number of states. Already the wave of accountability has resulted in some fundamental shifts in the ways that counselors view their jobs. There is more emphasis on behavioral objectives and the need to define specifically the desired results of counseling (Hannon, 1977; Knapper, 1978).

Current criticisms of counseling and human services and related demands for accountability reflect a variety of societal factors: the escalating cost of counseling and human services; developments in management techniques that have spurred the sharpening of goals, specificity in planning, and the establishment of cost-effectiveness measures; the politicization of communities; and rising expectations among minority groups. One can also speculate that the accountability movement is related to the American obsession with rendering every human activity—intellectual, physical, moral, social, and even sexual—accountable in terms of dollar expenditures. Behavioral objectives, systems analysis, and performance contracting fit the American philosophy of things. They are logical, ordered, objective, pragmatic, and precise, and they lend themselves to mechanized and computerized ways of measuring outcomes.

The supporters and advocates of accountability are not all of one mind. Some view accountability as a process inspired primarily by a desire to see worthwhile goals regularly attained in large measure. For others, accountability may be motivated by the wish to economize on costs. And for still others, accountability may reflect a belief that society should control, discipline, and indoctrinate on behalf of a given dogma or the status quo. Accountability has so many meanings, and has been used in so many ways for so many different ends that the net result has been professional and public confusion. There is a rush to easy answers, accessible plans of action, and methods of evaluation, and consequently there is a developing mythology of accountability. We are seeing more efforts to establish systematic accountability procedures and many of these attempts will not be successful. There is an obvious need for careful examination of the mythology, the confusion, and the fundamental questions of accountability in order to develop recommendations for an effective client-centered accountability process.

THE MYTHOLOGY OF ACCOUNTABILITY

Myth 1: *The management and business practices introduced through accountability will increase the efficiency and effectiveness of counseling services.*

Some people feel that counseling agencies should incorporate the precise accountability methods that produced "zero fault" aerospace systems. However, the question remains as to whether accountability methods alone produced zero fault systems or whether a *combination* of these methods and national commitment, legislative and executive branch support, and billions of dollars produced such results. Would that the field of counseling had the same commitment, the same executive and legislative branch support, and billions of dollars for meeting human needs. But what of the accountability methods that led to such fiascoes as the Edsel, and the F-111, or the Lockheed and Grumman aircraft debacles that required government intercession? What about the overrruns of 200% in the Pentagon industrial complex amounting to millions of dollars each year? Management techniques have been available to business and government for years, but they have not prevented poor performance, inefficiency, costly expenditures, or some colossal failures. Will the techniques do any better in counseling and human services?

Many of our rivers are polluted, food companies are selling their below-standard reserves overseas, the major car companies recall thousands of defective cars each year, certain products have been removed from the market, dangerous toys and flammable clothing maim and injure children, and obsolescence is part and parcel of consumer products. This is the humanitarian record corporations have compiled in their race to make America productive. Although a wholesale indictment of business and industry would be unfair, it is a fact that the industrial mind-set (profit first, humanity second) has led to some appalling behavior that should be totally unacceptable to counselors (Hottleman, 1971).

Indeed, the application of corporate management practices to human problems could lead to some bizarre results. The following story of a satirical and apocryphal study conducted by a management consultant on the efficiency of a symphony orchestra has been circulating at the University of Wisconsin for some time. If we view the music and musicians as analogous to clients and counselors, a telling point can be made about the myth of management techniques. After carefully studying the orchestra, the consultant had several observations and recommendations:

1. *Observation*: For considerable periods, the four oboe players have nothing to do. *Recommendations*: Their numbers should be reduced and the work spread more evenly over the whole of the concert, thus eliminating peaks of activity.
2. *Observation*: All the violins were playing identical notes. This seems unnecessary duplication. *Recommendation*: The staff of this section should be drastically cut. If a large volume of sound is required, it could be obtained by means of electronic amplifier apparatus.
3. *Observation*: There seems to be too much repetition of some musical passages. Scores should be drastically pruned. No useful purpose is served by repeating on the horns a passage which has already been played by the strings. *Recommendation*: It is estimated that if all redundant passages were eliminated, the whole concert time of two hours could be reduced to 20 minuntes and there would be no need for an intermission. The conductor isn't too happy with these recommendations and expresses the opinion that there might be some falling off in attendance. In that unlikely event, it should be possible to close sections of the auditorium entirely with a consequential saving of overhead expense, lighting, salaries for ushers, etc.

No more needs to be said. This satire speaks for itself and for a substantial number of counselors concerned about the complexities of counseling.

Myth 2:   *All professionals are accountable—why shouldn't counselors be?*

We are told society is about to start holding professional counselors accountable and that measurable success is the mark of the true professional. If accountability is the mark of the true professional, then as Taylor and Zahn (1972) suggest, we can expect to find that all professionals are accountable in the sense the word has been used. For instance, they speculate on how medicine can be fitted to accountability. A behavioral objective for the recipient of an appendectomy might read something like this:

At the end of 120 hours following the removal of the appendix, the patient will, without aid, rise from his bed, walk to the window and open the shade without pain. Furthermore, the length of the scar will be within 7 to 11 centimeters long, and the top of which will not be visible with the patient clothed in a bikini covering the anterior of the lower body from the mons pubis to 24–30 centimeters below the umbilical scar.

If the patient performs as outlined in the clearly stated objective, the physician gets paid. If the patient does better, the surgeon gets a bonus. If the performance does not meet the objectives set up in the contract, the surgeon must forfeit the amount paid.

Let's turn to another profession, say, law. Imagine that a woman has been practically wiped out in an auto accident: lost her car, her nerve, and time on the job. She attempts to recoup her losses through the courts and with her attorney sets up a clearly stated objective.

The claimant will, unaided by any springy step, leave the courtroom with a check in her pocket for damages, with said check amounting to no less than $100,000.

Again, being professional, her attorney will accept payment on the basis of the preceding performance contract.

If we look further in American life, we would have to grant that we have certain expectations in other areas as well. Let's look back at the role of a member of the clergy. We have long-range expectations that would probably come out something like this if expressed in clearly stated objectives:

The soul will leave the body within 5 seconds of death and will be welcomed into the Kingdom of God as evidenced by the playing of soft music by Handel and rays of sunshine emanating through the narthex on an overcast day.

Suppose we were to examine one of the oldest professions. What might one reasonably expect here? Consider this clearly stated objective.

The client will, at the end of 15 minutes, leave the house at an obviously slower rate than when the client entered, footsteps will be of a slow and shaky nature, the knees slightly bent, with the face carrying a beatific smile. All previously noticed lines on the client's forehead will be diminished so as not to be noticeable within five feet, and eyes will have a glazed and disoriented look.

Our lesson need not be limited to pursuits usually regarded as professions. We have been assured that this sort of thing pervades almost all the rest of American life (Taylor and Zahn, 1972). These examples of clearly stated objectives may be outrageous but they make a salient point.

Myth 3: *There are no existing procedures and practices of accountability.*

There are a variety of procedures and practices currently available for use by supervisors and boards of directors to evaluate counselors and hold them accountable. They include such devices and approaches as video taping, interaction analysis, observations, logs, rating scales, probationary periods, in-service training, and written examinations. The relationship between what exists now and what is proposed in the way of new accountability procedures should be spelled out (Landers, 1973). Maybe our efforts should be turned not only toward the design of new accountability systems but also to making what we already have work.

Many counselors have not been inclined to assess themselves and what they are doing because their employers have: (1) developed arbitrary evaluative criteria and imposed those criteria on counselors without regard for or recognition of the counselor's involvement in the evaluation process, (2) employed criteria developed in other organizations without making adjustments for the essential differences between other organizations and their own, (3) utilized haphazard approaches to evaluation, thus not inviting the confidence or professional respect of counselors, or (4) established adequate criteria but failed to implement the evaluation process in a manner consistent with the principles of democratic and humanistic interaction.

The procedures available now will work when counselors have a significant voice in designing and carrying out plans of accountability and evaluation. Counselors need the opportunity to work with administrators, community representatives, and others in developing a philosophy of and approach to a person-centered evaluation characterized by an emphasis on positive and constructive feedback promoting counselor growth and enhancing client behavior. Without counselor involvement, new approaches will work no better than current methods.

EVALUATING COUNSELING *

The counseling profession cannot move forward on the basis of gratuitous statements regarding the outcomes and effectiveness of counseling. What can be gratuitously asserted can be gratuitously denied, and incidental and haphazard approaches to evaluation contribute very little to our understanding of counseling or to its improvement. What is needed are well-designed action research types of evaluative studies conducted at the local level to demonstrate the effectiveness of counseling in the total helping process (Frey, Raming, & Frey, 1978; Oetting 1977).

Diverse and complex problems confront the counselor who wishes to measure counseling outcomes and process. An understanding of these problems is necessary if counselors are to carry out meaningful studies of counseling theory and practice (Lewis, 1970). The existence of these problems does not mean that the counselor should be a professional researcher. An effective counselor who is rendering meaningful assistance to clients will not have the time to conduct an elaborate research study regarding the counselor's effectiveness. The more effective the counselor, the greater will be the demand for his or her services as a counselor and consultant. The counselor's primary obligation is to provide a counseling service to clients; the counselor is not a researcher. Too much emphasis on researching counseling can lead to a diminution of counseling effectiveness. It is interesting to note that some of the most thoroughly researched populations

*The remainder of this chapter has been adapted with permission, from A. V. Boy and G. J. Pine, *The Counselor in the Schools: A Reconceptualization* (Boston: Houghton Mifflin, 1968), pp. 256–257, 261–271.

in the country for a number of years received the least assistance in the form of such services as education, counseling, family assistance, and job placement. As one man in Harlem put it, "We have been researched inside and out, we have had psychologists, sociologists, criminologists, educators, and cultural anthropologists under us, over us, and all around us. But what has been done to help us?" Counselors bitten by the "research bug" need to exercise caution lest they become so involved in measuring clients and their behavior that they lose sight of the importance of counseling.

In most settings the counselor would need the help of a research consultant to design studies that would meet the criteria suggested in the literature of counseling psychology as a definition of valid research. Like the practicing physician, lawyer, or dentist, the practicing counselor will leave rigorous research to rigorous researchers. However, this does not mean the professional counselor cannot become involved in designing and carrying out simple action research and evaluative studies that would have value at the local level. Simplicity of design and execution are not necessarily exclusive of validity and meaning. Simple, clear, and well thought-out studies can provide valuable data to the counselor to help in gauging and improving the effectiveness of the counselor's work.

Evaluative Objectives

The objectives of evaluation revolve around two pivotal concerns: Are we helping clients? How can we improve counselor and counseling effectiveness to be of greater assistance to clients? These are not only the concerns of counselors but also of the community at large. It is well for counselors to bear in mind that community members are not unreasonable in the quest for evidence that demonstrates the value of counseling. Altogether too many counselors feel it is impossible to evaluate counseling and have avoided planning any procedures to verify its worth (Shertzer & Stone, 1980). Counselors, through the use of audio and video tape recordings, case studies, and opinion surveys, can gather the kinds of information needed to answer their questions and the questions rightfully raised by a community. Although such evaluation techniques have their limitations, this does not mean that they are of little value. On the contrary, they provide reasonable evidence, which can be used to improve counseling and to inform the public and professionals of the benefits of a counseling service (Tolbert, 1972).

What are the purposes and objectives of evaluation? We view the following objectives as being appropriate for evaluating client-centered counseling:

1.   To increase the growth of those being evaluated
2.   To help the counselor gain new insights into counseling
3.   To improve the counseling process
4.   To provide a basis for improving a total human services program

5. To clarify and validate hypotheses underlying counseling activities
6. To provide data upon which a sound program of public information and public relations can be built
7. To increase the psychological security of professional staff by letting them appraise the results of their efforts
8. To provide evidence to convince critics of the value of counseling
9. To facilitate smoother intrainstitutional and interinstitutional relationships
10. To persuade administrators of the value of counseling services so that additional services can be provided, when needed
11. To facilitate improved client behavior
12. To help programs to gain acceptance
13. To determine the effectiveness of counseling as a process of assisting clients to achieve social and personal goals
14. To help to effect larger institutional contributions to social progress
15. To determine which approach to counseling will produce a desired result, under what conditions, and with which clients.

Establishing Criteria

Measuring the outcomes of counseling is basically a question of measuring human behavior, for, if counseling has been successful, positive behavioral changes have taken place. But objectively measuring behavioral changes involves first selecting objective evaluative criteria. What are the criteria we use to establish that a change in behavior has occurred through counseling?

We view the following as appropriate criteria for evaluating the effectiveness of counseling, as it pertains to client behavior:

1. Reduction in number of personal problems
2. Increase in the voluntary use of the counseling service
3. Reduction in number of norm-violating behaviors
4. Development of personal goals
5. Reduction in court appearances
6. Increase in participation in community activities
7. Degree of job satisfaction
8. Increase in insight and self-understanding
9. Increase in self-acceptance and self-respect
10. Increase in self-sufficiency
11. Increase in acceptance of and respect for others
12. Assumption of responsibility
13. Improved behavior, generally
14. Reduction in personal tension.

The criteria for judging successful outcomes are related to our subjectivity regarding what we think is appropriate. Rogers (1951, pp. 179–180) has given an illustration of the complexity involved in selecting objective evaluative criteria:

> While there is ample clinical evidence that behavior frequently changes during or after therapy, it is difficult to prove that this change resulted from therapy or to show that it represents improvement. Improvement, for one client, may mean a new willingness to differ with his wife, while for another it may mean fewer quarrels with his spouse. For one client improvement may be indicated by the fact that he now gets an A in courses where he formerly received C or D, but another client may show his improvement by a lessened compulsiveness, by taking a B or a C in courses where he formerly received nothing but A. One man may show that he has profited from therapy by a smoother and more adequate adjustment to his job, another by achieving the courage to leave his job for a new field. Clinically, each of these behaviors may seem to be clearly an indication of improved adjustment, but there is no doubt that such judgments are subjective and hence open to question.

The criterion problem is perhaps the single most vital issue affecting the process of evaluation (Shertzer & Stone, 1980). Generally speaking, the application of most criteria that have been identified in the literature of counseling research has not yielded data to validate that counseling is helpful. This is because criteria have not been derived from the individual client and the client's unique situation. Each client has different needs and goals, and what may be needed in evaluating the effectiveness of counseling is sufficiently subjective criteria that can also encompass the diversity and complexity of human behavior. The uniqueness of each individual, and the distinctiveness of each counseling relationship, suggest that the case study or individual longitudinal approach may represent the best approach for measuring the outcomes and values of counseling (Goldman, 1977). For example, client A's growth may best be measured in terms of increased self-sufficiency; client B may be self-sufficient and this client's growth may best be measured in terms of an increase in insight; and so on. The application of three or four common criteria in evaluating the effectiveness of counseling with clients A, B, and C would most likely reveal minimal success. However, the utilization of particular and different criteria, defined in accordance with the singular growth needs of each client and the client's idiosyncratic concerns, would most likely indicate optimal success—assuming, of course, that counseling has been effective.

Evaluative Methods

Evaluative methods and approaches vary in degree of validity in ascertaining the significance of the relationship between personal growth and counseling. Following are some of the approaches and tools that can be utilized for purposes of evaluating counseling effectiveness:

1. The experimental approach which includes the "after only" design, the "before and after" design, and the "before and after with control group" design

2. The tabulation approach—the number of clients, the number of counseling sessions, and the nature and kinds of problems discussed
3. The follow-up approach
4. The expert opinion, the "information please" method—a subjective evaluation by experts
5. The client opinion ("what-do-you-think?" method) characterized by opinionnaire surveys of counselees
6. The external criteria, the "do-you-do-this?" method, in which the first step is to set up certain standards against which the program to be evaluated is compared
7. Opinionnaire surveys
8. The descriptive approach in which practices are analyzed and described
9. The case-study approach characterized by a longitudinal view of each client.

Among the tools that have been discussed in the counseling journals are audio- and video-tape recordings, health records, sociometric devices, logs and diaries, standardized tests, checklists, rating scales, inventories, questionnaires, anecdotal records, stenographic reports, case studies, and tally sheets.

A variety of evaluative approaches and tools are at the disposal of the counselor. Some counselors may not have the competencies necessary to do an adequate job of evaluation with a number of the methods and instruments previously mentioned. Others, who do have the necessary competencies, do not have the time or the energy to use some of the methodologies described. It is suggested that three approaches can be reasonably used by the practicing counselor without taking an unreasonable amount of time and energy away from counseling and consultation and without demanding an unusually high degree of sophistication.

Case Study Method

The case study method represents a viable approach for measuring the specific outcomes of counseling. We have specific behaviors and changing them may be a specific operation; and what is to be changed at a given time is unique to the person. The case method represents a many-sided approach to understanding and measuring the unique behavior of a particular person. Qualitative data for the case study can be obtained through audio- and video-tape recordings of counseling sessions; observation of client behavior; and client self-reports.

Audio and video recordings provide the most appropriate and useful means for evaluating the quality of counseling. The foremost research concern of the professional counselor is the *quality*, not the quantity, of counseling relationships. From tapes, the counselor will harvest a richness of data yielded by no other psychometric source. Personal growth on the part of the client can be discerned by the contrast between the client's recorded behavior at the beginning of counseling and the client's recorded behavior in the terminal stage.

Of course, the case study method will require more than the use of tape recordings since behavioral outcomes require some kind of measurement following the termination of the counseling relationship. It would also be helpful to have an independent observer appraise the data collected in order to objectively verify the effectiveness of counseling. The case study method provides versatility and flexibility, and a number of other methods and tools can be used to complement this approach.

Although the case study is a valuable method for determining the effectiveness of counseling, Goldman (1977, p. 367) points out why it has not been used in recent years:

> The case study used to be regarded as a method of research but appears to have been little used for research purposes in recent years or even decades, perhaps because of the exclusive emphasis placed on quantified methods and group data. Now one sees case vignettes used, if at all, only to illustrate the kinds of changes that occurred during a study. But even that kind of use is rarely found; it is almost as if numbers are the only acceptable kind of research data, all else being subject as "subjective" and therefore contaminating the purely scientific study of the phenomenon. How ironic, that a field whose invention and growth were in large measure intended to humanize institutions has set up criteria for research that value most highly the nonliving number.

Survey Method

Through the use of questionnaires, clients and others can evaluate the effectiveness of counseling. Although some specific outcomes could be measured with this approach, the survey method would seem to be more appropriate for evaluating the global outcomes of counseling. It represents a practical way to elicit the data needed to confirm or disconfirm a hypothesis. Isolating specific questions for consideration tends to objectify, intensify, and standardize the observations that respondents make. Questionnaires and other survey methods have been subject to severe criticism, but many of their common weaknesses can be avoided if this method is structured carefully and administered effectively. Business, industry, and political parties make frequent use of the opinionnaire approach with a high degree of effectiveness and utilize the results to make some very important decisions. Although it has its limitations, the survey method yields the kind of data in which community members are interested. It is a means of collecting reasonable information.

The following questionnaire (Figure 9-1) is suggested for use in surveying clients. It is simply designed and easy to administer. It yields both quantitative and qualitative data, and also serves as a coding sheet. In checking the answer boxes, the client automatically codes the data so that a punch-card operator can use the questionnaire to punch in the data on

Figure 9–1
Questionnaire Regarding Effectiveness of Counseling

1. Sex

   Male   Female
   ☐   ☐
   1   2

2. How many times did you volunteer for counseling?

0	1	2–3	4–5	6–7	8–9	10	more than 10
☐	☐	☐	☐	☐	☐	☐	☐
1	2	3	4	5	6	7	8

3. How many times were you referred to the counselor?

0	1	2–3	4–5	6–7	8–9	10	more than 10
☐	☐	☐	☐	☐	☐	☐	☐
1	2	3	4	5	6	7	8

4. How often did you see the counselor individually?

0	1	2–3	4–5	6–7	8–9	10	more than 10
☐	☐	☐	☐	☐	☐	☐	☐
1	2	3	4	5	6	7	8

5. How often did you as a member of a group see the counselor?

0	1	2–3	4–5	6–7	8–9	10	more than 10
☐	☐	☐	☐	☐	☐	☐	☐
1	2	3	4	5	6	7	8

6. Has counseling been helpful to you?

Extremely helpful						No help at all
1	2	3	4	5	6	7
☐	☐	☐	☐	☐	☐	☐

7. Did you find the counselor to be understanding?

Extremely understanding						Not understanding at all
1	2	3	4	5	6	7
☐	☐	☐	☐	☐	☐	☐

8. Did the counselor listen to you?

Listened to everything I had to say						Didn't listen at all
1	2	3	4	5	6	7
☐	☐	☐	☐	☐	☐	☐

Figure 9–1
(continued)

9. Did you feel the counselor was interested in you, your feelings, your opinions, in you as a person?

Extremely interested in me   Not interested in me at all

1	2	3	4	5	6	7
☐	☐	☐	☐	☐	☐	☐

10. Did the counselor respect you and your opinions?

Always respected me and my opinions   Did not respect me and my opinions

1	2	3	4	5	6	7
☐	☐	☐	☐	☐	☐	☐

11. In counseling, did you feel you could talk freely?

Always felt I could talk about anything   Felt I could not talk about anything

1	2	3	4	5	6	7
☐	☐	☐	☐	☐	☐	☐

12. Did counseling help you to learn anything about yourself?

Learned a great deal about myself   Learned nothing about myself

1	2	3	4	5	6	7
☐	☐	☐	☐	☐	☐	☐

13. Did counseling bring about any change in you as a person? (Did it change your behavior, ideas, attitudes, or anything like that?)

Changed me greatly. I became a new person   Did not change me at all

1	2	3	4	5	6	7
☐	☐	☐	☐	☐	☐	☐

14. Did counseling help you to ''blow off steam,'' ''to get things off your mind,'' to talk about things that really ''bugged'' you?

Counseling helped me to blow off steam, whenever I wanted to   Never helped me to blow off steam, to get things off my mind

1	2	3	4	5	6	7
☐	☐	☐	☐	☐	☐	☐

Figure 9–1
(continued)

	Extremely helpful						Of no help
15. Has counseling been help-ful to you in personal planning?	1	2	3	4	5	6	7
	□	□	□	□	□	□	□

	Extremely helpful						Of no help
16. Has counseling been help-ful to you in general plan-ning?	1	2	3	4	5	6	7
	□	□	□	□	□	□	□

17. In a few paragraphs or so please tell us what you think about the counseling service. What are its strengths and weaknesses? How can it be improved?

18. If counseling has been helpful to you please tell us in what way it has been helpful. If it has not been helpful to you, please tell us why it hasn't.

computer cards. Each question represents a column on a computer card, and the number below each answer box represents the punch to be made in the column. The information punched in on computer cards enables the counselor to store data conveniently and presents innumerable possibilities for statistical analysis.

Tabulation Method

The tabulation method provides a quantitative descriptive analysis of counseling and gives information from which inferences about the quality of counseling can be drawn. Professional counselors can keep track statistically of the counseling program's trends by maintaining daily tally sheets and statistics to determine quickly and easily the types of problems clients are bringing into counseling, and whether clients are becoming voluntarily involved or whether counseling is initiated from other sources. Additional statistics could include the number of individual and group counseling sessions, the number of consultations, the number of clients using the counseling service, the mean number of counseling sessions per client, and the ratio of male and female counselees to male and female counselors (Boy & Pine, 1963).

Experimental Method

Controlled experimentation is one of the most scientific and rigorous procedures for evaluating a counseling program and measuring the outcomes of counseling (Pietrofesa, Hoffman, Splete, & Pinto, 1978). In the experimental method, two or more groups of subjects are matched on all but one variable; one group is provided with a specific experience (the experimental group) and the other is not (the control group). Comparisons between the groups are made to determine whether any statistically significant differences occur after the experimental group has undergone the particular treatment. Controlled experiments in counseling usually center on matching a group of counseled persons with a group of non-counseled persons, or matching a group of clients counseled by one approach, a group of clients counseled by another approach, and a third group of persons not counseled.

The problems of experimental design are randomization of sampling, equating groups, controlling relevant variables, and defining the nature of the treatment variable and operating within the definition of the treatment variable. Such problems can be overcome, but they require sophistication and skills usually not possessed by the professional counselor. What is needed in organizations, institutions, and agencies in which counseling is practiced is a research person who is knowledgeable about the counseling process and who has the high-level skills, competencies, and know-how to conduct experimental studies. A person of this caliber could function primarily as a researcher and perhaps serve several human services groups as a consultant. This person could design the experiments, analyze the data, and give an objective appraisal of the services. Until such a person is available, it is doubtful that counselors can employ the experimental method in a reasonable and realistic way in most work settings.

Even in the hands of an exceptionally skilled researcher, the experimental method of evaluating a counseling program still contains two major problems. First, the application of the experimental design requires that treatment and control conditions be held constant throughout the length of the experiment (Shertzer & Stone, 1980). This means that all clients must receive the same amount of the treatment to which they are assigned, so that clients receiving one type of treatment are not contaminated by the other (Pietrofesa, Hoffman, Splete, & Pinto, 1978). If data about differences between treatments are to be meaningful, treatments cannot be modified while the experiment is in progress. In accepting the rigorous conditions of the experimental method, one is asked to fit the treatment to the design, rather than vice versa. Therefore, the use of the experimental method conflicts with the fundamental principle that evaluation should encourage the continual improvement and modification of a counseling program. Counselors cannot be expected to limit their counseling service to accommodate the constraints of a design just to guarantee internally valid data. As counselors learn about the strengths and weaknesses of their counseling, they may have to change and sometimes radically alter a counseling program in order to do justice to their clients.

A second major weakness of the experimental method is that it yields data about the effectiveness of two or more treatments after the fact. Therefore, it is useful as a judgmental device but has little value as a decision-making tool. After-the-fact data are not provided at appropriate times to enable the counselor to determine what a counseling service should be accomplishing or whether it should be altered in process. Often, by the time experimental data have come in, it is too late to make decisions about plans and procedures whose nature often determines the difference between the success or failure of a service to begin with.

Evaluative Obstacles and Problems

Obstacles one might encounter when evaluating counseling programs fall into three problem areas: problems in connection with the selection of evaluation devices, problems in connection with the interpretation and use of data secured through the employment of evaluative devices, and problems in connection with the organization and administration of the program. There are obstacles inherent in the counseling function that are indicative of lack of a research "breakthrough." These obstacles are:

1. The specific objectives of counseling are stated in generalities rather than in specific behavioral outcomes.
2. Counseling terminology requires strict adherence to precise definitions. These are lacking.
3. Many variables outside of counseling may influence the behavior believed to be resultant from counseling.
4. There is confusion over process evaluation and product evaluation. Too often the latter is neglected.
5. Counselors enter into research hesitantly.

The problems of evaluation group themselves as follows:

1. Lack of a clear, acceptable statement of objectives in terms of observable client characteristics and behavior
2. Failure to relate counseling objectives to institutional objectives
3. The use of immediate and easily available criteria accompanied by failure to validate the immediate criteria against long-term goals
4. The tendency to regard certain goals as equally desirable for all clients, thereby ignoring individual differences
5. Confusion of means with ends or of process with outcomes
6. Excessive use of subjective reactions
7. Little or no attention to determining a satisfactory experimental design.

The existential counselor is confronted with the problem of clarifying and defining terminology so that certain meaningful hypotheses, ideas, and concepts can be scientifically tested and verified. Landsman (1965, p. 570) has stated that the following concepts "cry out for clarification" and this is still true today:

1. Being, becoming, non-being and nothingness, being-in-the-world, being there
2. Anguish, agony, anxiety, and angst

3. Loneliness and encounter
4. Despair and dread
5. Commitment
6. Being-able-to-be, being-allowed-to-be, having-to-be-in-this-world.

Landsman points out that "of all these terms, only one appears in Verplanck's *Glossary of Some Terms Used in the Objective Science of Behavior.*" However, he does cite studies by Jourard (1963), Blazer (1963), Privette (1964), and Puttick (1964), as representing rigorous experiments which included operational definitions that met the standards of behavioral science.

The obstacles that have been presented are not insurmountable. The professional researcher who has the time and the facilities can produce well designed experimental studies and long-term longitudinal and developmental studies. Often such studies require a team of researchers, paraprofessionals, and computer facilities. The practicing counselor who is expected to render a counseling service daily and who does not have the facilities and time can still gather meaningful data to validate the efficacy of counseling. What prevents most counselors from accomplishing evaluation studies is the obstacle of internal attitudes toward research and evaluation. Counselors have been so inundated with publications pleading for high-level research studies that they have developed the feeling that there is virtually little they can do to validly evaluate their counseling and its outcomes. As we pointed out earlier, this need not be the case.

If we regard evaluation as the process by which we determine the degree to which client and program objectives have been achieved, we can safely measure the attainment of these objectives through the use of statistics gathered in the local program, by studying recordings of counseling sessions, and by the skillful employment of questionnaires. Although the statistics gathered may not be elaborate or sophisticated and the qualitative data may be subjective, they will provide an adequate and fair measure of the substance and the effects of counseling.

C. H. Patterson (1962, p. 150) has recommended the following procedures for evaluative studies:

1. Select and describe the objectives or outcomes that the program or service should achieve. Define client and program goals in terms of measurable outcomes.
2. Define the criteria that are acceptable as indicators of the achievement or lack of achievement of these objectives.
3. Select or devise instruments to measure the defined criteria.
4. Design the experiment in terms of the samples and their selection, the experimental or statistical controls, the administration or identification of the treatment or independent variable, and the application of the criterion measures.
5. Perform a statistical analysis of the data to determine the effectiveness of the treatments in terms of the outcome criteria.

Patterson's recommendations would seem to be more applicable to the experimental approach, but they also constitute general principles that can be modified by the practicing counselor who wishes to use the survey, case study, or tabulation methods of evaluation.

Conditions for Accountability and Evaluation

The following items appear to be the minimal and necessary client-centered conditions for the development of accountability and evaluation programs that will improve counseling skills and facilitate improved behavior for clients:

1. A plan of accountability and evaluation that is developed by counselors, supervisors, and clients working together, and has evolved from a free and open discussion of the philosophical, theoretical, and empirical considerations that influence behavior

2. A clearly stated philosophy and rationale for accountability and evaluation developed by counselors, supervisors, and clients

3. A continuous, on-going process of accountability and evaluation characterized by continuous feedback and established monitoring points so that the counselor and appropriate supervisory personnel have specific time referents for gauging and discussing the progress of the counselor and the behavior of the counselor's clients

4. A clear statement of performance standards and criteria that is understandable and acceptable to counselors, supervisors, and clients

5. A plan of accountability and evaluation that accommodates judgments and observations from both the internal (counselor) and external (supervisor) frames of reference

6. A plan of accountability and evaluation that includes an annual review of processes, performance criteria and standards, roles, and responsibilities

7. A plan of accountability and evaluation that takes into consideration local conditions, needs, and resources

8. Clearly defined but flexible methodological procedures for collecting data to test performance criteria used in evaluating and supervising counselors; for instance:

    a. Counselor and supervisor analyze and critique audio- and/or video-tapes of the counselor's counseling skills

    b. Counselors and colleagues analyze and critique audio- and/or video-tapes of each other's counseling

    c. Counselor conducts research into personal effectiveness as a counselor and shares the results for critique with supervisor and colleagues

    d. Periodically, the counselor prepares a self-evaluation and the supervisor writes an evaluation of the counselor. Together they share the results and discuss areas of agreement and disagreement.

9. A plan of accountability and evaluation that can be defined and modified on the basis of periodic feedback from all who are affected

10. A plan of accountability and evaluation in which all participants accept some responsibility. For each goal the parties involved would decide not only what is to be accomplished but also what they are to be responsible for

11. A plan of accountability and evaluation based on needs assessments, philosophical considerations, and goal formulations that is the result of collaborative efforts.

A sensible plan of accountability and evaluation calls for the establishment of new relationships and the reshaping of traditional roles. Many more individuals will be involved. When the community and the counseling agency move into real partnerships the issues of accountability and evaluation will not be viewed within a framework of superior-subordinate relationships. Shared responsibility is the key to successful and sensitive accountability and evaluation.

EVALUATING THE COUNSELOR

A counselor who is judged to be competent achieves this status as the result of how people who work with the counselor generally feel about him or her. This situation is not unusual in that the public generally tends to judge the physician and dentist in the same manner. No one outside the field of medicine really knows much about the medical skills of the physician; they tend to judge the physician's competency according to how they generally feel about the physician. If their feeling tends toward the positive, the physician achieves a community image of competency. Even in a national presidential election, the typical voter casts a vote for one candidate instead of another out of a feeling that gravitates the vote toward a particular candidate. Very few people vote as a result of a logical and scientific evaluative procedure.

Competency Criteria

The professionalization of counseling demands the development of certain competency criteria whereby the counselor can be evaluated with a higher degree of sophistication than at present (Carr, 1977). In fact, the development of such criteria is currently the missing link in the professionalization of counseling. More adequate state certification and licensing standards are beginning to emerge for the counselor; a code of ethics exists that serves as the standard for professional behavior; national concepts of the counselor's proper role have emerged; and national standards for the preparation of a professional counselor have become more clarified. These accomplishments have been steps forward in the professionalization of counseling, but another task remains to be accomplished: the development of criteria whereby the on-the-job competency of the counselor can be determined.

There are some counselors who might object to the development of such criteria, preferring instead to exist in the current nebulous state in which the evaluation of their competency is essentially left to chance. Sometimes there is more safety in having no criteria, because then no one really knows what to expect. But, unless the profession of counseling begins to identify some criteria denoting counselor competency and to evaluate itself against such criteria, the full professionalization of counseling will never be achieved.

Who is to judge the competency of the counselor? Those who align themselves with the internal-frame-of-reference concept would argue that the counselor is the best source of information regarding competency. Those who align themselves with the external-frame-of-reference concept would argue that the counselor's competency, if it is to be known in any true sense, must be evaluated by sources external to the counselor since a self-evaluation may be distorted by personal and professional defensiveness. The logical solution is to evaluate the competency of the counselor from both the internal and external frames of reference. That is, the counselor must be a participant in determining professional competency, but, at the same time, the counselor must allow evaluations by those significant co-workers who are in a position to adequately judge the counselor's competency. A counselor may possess a personal perception of competence that enables the counselor to function easily and well but this perception may be limited because his or her frame of reference is only personal. Upon engaging in personal perceptions, the counselor is able to see much, but often this perception is obscured because he or she has no frame of reference external to the self. Therefore, counselors can learn much about how others view their competency by participating in a cooperative evaluative process whereby both the counselors' self and exterior-to-self concepts of competency are blended into a composite picture.

Who will evaluate the counselor's competency from an external frame of reference? It appears that the significant co-workers who would be in the best position to render such an external evaluation would be the director of the institution or organization that employs the counselor, provided that this person possesses a sufficient degree of professional sophistication to be adequately involved in such an evaluative process. Acquiring evaluations beyond such a director would be left entirely to the counselor. If the counselor felt that it might be profitable to secure the evaluations of other significant co-workers, these evaluations could be incorporated into a wider external-to-self picture.

The counselor's self-evaluation and external-to-self evaluations can then be synthesized in a meeting between the counselor and those who are performing the external-to-self evaluations. In an open and free discussion, the areas of strength and weakness could be identified, and both the counselor and external evaluators can become involved in firming up the strengths and identifying the weaknesses. In fact, the counselor could vastly improve a functional role if, when a weakness was identified, discussion could center upon whether this weakness was lodged in the personhood or professional competency of the counselor or was due to administrative patterns or procedures that inhibited the role of the counselor. For example, if the counselor was externally evaluated to have weak rapport with clients, was this condition due to the personal or professional attitudes and behaviors of the counselor or was it due to the fact that the counselor was so involved in administrative functions that clients saw him or her more as an authority figure than as a counselor? The pursuit of this question would shed much light upon the counselor's proper role and how it affects functional competency.

At first glance, defining the criteria for evaluating a counselor appears to be a difficult problem; but the lack of specific definitions for some criteria may lend itself to the initiation, at a local level, of meaningful discussions of what constitutes, for example, a facilitating counselor. Such discussion among administrators, staff members, and counselors could lead to the development of a common language and understanding regarding the complex dimensions of counseling. If such dialogues took place in local organizations with some specific areas of agreement emerging, they would constitute the first step toward a conceptualization of measurable and understandable criteria. When the problem of evaluating practicing counselors is tackled at the grass roots level and local criteria are developed, then, slowly but surely, through the collection, analysis, and synthesis of locally conceived evaluative instruments, usable competency criteria will emerge. Such criteria would be applicable in a variety of community and agency settings, and would mirror the commonalities of effective counseling regardless of different theoretical orientations.

Criteria are intended to reflect what members of the profession agree are common bases of practice among effective counselors. The criteria should be flexible enough to accommodate different theoretical positions. Thus, the behavior modification counselor or the client-centered counselor, for example, can be evaluated and can also engage in self-evaluations although they possess different theoretical and application concepts.

Counselor Involvement

The use of an evaluative instrument as part of the total evaluation process (with particular emphasis on counselor self-evaluation) may motivate counselors not only to examine their practice but also to look inwardly at themselves as persons. If counselors in a particular organization develop an evaluative instrument with their supervisor, and have an opportunity as individuals and as a group to modify and refine it so that there is general agreement regarding criteria, the counselors have a point of reference for continuous self-evaluation. For some it would not be an especially easy task to look at themselves and at their practice according to external criteria agreed upon by the group. Many counselors have not been disposed to view themselves and what they are doing because they have operated in settings that have:

1. Developed arbitrary evaluative criteria and imposed these criteria on counselors without due regard or recognition of the counselor's involvement in evaluation, thus creating negative attitudes about any kind of evaluation
2. Employed criteria used to evaluate other staff members as "suitable" criteria for evaluating counselors without recognizing and accommodating the essential differences between other staff functions and counseling, thus creating resistance to evaluation
3. Utilized a haphazard and "willy-nilly" approach to evaluation, thus not inviting the confidence and the professional respect of counselors
4. Established adequate criteria but have not implemented the evaluation process in a way consistent with the principles of democratic supervision.

Evaluative Conditions

To effectively evaluate and supervise counselors so that they will improve their counseling and render more meaningful and effective assistance to clients, it would seem that the following would constitute minimal and necessary conditions:

1. The use of appropriately designed evaluative instruments that include criteria reflecting the body of theoretical and empirical knowledge derived from professional literature and research
2. The establishment of evaluative criteria flexible enough to encompass varied theoretical positions
3. The establishment of criteria that would be applicable within varied settings
4. A statement of criteria understandable to counselors, administrators, and supervisors
5. A plan of evaluation that includes judgments from both the internal and external frames of reference
6. A continuous on-going process of evaluation with established monitoring points so that the counselor and the appropriate supervisory personnel have some specific time referents for gauging and discussing individual progress
7. A plan of evaluation consistent with the democratic and psychological principles of supervision and counseling

8. A clearly stated philosophy and rationale for evaluation and super-
    vision derived from the contributions of counselors and supervisors
9. A clearly defined but flexible methodological procedure for collect-
    ing data to test evaluative criteria for the evaluation of each
    counselor, such as:
    a. Counselor and supervisor listen to and analyze the audio- and/
        or video-tapes of the counselor's counseling
    b. Counselor and colleagues listen to and analyze the tapes of the
        individual counselor's counseling
    c. Supervisor observes the counselor through one-way observa-
        tion mirror
    d. Counselor conducts personal research regarding effectiveness
        and shares the results for critique with a supervisor and/or col-
        leagues
    e. Counselor writes a self-evaluation, and supervisor writes an
        evaluation of the counselor periodically
    f. Counselors statistically keep track of their work by maintaining
        tally sheets and detailed statistics to let them know quickly and
        easily the types of problems that clients are bringing into
        counseling; whether these clients are coming in on their own or
        counseling is initiated from other sources; the number of in-
        dividual and group counseling sessions; the number of con-
        sultations; and the number of different clients using the
        counseling service
10. A plan of evaluation that includes an annual review by counselors
    and supervisors of evaluative processes and criteria
11. An annual orientation by supervisory personnel and counselors to
    inform the public of how counselors are evaluated
12. A plan of evaluation characterized more by a horizontal super-
    visory relationship between counselor and supervisor than by a
    vertical relationship
13. A plan of evaluation that has been developed by counselors and
    supervisors working together, and which has evolved from a free
    and open discussion of the philosophical, theoretical, and empirical
    considerations that influence the work of the counselor
14. A plan of evaluation that takes into consideration local conditions,
    needs, and resources.

Following is a sample instrument (Figure 9-2) for evaluating counselor
competency. It represents a fundamental step in developing an evaluative
instrument that can be used locally, as well as nationally. The instrument
can be easily quantified and the data derived from its use can furnish a picture of the counselor's on-the-job competency. Such a picture is necessary
if counseling is to become more professionalized.

Evaluative instruments may have national implications as the counseling profession moves toward determining competency criteria and the

Figure 9–2
An Instrument for Evaluating the Counselor

Check relative position on the line	
Strong Weak	**Personal Characteristics**
1 2 3 4 5	Is alert and enthusiastic
1 2 3 4 5	Is professionally ethical
1 2 3 4 5	Is professionally involved
1 2 3 4 5	Is self-motivated
1 2 3 4 5	Is emotionally balanced
1 2 3 4 5	Relates easily to others
1 2 3 4 5	Is genuine
	Relations with Clients
1 2 3 4 5	Is sensitive to clients
1 2 3 4 5	Motivates clients to seek counseling
1 2 3 4 5	Has rapport with clients
1 2 3 4 5	Is a facilitating agent
1 2 3 4 5	Respects the dignity and worth of the individual
1 2 3 4 5	Has a facilitative image in the community
1 2 3 4 5	Has ability to handle a wide range of client problems

Figure 9–2
(continued)

Strong				Weak	Relations with Referents
1	2	3	4	5	Is sensitive to referents
1	2	3	4	5	Is cooperative with referents
1	2	3	4	5	Attends to referrals
1	2	3	4	5	Is available to referents
1	2	3	4	5	Has a professional image among referents
1	2	3	4	5	Provides referents with an opportunity to be heard
1	2	3	4	5	Is conscientious in following through with referents

Relations with Staff

1	2	3	4	5	Is sensitive to the roles of other staff
1	2	3	4	5	Communicates easily with staff
1	2	3	4	5	Is a facilitating agent with staff
1	2	3	4	5	Is aware of the demands made on staff
1	2	3	4	5	Is receptive to staff
1	2	3	4	5	Has good rapport with staff
1	2	3	4	5	Attends to staff referrals

Relations with Administration

1	2	3	4	5	Is sensitive to the role of the administrator

Figure 9–2
(continued)

Strong   Weak   Relations with Administration

1   2   3   4   5
|___|___|___|___| Has a professional rationale for counseling

1   2   3   4   5
|___|___|___|___| Meets with the administrator regarding program
                       development

1   2   3   4   5
|___|___|___|___| Communicates easily and effectively

1   2   3   4   5
|___|___|___|___| Functions effectively as a resource consultant

1   2   3   4   5
|___|___|___|___| Attends to administrative referrals

1   2   3   4   5
|___|___|___|___| Functions in a well-organized manner

Professional Attitudes and Activities

1   2   3   4   5
|___|___|___|___| Is sensitive to research findings

1   2   3   4   5
|___|___|___|___| Contributes to the counseling profession

1   2   3   4   5
|___|___|___|___| Periodically evaluates own counseling skills

1   2   3   4   5
|___|___|___|___| Is aware of both the art and science of counseling

1   2   3   4   5
|___|___|___|___| Has a professional balance between theory and
                       practice

1   2   3   4   5
|___|___|___|___| Is professionally enthusiastic

1   2   3   4   5
|___|___|___|___| Is aware of the counselor's professional role

General Rating

                1   2   3   4   5
Strong |___|___|___|___| Weak
        (Check relative position
              on the line)

degree to which counselors meet these criteria. When used in harmony with the counselor involvement and evaluative conditions suggested in this chapter, it has much potential for improving the counselor's competency in a variety of professional settings.

REFERENCES

Blazer, J. A. An experimental evaluation of transcendence of environment. *Journal of Humanistic Psychology*, 1963, *3*, 49–53.

Boy, A. V., & Pine, G. J. *Client-centered counseling in the secondary school.* Boston: Houghton Mifflin, 1963, 78.

Boy, A. V., & Pine, G. J. *The counselor in the schools: A reconceptualization.* Boston: Houghton Mifflin, 1968.

Carr, R. The counselor or the counseling program as the target of evaluation? *The Personnel and Guidance Journal*, 1977, *56*, 112–118.

Frey, D. H., Raming, H. E., & Frey, F. M. The qualitative description, interpretation, and evaluation of counseling. *The Personnel and Guidance Journal*, 1978, *56*, 621–625.

Goldman, L. Toward more meaningful research. *The Personnel and Guidance Journal*, 1977, *55*, 363–368.

Hannon, J. C. Counselor's alternative to retrenchment and accountability. *The Personnel and Guidance Journal*, 1977, *56*, 50–52.

Hottleman, G. D. Performance contracting is a hoax. *Education Digest*, 1971, *37*, 1–4.

Jourard, S. *The transparent self.* Princeton, N.J.: Van Nostrand, 1963.

Knapper, E. Q. Counselor accountability. *The Personnel and Guidance Journal*, 1978, *57*, 27–30.

Landers, J. Accountability and progress by nomenclature: Old ideas in new bottles. *Phi Delta Kappan*, 1973, *54*, 538–540.

Landsman, T. Existentialism in counseling: The scientific view. *The Personnel and Guidance Journal*, 1965, *43*.

Lewis, E. C. *The psychology of counseling.* New York: Holt, Rinehart and Winston, 1970, 202.

Oetting, E. R. The counseling psychologist as program evaluator. *The Counseling Psychologist*, 1977, *7*, 89–91.

Patterson, C. H. *Counseling and guidance in schools.* New York: Harper, 1962.

Pietrofesa, J. J., Hoffman, A., Splete, H. H., & Pinto, D. V. *Counseling: Theory, research and practice.* Chicago: Rand McNally, 1978, 351–352; 363–365.

Pine, G. J. Teacher accountability: Myths, realities and recommendations. *Educational Forum*, 1976, *51*, 49–60.

Privette, G. *Factors associated with functioning which transcend modal behavior.* Unpublished doctoral dissertation, University of Florida, 1964.

Puttick, W. H. *A factor analytic study of positive modes of experiencing and behaving in a teacher college population.* Unpublished doctoral dissertation, University of Florida, 1964.

Rogers, C. R. *Client-centered therapy.* Boston: Houghton Mifflin, 1951 (renewed 1979).

Shertzer, B., & Stone, S. C. *Fundamentals of counseling* (3rd ed.). Boston: Houghton Mifflin, 1980, 414–441.

Taylor, A. J., & Zahn, R. D. Accountability for the professional. *The Clearing House,* 1972, *46,* 356–358.

Tolbert, E. L. *Introduction to counseling* (2nd ed.). New York: McGraw-Hill, 1972, 364.

Chapter 10

COUNSELOR EDUCATION: A STUDENT-CENTERED VIEW

The process of preparing persons to become professional counselors has received the attention of authors whose concepts range on a continuum from the strict scientific requirements of operations research to those that border on the supernatural requirements of extra-sensory perception.

Zifferblatt (1972, p. 16) represents one end of the continuum when he recommends that counselor education programs be based on operations research or management science. He presents his view in the following definition:

> Operations research (OR) or "management science" is a very successful cybernetically based model for analyzing complex problems in technology. A scientific method is employed in analyzing the actual operations of a specific setting with emphasis on the solution of problems relating to flow inventories and cost benefit analysis. Operations research strategies emphasize the need for an organization or system wide view of analysis. Operations research takes the system view by developing an analytic model which represents the entire system and its interrelationships in relation to a pre-specified mission. This specification is usually done mathematically.

Zifferblatt (1972, p. 17) goes on to indicate that the analytical strategy in operations research involves six steps:

1. Formulating the problem (mission)
2. Constructing a model to represent the system variables possibly related to the problem or affected by it
3. Deriving an optimal solution
4. Deriving alternative solutions
5. Maximizing a solution (efficiency-effectiveness ratios)
6. Implementing and maintaining a maximal solution
7. Ongoing re-cycling of steps 1–6.

Arbuckle (1971, p. 34) represents the opposite end of the continuum when he recommends that the following be added to a counselor education staff:

If we say we can accept the reality of the irrational in life, if we can live comfortably with important aspects of our life being felt and sensed, but basically remaining forever unknown, then students should have experiences with human beings who are already there. Witches and warlocks, for example, might prove to be an interesting, though possibly bothersome addition to the staff of counselor education departments.

Those who support a systems analysis approach to counselor education have received a receptive ear from counselor education programs that desire to produce an organized, unified, systematic, and scientifically accountable method for producing counselors. Such counselor education programs feel that the performance of the product will be better known and guaranteed if the system through which the product is developed is better organized and accountable for outcomes (Bergland & Quatrano, 1973; Horan, 1972; Yelon, 1969).

The counselor education approach that has attracted recent attention has been skill training (Carkhuff, 1969; Ivey, 1974; Kagan, 1972b). In this approach, the counselor learns facilitative skills and techniques that are precisely designed to meet the behavioral needs of clients. These skills are defined, teachable, and their development, implementation, and effectiveness can be closely monitored. Kagan (1972a, p. 42) represents the enthusiasm for skill training when he states:

> This new psychology has not abandoned analytic insights and existential goals but is dedicated to finding precise ways to define very complex human dynamics and relationships. Methods have been developed which not only serve as effective and reliable ways of helping people learn to live better with themselves and others, but which are designed so that large numbers of people can be helped. Potential for mass dissemination is one of the hallmarks of the new psychology. Emphasis on controlled evaluation and reformulation is another.

As with all new ideas, criticism and negative evidence begins to appear that counterbalances enthusiasm. Inconclusive skill training results have emerged. The Carkhuff model (1969) was found to be limited in applicability in the research done by Resnikoff (1972), Miller (1973), and Gormally and Hill (1974). The Kagan model (1972b) was found to produce inconclusive results in the research conducted by Bradley (1974) and Kingdon (1975). The Ivey model (1974) also produced inconclusive results according to the research conducted by DiMatta and Arndt (1974) and Authier and Gustafson (1975).

Mahon and Altmann (1977, p. 47) indicate that skill training is ineffective because:

> . . . altering a behavior, without altering beliefs or values associated with that behavior is not likely to result in lasting behavior change. Thus skill training might indeed produce some behavior changes, but the permanence of these changes will depend upon the extent to which they are accompanied by meaningful and relevant changes in perception. When perceptions do not change,

newly acquired skills can be expected to fade out. This is very likely what happens in many skill training programs.

. . . the effectiveness of the skill approach is limited, and it appears to neglect certain important personal qualities.

Mahon and Altmann (1977, p. 48) go on to draw from the field of perceptual psychology and indicate what they consider to be a missing dimension in skill training:

Perceptual psychology (Combs, A. W., Richards, A. C., and Richards, F., 1976) does not deny the importance of skills or techniques—rather it adds to them. It adds the integrating basis from which the skills emerge. It is not the skills themselves which are all important, it is the *control* of their use, the *intentions* with which they are used, and their flexibility or changeability that is so crucial. In this view, using one's self as instrument represents a dynamic rather than static process, a direction of movement rather than point of arrival.

In an article, written in the form of a letter in response to Carkhuff's support for skill training (1972), Korn and Korn (1972, p. 77) make the following observations regarding the limitations of skill training:

Your emphasis on developing an extensive repertoire of responses in the counselor somehow removes you from the inner phenomenological life of the individual, both client and counselor.

. . . your emphasis on teaching skills does not come to grips with the task of encouraging the individual to focus on himself as an integrated whole and to find meaning in his life. To put it succinctly, you seem to be concerned with giving people answers while we believe it is more important to teach people how to ask questions about themselves and their responsibilities to others.

While addressing himself to the components of an existential-humanistic program of counselor education, Arbuckle (1975, p. 171) has the following to say about counselor skills: ". . . competency is measured less by skills than it is by the quality of the person called counselor."

Kemp (1971, p. 18), from an existential viewpoint, says the following regarding the use of techniques by the counselor:

Customarily, it is assumed that if the right technique is used, we can then understand the uniqueness of the counselee. The existential counselor's primary goal is to understand the counselee as a person, a being and as being-in-the-world. This does not mean that he has a low respect for technique, but rather that technique takes its legitimate place in a new perspective. The new perspective is to help the counselee recognize and experience his own experience.

In the preceding statement, Kemp indicates that he is not against counseling techniques, as such. He implies that techniques are applicable when they are sensitive to a deeper and more meaningful concept of the counseling relationship and the process of helping. Melnick and Brandsma (1977, p. 197) indicate a blending of the self of the counselor with the use of techniques. They emphasize the development of the self as a counselor as a therapeutic catalyst by stating the following goals that should characterize a program of counselor preparation:

> . . . providing the students with a grounding in the phenomenology of therapy.

> . . . teaching them the parallel between therapy and real life and helping them to learn to deal with the initiation and termination of therapy as well as the pitfalls in between.

> . . . allowing them to learn to identify their assumptions about the world and psychotherapy and to become aware of how these assumptions color the therapeutic experience.

They also desire to blend the preceding goals with the goal of assisting students to acquire techniques: ". . . teaching techniques such as paraphrasing, descriptive observation, and self disclosure."

In a student-centered concept of counselor education skill development also occurs but it is a secondary emphasis. The primary emphasis is on developing a realization among student counselors that one's selfhood, one's psychological wholeness, the totality of one's being, is the influence to which clients respond in their movement toward personal reorganization and the accompanying behavioral change. That is, both the counselor and client must *first* improve themselves as persons. When the counselor does this, skills flow from the improved self in a natural way that is beneficial to clients. When the client does this, behaviors flow from the improved self that are beneficial to the client. The improved self, for both the counselor and client, is the catalyst that influences the evolvement of therapeutic behaviors. The influence of an improved or actualized self upon behavior has been identified by Rogers (1962), Combs et al. (1971), Webb (1971), Pulvino & Sanborn (1972), Calia (1974), and Bartlett (1978).

Arbuckle (1975, p. 170) states that the student counselor's self-awareness is of critical importance if we expect that student counselor to become an effective counselor:

> . . . it is essential that counselors have an awareness of self. It is, of course, very important to understand the client, but counselors who are unaware of who they are are not likely to be very helpful with clients who are trying to answer similar questions. The goal is to help student counselors better understand themselves so that they may do the same for clients.

Boy and Pine (1978, p. 142) have stated that counselor educators will influence student counselors to become quality persons if counselor educators themselves model the behaviors of quality persons:

> . . . model the behaviors of caring, understanding, empathy, acceptance, and concreteness. Such counselor educators will develop colleague relationships with students rather than foster aloof and guarded professor-student relationships. If counselor educators expect student counselors to become quality persons, then they themselves must model the behavior of quality persons.

Boy and Pine (1978, p. 142) go on to identify program experiences that will enable student counselors to expand, refine, and develop the quality of their personhoods: ". . . self awareness workshops, encounter groups, microcounseling, individual counseling, independent study projects, and individualized self development projects."

A student-centered counselor education program begins with the development of the therapeutic potential of the student counselor's personhood. From this base the student counselor is able to learn skills that flow naturally from the humanness of that personhood and positively affect both the attitude and behavior of the client. The student counselor must be exposed to both self-development opportunities and skill training in order to become a competent counselor. Each is insufficient preparation without the complementary contribution of the other.

CRITERIA OF A THEORY

Although many ideas exist regarding the process of preparing a person to become a counselor, there has been little evidence that these ideas have been translated into a theory of counselor preparation. This is essentially because ideas do not often lend themselves to being converted into the strict requirements of becoming a theory. A theory must be more than an idea or hunch regarding the best way to do something. A theory must be more than a gratuitous assertion or cybernetically based flow chart.

Blocher and Wolleat (1972, p. 39) recognize the absence of theories of counselor education when they state:

> There have been few attempts to formulate theories of counselor education or to develop models for counseling training which could systematically guide content, methods, or evaluation.
>
> . . . A theory of counseling provides direction for the counselor in his interaction with clients, whereas a counselor education theory guides the interaction of a counselor educator with his students. (p. 40)

Few attempts have been made to develop a theory of counselor education because the criteria, which outline the requirements that must be met in order to have a theory, are difficult standards.

There are criteria, however, that must be met if one desires to judge whether an idea meets the requirements of being a theory. These criteria of a theory have been identified by Stefflre and Grant (1972) and have been used primarily to judge whether a theory of counseling meets certain standards. The essence and intentionality of these criteria can be applied to judging a theory of counselor education and can be converted as follows: (1) assumptions regarding the nature of the person, (2) beliefs regarding learning theory and changes in behavior, (3) a commitment to certain goals of education, (4) a definition of the role of the educator, and (5) research evidence supporting the theory. These criteria of a theory have also been generally identified and supported in the writings of Dimick and Huff (1970), Patterson (1973), and Hansen et al. (1977).

In the following restatements of the Stefflre and Grant (1972) criteria of a theory, and the accompanying references indicating the evidence that supports the fact that each criteria has been met, student-centered teaching emerges as a bona fide theory of instruction that can be applied to counselor education:

1. Assumptions regarding the nature of the person (Coulson & Rogers, 1968; Rogers, 1951, 481-533; 1969, 221-297)
2. Beliefs regarding learning theory and changes in behavior (Anderson, 1974, 21-48; Pine & Boy, 1977, 75-139; Rogers, 1951, 481-533)
3. A commitment to certain goals of learning (Boy & Pine, 1971, 107-118; Rogers, 1951, 399-414; 1969, 103-145, 157-166, 279-297)
4. A definition of the role of the educator (Lyon, 1971, 183-230; Pine & Boy, 1977, 3-33; Rogers, 1951, 399-414; 1969, 29-97; 1970, 468-483)
5. Research evidence supporting the theory (Blocksma & Porter, 1947; Faw, 1949; Graves, 1977; Gross, 1948; Lyon, 1971, 263-289; Pine, M. A., 1977; Rogers, 1969, 327-342; Schwebal & Asch, 1948).

A STUDENT-CENTERED VIEW

The cohesiveness of the client-centered viewpoint gives it a decided advantage. It can be applied as student-centered teaching in counselor education and it can be applied by enrollees and graduates of a counselor education program as client-centered counseling. When it is applied in both the educational and counseling processes it takes on a comprehensive unity.

Client-centered theory is essentially a counseling theory but early adherents saw it as being logically convertible and applicable to the process of education. Soon after the appearance of Rogers' first major contribution, *Counseling and Psychotherapy* (1942), there emerged an awareness that the viewpoint was also applicable to teaching (Blocksma & Porter, 1947; Faw, 1949; Gross, 1948; Schwebel & Asch, 1948). Rogers (1951) confirmed this interest in his book, *Client-Centered Therapy*, by devoting Chapter 9 to "Student-Centered Teaching." This applicability to teaching was further extended and confirmed by Rogers (1969) in his book, *Freedom to Learn,* and is evident in more recent contributions (Rogers, 1977, 1980). The convertibility and applicability of the client-centered counseling view has also, of course, been recognized in organizational behavior, families, parenting, groups, marriage and its alternatives, leadership, pastoring, and general interpersonal relationships.

Rogers (1951, p. 384) has traditionally recognized the applicability of the concepts of client-centered counseling to the teaching and learning process: "If the creation of an atmosphere of acceptance, understanding, and respect is the most effective basis for facilitating the learning which is called therapy, then might it not be the basis for the learning which is called education?"

What will be the behavior of the counselor educator who has internalized the attitudes of student-centered teaching? Rogers (1951, p. 427) has identified that behavior as follows:

> He creates a classroom climate which respects the integrity of the student, which accepts all aims, opinions, and attitudes as being legitimate expressions of the student's internal frame of reference at that time. He accepts the feelings and emotionalized attitudes which surround any educational or group experience. He accepts himself as being a member of a learning group, rather than an authority. He makes learning resources available, confident that if they meet the needs of the group they will be used. He relies upon the capacity of the individual to sort out truth from untruth, upon the basis of continuing experience. He recognizes that his course, if successful, is a beginning in learning, not the end of learning. He relies upon the capacity of the student to assess his progress in terms of the purposes which he has at this time. He has confidence in the fact that, in this atmosphere which he has helped to create, a type of learning takes place which is personally meaningful and which feeds the total self-development of the individual as well as improves his acquaintance with a given field of knowledge.

Rogers (1951) identified certain characteristics of student-centered teaching which he presented as principles and hypothesis:

1. We cannot teach another person directly; we can only facilitate his learning. (p. 389)
2. A person learns significantly only those things which he perceives as being involved in the maintenance of, or enhancement of, the structure of self. (p. 389)
3. Experience which, if assimilated, would involve a change in the organization of self tends to be resisted through denial or distortion of symbolization. (p. 390)
4. The structure and organization of self appears to become more rigid under threat; to relax its boundaries when completely free from threat. Experience which is perceived as inconsistent with the self can only be assimilated if the current organization of self is relaxed and expanded to include it. (p. 390)
5. The educational situation which most effectively promotes significant learning is one in which threat to the self of the learner is reduced to a minimum and differential perception of the field of experience is facilitated. (p. 391)

Rogers (1962, p. 420) indicates that counselor education is a process in which the student counselor exists in an atmosphere where authenticity can emerge. He places the creation of such an atmosphere directly in the hands of the counselor educator, who must be free of the facades generally characteristic of the endeavor we call education:

We would also endeavor to plan the educational program for these individuals so that they would come increasingly to experience empathy and liking others, and that they would find it increasingly easier to be themselves, to be real. By feeling understood and accepted in their training experience, by being in contact with genuineness and absence of facade in their instructors, they would grow into more and more competent counselors.

For the counselor educator who feels that the concept of student-centered teaching has merit theoretically but is not operative because of the limitations imposed by a particular institution, Rogers (1951, p. 396) offers the following: ". . . every group has some limitations, if only the fact that they meet for a limited rather than an unlimited number of hours per week. It is not the fact that there are limitations, but the attitude, the permissiveness, the freedom which exists within those limitations, which is important."

In an attempt to identify what happened to the student as a result of the student's experience with student-centered teaching, Gordon (1955, p. 100) reviewed 11 historic studies and found that:

> Students seem to learn as much or more factual information; they participate more; they enjoy the experience; and they acquire certain other important learnings, such as clinical insight, greater personal adjustment, socially integrative behavior, skills of working cooperatively with others, and the freedom to communicate their deeper feelings and attitudes.

Gordon (1955, p. 154) also identified certain attitudes which, when housed in a teacher, will inhibit a learning group's thrust toward self-generated and personally relevant knowledge: ". . . our own insecurities, our lack of faith in people, our tendencies to use others for our own ends, our needs for prestige and status, our lack of tolerance of ambiguity, our fear of hostility expressed toward us, and the inconsistencies that often appear in our systems of values."

In describing the interpersonal relationship that facilitates learning, Rogers (1970) indicates that it is characterized by realness, prizing, acceptance, trust, and empathic understanding. These characteristics are identical to those Rogers has described as being characteristic of an effective counseling relationship. The Rogerian message, for both counseling and teaching, is basically the same. A counselor or teacher who possesses these characteristics will create a counseling or learning environment that facilitates the development of the self of the client or student. Once again, the counselor or teacher must model these human and facilitative qualities in order for them to emerge in a client or student.

In commenting upon empathic understanding, Rogers (1975, p. 7) states that: "An empathic way of being can be learned from empathic persons."

Rogers (1977, pp. 7–22) sees the educational process as occurring along a continuum. One end of the continuum represents a teacher-centered approach to teaching while the other represents a student-centered approach.

Following is a summary of what Rogers considers to be characteristic of a teacher-centered approach to teaching:

1. The teacher is the possessor of knowledge, the student the expected recipient.
2. The lecture, or some means of verbal instruction, is the major means of getting knowledge to the recipient. The examination measures the extent to which the student has received it.
3. The teacher is the possessor of power, the student is the one who obeys.
4. Rule by authority is the accepted policy.
5. Trust is at a minimum.
6. The students are best governed by being kept in an intermittent or constant state of fear.
7. Democracy and its values are ignored and scorned in practice.
8. There is no place for the whole person in the educational system, only for his or her intellect.

Following is a summary of what Rogers considers to be characteristic of a student-centered approach to teaching:

1. The facilitative teacher shares with students the responsibility for the learning process.
2. The student develops his or her own program of learning, alone or in cooperation with others.
3. A facilitative learning climate is provided.
4. The focus is primarily on fostering the continuing process of learning.
5. The discipline necessary to reach the student's goals is a self-discipline.
6. The evaluation of the extent and significance of the student's learning is made primarily by the student.
7. In this growth-promoting climate, the learning tends to be deeper, proceeds at a more rapid rate, and is more pervasive in the life and behavior of the student, than traditional learning.

Pine and Boy (1977, pp. 115–121) have identified certain principles of learning that undergird the process of student-centered teaching. These principles are summarized as follows:

1. Learning is the process of changing behaviors in positive directions.
2. Learning is an experience that occurs inside the learner and is activated by the learner.
3. Learning is the discovery of the personal meaning and relevance of ideas.
4. Learning is a consequence of experience.
5. Learning is a cooperative and collaborative process.
6. Learning is an evolutionary process.
7. Learning is sometimes a painful process.
8. One of the richest sources for learning is the learner himself or herself.

9. The process of learning is affective as well as cognitive.
10. Learning is enjoyable.
11. Learning is an experience that expresses values.
12. The learner is a free and responsible agent.
13. The process of problem solving and learning are highly unique and individual.
14. Teaching is learning.

In commenting on the last of the preceding principles, Arbuckle (1975, p. 170) states that: ". . . the goal of the program will be student and staff learning rather than staff teaching."

Arbuckle reinforces the idea that *both* students and staff are involved in the learning process in a student-centered counselor education program. In more traditional programs, the emphasis is strictly on staff teaching and student learning; a decidedly superior-subordinate process that is directly opposite the process that characterizes student-centered teaching.

Pine and Boy (1977, pp. 122–127) also have identified conditions that facilitate learning in the process of student-centered teaching. These conditions indicate that learning is facilitated in an atmosphere:

1. Which encourages students to be active
2. That facilitates the student's discovery of the personal meaning of ideas
3. That emphasizes the uniquely personal and subjective nature of learning
4. In which difference is good and desirable
5. That constantly recognizes the right to make mistakes
6. That tolerates ambiguity
7. In which evaluation is a cooperative process with emphasis on self evaluation
8. Which encourages openness to self rather than a concealment of self
9. In which students are encouraged to trust in themselves as well as external sources
10. In which students feel they are respected
11. In which students feel they are accepted
12. Which permits confrontation
13. In which the teacher creates conditions by which the teaching function is lost.

We have summarized what Rogers (1969, pp. 109–202) considers as a rationale that should undergird a graduate program in counseling. Rogers sees this rationale as applicable to any program of graduate education, not just in the field of counseling.

1. The student has the potentiality and desire to learn.
2. The program is rooted in reality.
3. The program provides opportunities for meaningful learning.

4. The program provides a psychological climate suitable for self directed and significant learning.
5. The teacher encounters the student as a person and reacts himself or herself as a person.
6. The program relies on the student's self-criticism and self-evaluation.
7. The program develops the whole person, ". . . not simply someone who is informed from the neck up but someone who exists in a significant relationship to others and to himself" (p. 201).
8. The program permits the person to become a fully professional person—a scientist, a practitioner, a facilitator of learning, ". . . not at some future date, after he has received his degree, but during every day and year of his graduate work" (p. 202)

Rogers (1969, p. 192) suggests three criteria for admission into a graduate program in counseling: intelligence, empathic ability, and a degree of spontaneous curiosity and originality. Regarding the first criterion, intelligence, Rogers defines it as a: ". . . high degree of ability in problem solving. My reason for this criterion is simply that, in general, intelligence 'pays off.' Of two professional individuals completely equal in every other respect, the brighter one of the two is probably more likely to make a lasting contribution."

Felker, (1973, p. 147) noted the same thing when he said: ". . . intellectual ability, and counseling effectiveness are not antithetical."

White (1978) conducted a study among 596 counselor educators in which their theoretical orientations to counseling were identified. In rank order, the four counseling theories that had the most adherents were eclectic, client-centered, humanistic, and behavioral. White, however, provides no information indicating that those counselor educators who are oriented toward client-centered counseling translate that orientation into student-centered teaching. We observe that if a counselor educator is oriented toward client-centered counseling, then such an orientation would naturally need to find its expression through student-centered teaching, if the orientation is intellectually and affectively real.

In one sense, all counselor educators are student-centered because they all appear to focus upon student counselors and their needs. What is distinctive about student-centered teaching is that the *process* as well as the objective is student-centered. Being student-centered is an *attitude* rather than a technique.

THE COUNSELOR EDUCATOR

Underlying our concept of counselor education is the basic idea that each one of us is both actuality and potentiality. As persons, we can become more than we are. We can become more adequate, more fully functioning, more psychologically whole, more creative, more productive, and more caring. Our world needs more adequate, fully functioning, psychologically whole, creative, and caring people; and indeed, our survival may depend upon the ability of our educational institutions to produce such people.

To develop student counselors with positive selves, counselor education must have teachers who are themselves in the process of becoming, and who can enter into meaningful and growth-facilitating relationships with students. This calls for teachers who are, first and foremost, persons. It is in response to and in relationship with a person that the student counselor's affective and intellectual growth occurs, and a substantive counselor education program is one which *integrates* the student's affective and intellectual development. As Hebert (1979, p. 29) has said: ". . . objectivity and subjectivity, cognition and affect, thinking and feeling are not antithetical, they are symbiotic."

Although much concern about the development of the individual within the context of counselor education has been articulated, there is a wide gap between what we want to do and what we are doing to enhance the development of professionally mature student counselors. We believe the critical factor that can narrow this gap is the teacher-student relationship. "It is the relationship that teaches rather than the text" (Goldhammer, 1969). Students feel the affective dimension of the teacher long before they feel the impact of the intellecutal content offered by that same teacher. Teachers and students are human beings and are reciprocally involved in personal and intellectual development. Students, in no small way, discover who they are and what they are as a result of their frequent interactions with each other and with their teachers. Teachers determine to a great degree the positive or negative effect of their teaching. Goldhammer (1969) states that the teacher's emotional capacities, cognitive styling, views of life and the world, values, the process of meeting anxiety, and the teacher's view of self determine the essence of teaching. In other words, teaching is a personal expression of the self.

Teaching: Personal Expression of the Self

As a personal expression of the self, effective teaching in counselor education is more than just doing something with students; it is being a fully functioning person, the most adequate person (Pine & Boy, 1977, pp. 4–5). It is our contention that the counselor educator who can be the most whole person will make the most significant contribution to the development of student counselors as self-actualizing persons. The counselor educator's role as a teacher is transcended by the counselor educator's existence as a human being. For the counselor educator, this means that first there must be comfort with the self before the counselor educator can be comfortable with others. The counselor educator/teacher who does not accept and respect the self will find it difficult to accept and respect students;

the one who is threatened by personal feelings may not be able to handle the feelings of others. The warm and secure counselor educator continually reflects warmth and security, and the counselor educator who values persons cannot help but communicate this prizing and valuing of people to others. Being a teacher and counselor educator requires an existential honesty with oneself and with others. It calls for the ability to become more aware of one's strengths and shortcomings and the effect they have on others.

Humanness in Teaching

Because the humanness of the teacher inevitably shows through in teaching, one implication that can be drawn for counselor educators is that they must become more sensitive and aware of their personal life styles. Counselor educators must be willing to involve themselves in the process of introspection so that they can become more aware of the influencing aspects of their personalities and how their personalities affect the teaching function. Each counselor educator must be; the counselor educator cannot deny the self, therefore, it is important that the self be known.

This does not mean that counselor educators can do away with personal values. As human beings, they have unique identities and values that are expressed in concrete behavior. But they can be free from defining the behavior of others in terms of personal values. Developing an awareness of cultural and subcultural stereotypes, of personal values, will enable counselor educators to sense the unique potentialities in those students who differ from the counselor educators in their perceptions. Each counselor educator's understanding of the self is the most important requirement in any effort made to gain healthy attitudes of self-acceptance which can be translated into an acceptance of students.

Self-Awareness Not Enough

Self-awareness is not enough in the development of the self-actualized counselor educator. Just as learners need positive enabling experiences to develop fully as persons, so do counselor educators. As teachers, they are no less valuable than the learner, no less alive, and, in many respects, no less needy (Goldhammer, 1969). Counselor educators need experiences in being treated as likable, wanted, accepted, and knowing persons. They need opportunities for emotional and intellectual enrichment and for experiences that expand the self. The self of the counselor educator can expand through a balanced, integrated, and continuous involvement in intellectual, therapeutic, facilitative, and enhancing experiences. As a consequence of these experiences, the counselor educator can become more human and real as a person and, in turn, more facilitative in fostering the growth and development of the student counselor as a unique person.

People *become* fully functioning and emotionally expanded, they are not born that way. The self-actualizing whole personality is an achievement that can be realized through growth-producing experiences. We are concerned about counselor educators as persons because we do not believe that, in themselves, good teaching strategies, techniques, curriculum, media, or materials produce fully competent student counselors. Although these things offer adjunctive help, we are convinced that it is the counselor educator's personhood that makes the difference in the development of professionally productive and positive student counselors. We believe that positive, fully functioning students are the crowning achievement of psychologically mature teaching emanating from psychologically whole counselor educators.

The Self-Actualizing Teacher

What is the self-actualizing counselor educator like? From our own observations and the major contributions of others (Combs & Snygg, 1959; Kelley, 1947; Maslow, 1954; Rogers, 1951; 1969), we would describe self-actualizing counselor educators in terms of the following behaviors (Pine & Boy, 1977, pp. 6–7):

1. Self-actualizing counselor educators think well of themselves. They have a positive self concept—they like themselves.
2. Self-actualizing counselor educators are unified and integrated. The dichotomies between real self and role self, between the selfish and the unselfish, between the conscious and the unconscious, between the inner self and the outer, between the affective and the cognitive, become resolved in psychologically whole counselor educators.
3. Self-actualizing counselor educators think well of others. Liking and accepting themselves, they like and accept others. While they can and do act independently, they realize their development and personhood are interdependent with the development and personhood of others. They engage in and like cooperative relationships and function harmoniously in such relationships.
4. Self-actualizing counselor educators develop, hold, and live human values. Their values are related to the welfare and enhancement of people. They tend to develop and to live values that enhance the self, enhance others, and enhance the human community.
5. Self-actualizing counselor educators see themselves in the process of becoming. They see life as a continuous process of becoming rather than a static state of being. They know that dealing with problems is a characteristic of living. They not only accept change, but they make change.
6. Self-actualizing counselor educators see the value of mistakes. They are adventurous, are not afraid to move forward, and are willing to test the unknown and tread new paths. They know they

cannot always be right. They make experience an asset and profit from their mistakes. They continually refine, modify, and redefine themselves as persons.

7. Self-actualizing counselor educators trust themselves. They trust their feelings and their intuitions. They trust their experiencing and the evidence of their senses. Their inner reactions and experiences serve them as a rich resource for behaving and for problem solving.

8. Self-actualizing counselor educators are open to experience. They are open to their feelings because they are less defensive. They are open to the data of their experiencing because they are less defensive. They are open to the stimuli of their environment. They are open to the data and points of view expressed by others in their environment. They are open to what is going on now, internally and externally.

9. Self-actualizing counselor educators are initiatory. They are more creative than reactive. While they can flow smoothly with their environment, they just don't react to it. They are initiators who exercise control over their lives and their environment. Self-actualizing counselor educators do not wait for others to do something. They move ahead and are often on the edge of change in their work, in their group, or in their profession.

10. Self-actualizing counselor educators are spontaneous, vibrant, and responsive. Their spontaneity and vitality are expressed in positive and enhancing ways. This does not mean that psychologically whole counselor educators are "hail fellow, well met" individuals. They enjoy life, are sensitive to the needs of others, and live optimistically and energetically.

Self-actualizing counselor educators are not perfect. They experience conflict, anxiety, guilt, and hurt. However, in self-actualizing counselor educators, there is movement from neurotic, superficial problems to the real, unavoidable problems inherent in the nature of the person. They feel troubled when the reality of the situation indicates that they should feel troubled; they feel guilt, anger, and anxiety. They ordinarily do not create their own problems, but when reality creates problems for them they respond in a very human way.

Because self-actualizing counselor educators trust themselves and are genuine, they are continually in touch with their feelings. At times they are confrontive in their relationships with others, they express anger. However, it is important to recognize that their genuineness and congruence are expressed in caring and facilitative ways that call for involvement and response. Their personal honesty is not destructive because they are involved and there is follow-up to any expression of honest anger in order to preserve the relationship and to make sure that anger serves as a constructive tool.

The Effects of Self-Actualizing Teaching

Counselor educators who create a meaningful teaching-learning relationship will find that intellectual and affective growth occurs among students as a result of their positive reaction to the communicating atmosphere in which they exist (Pine & Boy, 1977, pp. 14–16). As a result of their involvement with a skilled, competent, and psychologically whole counselor educator:

1. *Students assume responsibility.* Students become involved in the pursuit of knowledge and assume the responsibility for their intellectual growth because of the teacher's attitude in the relationship. Since the teacher has freed them to learn, they learn.

2. *Students are accepted.* Students feel that they are respected as persons who have a worthy contribution for both today and tomorrow. The positiveness of the teacher's attitude enables students to feel an acceptance that encourages them to relate comfortably to the teacher. It is this attitude that enables students to sense a comfort in the relationship, which facilitates their development.

3. *Students are motivated.* As a result of their experience with a teacher's enthusiasm for knowledge, students develop a desire to delve into the elements of knowledge. They sense a value in knowledge and acquire a desire to learn those things that are pertinent.

4. *Students are actively involved in the process of growth.* Intellectual maturity occurs for students because the teacher's educational process is focused upon students and their needs. In such a relationship the teacher is not the dominant figure, since the educational process is designed to produce an active, participatory involvement on the part of the student.

5. *Students interact on a human level.* Because of their association with a communicating teacher, students do not assume a superficial role but react to learning at an affective level. Anyone who has deeply learned anything has learned it because there was an accompanying emotionality to the process. What was being learned was deeply significant; the learner felt its importance in a visceral manner.

6. *Students exist in a safe atmosphere.* Students must feel free from threat or coercion if they are to be secure enough to respond to the learning process. No one has ever been coerced into learning or changing behavior. Such changes have occurred because one has felt safe enough to inquire into knowledge or into oneself. When the teacher provides an emotionally safe atmosphere, students are able to find progressive significance in the association.

7. *Students are understood.* The psychologically integrated teacher is vitally concerned with the learners' frame of reference. The teacher's

awareness of students finds its expression in an understanding attitude that enables students to be hesitant or confident, aware or insensitive, courageous or fearful. An understanding of how students feel about the various dimensions of existence is part of the attitude of an effective teacher. When students feel understood, they are able to move in an unfaltering manner in the learning process.

8. *Students are self-disciplined.* They find the resources within themselves to be their own masters because they have existed in learning relationships that facilitated their awareness of the importance of managing themselves. Teachers bring this into awareness by providing an atmosphere in which students learn to rely upon themselves for control rather than upon an external source. Teachers furnish students with the opportunity of self-management by providing an atmosphere in which students engage themselves in the more difficult task of looking to themselves rather than to authority figures for answers.

9. *Students communicate with ease.* When students associate with an effective teacher, they are able to communicate comfortably and honestly. They feel no need to be defensive in a relationship in which they know that they can be themselves. Such comfort enables them to respond to learning with much more accuracy, since their verbalizations and questions are not couched in language designed to protect rather than to reveal. They are able to discuss issues of relevance rather than what they feel the teacher wants to hear.

10. *Students achieve insight.* As a result of their association with a psychologically whole teacher, students are able to discover the fundamentals of learning or of themselves. They are able to bring meaning into their experiences because the relationship provided them with an opportunity to weigh and sift, and eventually come to grips with the deeper components of learning or of the self. They achieve a spiritual awareness of their existence because they are involved in a communicative process that gradually enables them to shed more light upon things to be learned and assimilated. Such an opening of one's self to experiences occurs because the teacher provides an atmosphere in which students' insights are far more relevant and significant than if the students were merely provided with the teacher's concept of appropriate insight.

11. *Students are more aware of facilitative attitudes.* Because of the qualitative nature of their association with a teacher, students do not have to be told directly what attitudes are facilitative and nonfacilitative. As human beings they are aware of which attitudes help or hinder their functioning as persons. They become sensitive to self-facilitating attitudes because they have had an opportunity to ponder those attitudes that either enhance them or cause them turmoil. They are not only more aware of self-facilitating attitudes, but they see themselves in relationship to others

and shape these attitudes so that they are able to function effectively in human relationships. They look beyond themselves rather than enclosing themselves. The feelings of others in response to their attitudes are more openly sensed and internalized.

12. *Students are valuing.* Students become involved in the development, processing, and synthesizing of values, ordering them in a hierarchy that is beneficial to their functioning and to others. Because of their association with a psychological whole teacher, they reject the values that hamper their behavior and move toward those that enable them to find more meaning from learning and life. This sifting and processing of values occurs because students exist in an open relationship in which they confront these values and are, in turn, confronted by them. It is only when students reject certain nonsustaining values that they move toward personal values that are of a higher order and have more personal significance. Effective teaching enables each student to become involved in the processing of values.

13. *Students respond to genuineness.* They sense the genuine quality of the teacher and react by becoming more genuine themselves. Students can easily sense a lack of genuineness. If the teacher has an unconditional, positive regard for students, this attitude finds its expression in a genuineness that the student internalizes. When students respond to the genuine quality of the teacher, they involve themselves in learning as a reaction to that quality. They trust the relationship and find that they are able to accelerate their progress. Such genuineness must exist if students are to have inner feelings of assurance in the relationship.

Student counselors respond primarily to the teacher as a person, and optimal intellectual learning and personal development occur through the relationship of the student with psychologically whole counselor educators.

The challenge for counselor educators is twofold: to seek and create the opportunities that will stretch and expand themselves as persons; and to create conditions whereby students also can grow and become more fully functioning persons and effective counselors. The latter task will be accomplished more easily and effectively as the counselor educator moves toward becoming a psychologically whole person.

A QUALITATIVE EVALUATION OF A STUDENT-CENTERED COUNSELOR EDUCATION PROGRAM

In an evaluation of a student-centered graduate program in counseling (Boy, 1978), enrollees and graduates were asked, among other items, to furnish statements regarding the program's contribution to their development as counselors. Following are their responses:

Fine faculty . . . excellent supervision . . . advanced practicum as fine as I have seen . . . taught me more about counseling than any place I've ever been . . . enabled me to refine my counseling skills and remain current . . . developed supervisory skills . . . developed advanced knowledge of counseling theory . . . developed a wider perspective on approaches to research . . . counseling experience . . . research experience . . . theoretical background gained in theories course . . . program gave me professional background of the highest quality . . . excellent faculty and curriculum . . . stimulated me to become interested in career education . . . broadened job options . . . improved counseling competencies . . . added stature and status to my chosen profession . . . format of program enabled me to explore issues that are important to me . . . I had the freedom to learn . . . kept my skills sharp . . . growth in counseling and research approaches . . . has aided me as no other program could do in helping me find myself and my place in the field of counseling . . . program allowed me much latitude in exploring my special interests . . . helped me to gain a broader perspective of the field and to improve my skills . . . given me a better foundation to continue my education . . . central to my personal development . . . program was more valuable than my doctoral program . . . the counselor education faculty is exceptional . . . it was more personal growth than just information . . . renewed confidence in counseling theory and techniques . . . served as a tremendous reinforcement to me as I was developing my new role as an elementary school counselor . . . broadened my counseling experience . . . helped develop counseling skills beyond "listening stage," . . . sound basic counseling skills and personal growth through experiences in a variety of encounter groups.

Excellent practicum experience . . . superior faculty . . . excellent advanced counseling theories course . . . one of the few places I have been where staff was congruent in their philosophical and theoretical orientations . . . I always felt important and valued as a person . . . the program's philosophy and its emphasis on "freedom to learn" . . . the counseling theories course . . . the advanced practicum . . . the high quality of instruction . . . experience in supervision within the advanced practicum . . . diversity of experiences in research course . . . a very good faculty . . . a solid and practical curriculum . . . generic nature of program . . . faculty's concern, interest, and knowledge . . . chance to supervise others . . . close knit nature of program . . . quality faculty, practicum, and curriculum . . . diversity of orientations among instructors . . . coordination with the department of psychology . . . flexibility of program . . . good solid practicum . . . seminar format . . . well qualified teaching staff, good facilities, availability of staff . . . quality of the practicum, variety of counseling approaches presented, staff very encouraging . . . freedom to explore areas of interest with the support of the faculty . . . humanistic confidence in our abilities and in ourselves . . . valuable associations with other students and faculty . . . personalized approach to learning . . . faculty's counseling skills . . . humanistic overview . . . faculty's commitment to student growth . . . professional and competent faculty . . . excellent staff-student ratio . . . excellent support from staff and students . . . supervision in advanced practicum was excellent . . . supervising masters students was broadening . . . excellent fellow students . . . allowing part-time study in conjunction with one's work . . . flexibility in interdepartmental programming . . .

humanistic and nurturant faculty who modeled counseling skills . . . practice in individual and group counseling . . . excellent preparation for my work.

The program stretched me . . . I have benefited from the research techniques learned, exposure to many varied areas of learning, close relationships with others—both staff and students . . . helped me with my intellectual competence, administrative skills, and especially my counseling skills . . . especially helpful were the practicum and group counseling courses . . . exposure to counseling theories and philosophies, the main elements in my growth as a counselor . . . excellent course in research . . . helped me in my career development . . . the synthesis of what appeared to be quite divergent schools of counseling into a more understandable and usable base of knowledge . . . the quality, and stimulation of, students and instructors . . . given me depth and scope in counseling . . . motivated me toward a confluence of theory and practice which challenges my knowledge and emotional integrity as I never thought possible . . . I experienced an unrelenting standard of excellence in the program . . . broadened the scope of my professional views . . . encouraged serious consideration of my theoretical base, values as a counselor, and techniques of therapeutic intervention . . . has afforded me the opportunity to explore the field of counseling more fully and to maximize my own potential as a counselor . . . developed my research skills . . . gave me experience in supervision . . . furthered my counseling experience in a new area (the elderly) . . . better understanding of people (including myself) . . . exposed to various ways of helping others in counseling or in teaching . . . assisted me in putting together a personal theory of counseling from a strong theoretical and personal base . . . the program has been intellectually stimulating so that now I'm considering doctoral studies . . . I am very confident in my skills as a counselor . . . the program has strengthened the theoretical base underlying my counseling . . . research skills have improved . . . theoretical depth in certain areas . . . supervised internship helps create and promote self confidence . . . broadened my theoretical base and enhanced my practical skills . . . enriched theoretical base of counseling . . . superb advanced practicum in which skills were increased . . . support in setting up an elementary school counseling program . . . important role model-mentor relationships with faculty; these have had a great impact on my professional growth . . . keeps me in touch with current theoretical thinkings and current happenings in other agencies and areas . . . has benefited my counseling skills and administrative abilities . . . expansive effect in terms of professional growth.

Exposure to many theories and philosophies . . . strong leadership from faculty . . . classes tailored to student needs . . . the faculty . . . program's structure toward particular goals . . . setting is intellectually stimulating . . . practicum courses . . . small classes . . . good discussions . . . professors seem well educated in their major subject . . . the chief strength of the program is the people . . . well organized . . . contains the elements needed for continued professional growth . . . the strengths are clearly its faculty . . . it would be difficult for a student to find elsewhere the faculty's commitment to the client, teaching, investigation and a unanimity of purpose which one finds in this program . . . small classes . . . superior faculty, academically . . . personable faculty . . . students are respected and treated as peers/equals . . . highly skilled and very professional faculty . . . selection process admits very human and capable students . . . faculty and students are stimulating and supportive . . . class sizes have stimulated intellectual exchange . . . the support of the program's staff . . . faculty is knowledgeable, capable, concerned, and extremely helpful . . . program provides intimate contact and support . . . provides opportunity to supervise . . . emphasis on research/professional experience . . . practicum with classmate participation in critiquing . . . professionalism and competence of faculty . . . small classes and stimulating learning environment . . . program information has immediacy and relevance . . . good courses in theory . . . strong internship provides application of theoretical principles and academic learning . . . small class sizes conducive to learning . . . supervised internship . . . the faculty and facilities . . . small faculty-student ratio . . . counseling practicum . . . diverse interests of the faculty . . . supportive environment in the department . . . excellent practicum supervision . . . a high level of ethical and professional consciousness . . . I am better prepared . . . the faculty . . . Advanced Counseling Theory and Practice, Advanced Human Development, Administration of Counseling . . . professional atmosphere . . . high level expectation courses . . . encourages research rather than directed learning.

REFERENCES

Anderson, W. Personal growth and client-centered therapy: An information-processing view. In D. A. Wexler & L. N. Rice (Eds.), *Innovations in client-centered therapy*. New York: John Wiley, 1974, 21–48.

Arbuckle, D. S. Reactions to Kemp. *The Counseling Psychologist*, 1971, *2*, 32–36.

Arbuckle, D. S. An existential-humanistic program of counselor education. *Counselor Education and Supervision*, 1975, *14*, 168–174.

Authier, J., & Gustafson, K. Application of supervised and nonsupervised micro-counseling paradigms in the training of paraprofessionals. *Journal of Counseling Psychology*, 1975, *22*, 74–78.

Bartlett, W. E. *Counselor accountability through personal credibility*. Unpublished manuscript, University of Notre Dame, 1978.

Bergland, B. W., & Quatrano, L. Systems evaluation in counselor education. *Counselor Education and Supervision*, 1973, *12*, 190–198.

Blocher, D. H., & Wolleat, P. L. Some reactions to Zifferblatt and a report of a practical attempt at the development and evaluation of a counselor education model. *The Counseling Psychologist*, 1972, *3*, 35–55.

Blocksma, D. D., & Porter, E. H., Jr. A short-term training program in client-centered counseling. *Journal of Consulting Psychology*, 1947, *11*, 55–60.

Boy, A. V. *1978 evaluation study of graduates and enrollees in UNH certicate of advanced graduate study in counseling*. Durham, N.H.: University of New Hampshire, mimeographed, 1978, 15 pages.

Boy, A. V., & Pine, G. J. *Expanding the self: Personal growth for teachers*. Dubuque, Iowa: Wm. C. Brown, 1971, 107–118.

Boy, A. V., & Pine, G. J. Effective counseling: Some proportional relationships. *Counselor Education and Supervision*, 1978, *18*, 137–143.

Bradley, F. O. A modified interpersonal process recall technique as a training model. *Counselor Education and Supervision*, 1974, *14*, 34–39.

Calia, V. F. Systematic human relations training: Appraisal and status. *Counselor Education and Supervision*, 1974, *14*, 85–94.

Carkhuff, R. R. *Helping and human relations* (Vols. 1 and 2). New York: Holt, Rinehart and Winston, 1969.

Carkhuff R. R. The development of systematic human resource development models and new directions for training for the helping professions: Toward a technology for human and community resources development. *The Counseling Psychologist*, 1972, *3*, 4–30.

Combs, A. W., Avila, D. L., & Purkey, W. W. *Helping relationships—Basic concepts for the helping professions.* Boston: Allyn and Bacon, 1978. (2nd ed.)

Combs, A. W., Richards, A. C., & Richards, F. *Perceptual psychology.* New York: Harper and Row, 1976.

Combs, A. W., & Snygg, D. *Individual behavior: A perceptual approach to behavior* (2nd ed.). New York: Harper and Row, 1959.

Coulson, W. R., & Rogers, C. R. (Eds.). *Man and the science of man.* Columbus, Ohio: Charles E. Merrill, 1968.

DiMatta, D., & Arndt, G. A comparison of microcounseling and reflective listening techniques. *Counselor Education and Supervision*, 1974, *14*, 61–64.

Dimick, K. M., & Huff, V. E. *Child counseling.* Dubuque, Iowa: Wm. C. Brown, 1970, 59.

Faw, V. E. A psychotherapeutic method of teaching psychology. *The American Psychologist*, 1949, *4*, 104–109.

Felker, S. Intellectual ability and counseling effectiveness: Another view. *Counselor Education and Supervision*, 1973, *13*, 146–150.

Fromm, E. *The art of loving.* New York: Bantam Books, 1963.

Goldhammer, R. *Clinical supervision.* New York: Holt, Rinehart and Winston, 1969, 365.

Gordon, T. *Group-centered leadership.* Boston: Houghton Mifflin, 1955, 154.

Gormally, J., & Hill, C. E. Guidelines for research on Carkhuff's training model. *Journal of Counseling Psychology*, 1974, *21*, 539–547.

Graves, D. H. Writing and the self: An examination of the writing processes of seven year old children. In G. J. Pine & A. V. Boy, *Learner-centered teaching: A humanistic view.* Denver: Love Publishing, 1977, 171–191.

Gross, L. An experimental study of the validity of the nondirective method of teaching. *Journal of Psychology*, 1948, *26*, 243–248.

Hansen, J. C., Stevic, R. R., & Warner, R. W. *Counseling: Theory and process.* Boston: Allyn and Bacon, 1977, 20.

Hebert, D. J. Faculty-student relationships: Fostering independence. *Oregon Personnel and Guidance Journal*, 1979, *3*, 27–29.

Horan, J. J. Behavioral goals in systematic counselor education. *Counselor Education and Supervision*, 1972, *11*, 162–169.

Ivey, A. E. Microcounseling and media therapy: State of the art. *Counselor Education and Supervision*, 1974, *13*, 172–183.

Kagan, N. Observations and suggestions. *The Counseling Psychologist*, 1972, *3*, 42–45. (a)

Kagan, N. *Influencing human interaction*. East Lansing: Michigan State University, College of Education and Human Medicine, 1972. (b)

Kaplan, M. F., & Singer, E. Dogmatism and sensory alienation. *Journal of Consulting Psychology*, 1964, *27*, 486–491.

Kelley, E. C. *Education for what is real*. New York: Harper and Brothers, 1947.

Kemp, C. G. Existential counseling. *The Counseling Psychologist*, 1971, *2*, 2–29.

Kingdon, M. A. A cost/benefit analysis of the Interpersonal Process Recall technique. *Journal of Counseling Psychology*, 1975, *22*, 253–257.

Korn, C., & Korn, H. A letter to Dr. Carkhuff. *The Counseling Psychologist*, 1972, *3*, 75–79.

Lyon, H. C., Jr. *Learning to feel—Feeling to learn*. Columbus, Ohio: Charles E. Merrill, 1971, 183–230, 263–289.

Mahon, B. R., & Altmann, H. A. Skill training: Cautions and recommendations. *Counselor Education and Supervision*, 1977, *17*, 42–50.

Maslow, A. H. *Motivation and personality*. New York: Harper and Row, 1954. Melnick J., & Brandsma, J. M. Teaching psychotherapy as an adventure. *Psychotherapy: Theory, Research and Practice*, 1977, *14*, 196–201.

Miller, J. P. The effects of human relations training on teacher interpersonal skills. *The Alberta Journal of Educational Research*, 1973, *19*, 37–47.

Patterson, C. H. *Theories of counseling and psychotherapy*. New York: Harper and Row, 1973, xv–xvi.

Pine, G. J., & Boy, A. V. *Learner-centered teaching: A humanistic view*. Denver: Love Publishing, 1977.

Pine, M. A. Reading, self-concept and informal education. In G. J. Pine and A. V. Boy, *Learner-centered teaching: A humanistic view*. Denver: Love Publishing, 1977, 143–169.

Pulvino, C. J., & Sanborn, M. P. Feedback and accountability. *The Personnel and Guidance Journal*, 1972, *51*, 15–20.

Resnikoff, A. Critique of the Human Resources Development model from the viewpoint of rigor. *The Counseling Psychologist*, 1972, *3*, 46–61.

Rogers, C. R. *Counseling and psychotherapy*. Boston: Houghton Mifflin, 1942.

Rogers, C. R. *Client-centered therapy*. Boston: Houghton Mifflin, 1951 (renewed 1979), Chapter 9, Student-centered teaching, 399–414; Chapter 11, A theory of personality and behavior, 481–533.

Rogers, C. R. The interpersonal relationship: The core of guidance. *Harvard Educational Review*, 1962, *32*, 416–429.

Rogers, C. R. *Freedom to learn*. Columbus, Ohio: Charles E. Merrill, 1969, 29–97, 103–145, 109–202, 157–166, 192, 221–297, 327–342.

Rogers, C. R. The interpersonal relationship in the facilitation of learning. In J. R. Hart & T. M. Tomlinson (Eds.), *New directions in client-centered therapy*. Boston: Houghton Mifflin, 1970, 468–483.

Rogers, C. R. Empathic: An unappreciated way of being. *The Counseling Psychologist*, 1975, *5*, 2–10.

Rogers, C. R. The politics of education. *Journal of Humanistic Education*, 1977, *1*, 7–22.

Rogers, C. R. *A way of being*. Boston: Houghton Mifflin, 1980.

Schwebel, M., & Asch, M. J. Research possibilities in nondirective teaching. *Journal of Educational Psychology*, 1948, *39*, 359–369.

Stefflre, B., & Grant, W. (Eds.). *Theories of counseling*. New York: McGraw Hill, 1972, 4–7.

Webb, D. Teacher sensitivity: Affective impact on students. *The Journal of Teacher Education*, 1971, *22*, 455–459.

White, L. Theoretical orientations of counselor educators. *College Student Personnel*, 1978, *19*, 132–135.

Yelon, S. T. Toward the application of systems analysis to counselor education. *Educational Technology*, 1969, *9*, 55–60.

Zifferblatt, S. M. Analysis and design of counselor-training systems: An operant and operations research perspective. *The Counseling Psychologist*, 1972, *3*, 12–31.

Chapter 11

BEYOND COUNSELING: EXPANDING THE SELF

Anyone attuned to the vibrancy of existence realizes that there are many persons who are synchronized with life, who deal with it in an easy and relaxed manner, and who have a highly positive self-concept. We're aware of their presence in restaurants, at the ocean, at religious services, at zoos, in taverns, on fire escapes, at parties, in our neighborhood, and in our homes; we're aware of them selling merchandise, building a highway, riding to work, walking in the park. They are psychologically contented people—people who have learned to absorb the self-enriching fullness of life. They don't have incapacitating personal, social, or economic problems. They know who they are, why they exist, and where they are going. They generally feel good about life, and they radiate a joy that others can easily feel and absorb. They love their families, find personal satisfaction in their livelihoods, and enjoy the simple pleasures of life. Life is not perfect for such people, but they deal with it, cope with it, confront it, manage it, and flow with it. They do what they should, at the time they should do it, by using their human intuition—an intuition based upon a profound self-awareness and sense of their presence in the world; their self-concepts have been fully and positively expanded.

As professional counselors, we have had therapeutic helping relationships with troubled people as individuals or as members of a group. In our capacity as reasonably observant persons, existing outside the context of professional counseling relationships, we have seen people who have never been professionally counseled living honest, open, and relatively untroubled lives. These people never need counselors, psychologists, or psychiatrists. They have learned, without professional assistance, how to bring full and satisfying meaning to their lives. They have expanded themselves so that they embrace life—they have penetrated the meaning of the nuances of their behavior. Certainly, they have personal problems, but they deal with them and solve them—they are not so overpowered by their problems that they become psychologically troubled to the point of needing professional assistance.

The genuineness of these persons captured our personal and professional interest and prompted us to devote this chapter to an understanding of the *gravitas* of their behavior. In essence, we desired to develop a profile of the psychologically healthy and happy person; a person who possesses an enriched, expanded, and enhancing perception of the self. As we began the study of why some persons who had never received professional assistance were handling life better than were some persons who had had assistance, we made some false starts and took many appealing primrose paths that led us nowhere. Certainly, the happy people we knew were not personifications of the personality theories espoused in the traditions of Freud, Jung, Adler, and Fromm. Many of the freewheeling people we knew had never heard of these persons, while those who had some familiarity with them had seldom read any of their works. They were too busy with life to have time for the hallowed truths regarding human nature as revealed in the real and the pop psychological literature. They were too busy going to ball games, watching TV, earning a living, camping, making love, talking, listening, meditating, dancing, and laughing. They were too deeply engaged in personally penetrating the substance of life to care about the august insights of the scholars. They didn't need anyone to explain what life was all about because they knew. They knew because of their sensitive contact with life.

These happy people came from a wide socioeconomic range and included construction workers, night watchmen, fishermen, barbers, plumbers, printers, housewives, businessmen, teachers, clergymen, physicians, engineers, and bartenders. But why were they able to lead such a psychologically full and balanced life? After all, as professional counselors, we believe in the viability of the therapeutic relationship as a catalyst for self-emergence—as a process that would enable people to discover the positive potential of the inner self and translate it into a more rewarding personal existence.

HUMAN THERAPEUTIC EXPERIENCES

The clients who were able to expand themselves and live a more personally rewarding existence used the counseling process as one mode of self-emergence. For them, counseling was a therapeutic human experience that made them feel alive, which made them feel like participating in life. But what about the vast majority of humanity who had never had any contact with members of the psychotherapeutic professions? Why were they making it while others needed professional assistance? What was the experience in their lives that was the equivalent of a professional counseling or a psychotherapeutic relationship? A professional psychotherapeutic relationship is based upon the client's existing in an atmosphere of liberality, honesty, acceptance, understanding, positive regard, concreteness, and empathy. Were these members of the human race getting help from sources who didn't possess degrees in counseling and psychotherapy? Of course they were! They were getting this human therapeutic experience from each other. Existing in the lives of these psychologically balanced persons were individuals and groups who cared for them and who expressed that caring attitude by being available to them when they needed to talk, to cry, to be happy, to emote, or to siphon off hostility.

In other words, a person needs human therapeutic experiences as a basic and necessary component of existence. Those who have no one with whom they can communicate at a human level seek out the therapeutic assistance provided by a professional. Those who have someone to whom they can turn receive therapeutic assistance because of the caring attitude of the person to whom they turn. Husbands and wives can receive such therapeutic assistance from each other, just as it can be derived from deeply human relationships between employer and employee, brother and sister, black person and white person, neighbor and neighbor, between co-workers, and between friends. The expanding self encompasses other people—it goes beyond itself not only in giving love to other people, but in receiving love from others; and this reciprocal caring for each other is a therapeutic human experience for both the one who is giving and the one who is receiving.

In the history of civilization, one component of the expanded self has always been provided through a process of interpersonal caring that has been passed from generation to generation and from culture to culture. When people care enough for each other to extend their caring to each other, then we possess a dimension of human existence and survival that not only is viable in a one-to-one relationship but is the basis for a variety of multilateral and caring relationships between and among nations.

VOCATIONAL THERAPEUTIC EXPERIENCES

If the self is to be truly expanded, however, it must not only embrace and engage in therapeutic human relationships, but it must also be involved in therapeutic work experiences. That is, the person who lives a full life finds relevance and meaning in the work that is performed to earn a living. The person realizes that the financial rewards of work are important, but he or she also realizes that the personal meaning of work is even more important. A plumber who feels that plumbing is a contribution to public health and sanitation finds that work is a therapeutic experience because it is a fulfillment of a basic urge to contribute to the well-being and development of humanity. The plumber may not be fully conscious of the importance of a work contribution, but it is the motivational dynamic that enables the plumber to gain therapeutic satisfaction when a leaking pipe is repaired. The printer who is sensitive to the historical importance of print to civilization feels fulfilled when a work order is finished, the outcome is examined, and the finished product is packaged for a customer. The musician who composes or performs derives a great deal of personal therapy from the knowledge that music is contributing to the relaxation and enjoyment of others.

Work can be therapeutic, and it is another dimension of the person who lives an enriched and expanded life. And so the people who exist without the need for professional therapeutic assistance not only have deep human relationships with certain people in their lives, but they also derive therapeutic satisfaction from their vocations. The wife who feels that warmth and human caring of her husband and who senses a personal fulfillment in her work is engaging in two activities that satisfy and expand the self. The child who feels parental love and respect and who is fascinated by the work of learning possesses two positive components of existence that contribute to an inner sense of psychological well-being.

Ashley Montagu (1950) has indicated that the personally relevant life is characterized by the presence of love, while dissatisfaction with life is characterized by the absence of love. Donald Super (1957) has indicated that a person, through work, can achieve psychological balance or imbalance; that those who work simply to earn the money to pay the bills are psychologically unfulfilled. One who engages in work that is a fulfillment of the self will derive psychotherapeutic benefits from that work, benefits that will permeate other phases of that person's existence.

We seemed to be headed in a direction that was beginning to make sense. Those who were able to deal and cope with life and who are not in need of professional psychotherapeutic assistance were certainly people who had human and work experiences that enhanced and fulfilled the self. But there was more to these people—a personal substance that went beyond their ability to gain satisfaction from therapeutically inclined human and work experiences. Being an alive and relevant person in the world surely demanded something more. But what?

RELIGIOUS THERAPEUTIC EXPERIENCES

Uncovering the third dimension of the expanded person was more difficult because the academic world was often so coldly empirical and logical that any consideration of the religious or spiritual nature of the person was a concept too simplistic to bear much fruit. After all, the revered Freud had deflated the whole concept of humanity's religiosity as being a neurotic need to identify psychologically with an idealized Authority Figure because of an unfulfilled need for parental love during childhood (Zilboorg, 1964). Karl Marx described religion as the opium of the people. George Bernard Shaw had sprinkled his writings with satire and diatribes aimed at anyone who might consider something beyond the self (Weintraub, 1969). Shakespeare had carried the recurrent and subtle theme that a person's belief in something beyond the self was often an impairment (Craig, 1931). The "God is Dead" movement was a startling reminder that religious people had historically stood aside and watched human deterioration—they were too busy constructing dogmas, organizational patterns, and edifices to be concerned with the needs of human beings. They were so entranced with raising their heads toward heaven that they were unaware of the human misery beneath their noses.

Academia had conditioned us to be skeptical about the place of religion in the life of the whole person. But as we began to desensitize ourselves from these historical and contemporary prejudices against religion and to look objectively at the other possible dimensions of persons who led full and personally meaningful lives, we began to realize that these people were indeed religious—not, perhaps, by being members of an organized church (although some were church members), but they were religious in their personal life style and in their attitude toward other persons. They possessed a sense of their position in the evolution and civilization of humanity. They wondered about the deeper issues of life and the meaning of existence in much the same way that the Jews evolved toward monotheism in a polytheistic world which, for countless centuries, had worshipped mountains, oceans, animals, the sun, and the moon.

The expanded person is religious in that such a person contemplates and meditates regarding the human condition. This person starts with the self and considers the universe, going beyond the self and consciously, through institutionalized theistic religion, or through a private stream of thought, contemplates a personal past and that of the universe, a current sense of personal presence within the universe, and a personal future and the future of the universe. Such an individual may reject organized theistic religions but, in a secular sense, is aware of the personal spirituality that affects one's personal existence. This person may consider absurd the idea of a life hereafter, but he or she does contemplate death and hopes that somehow there will be an eternity in the memory of others. In other words, the whole person desires that one's existence becomes a contribution to posterity. This person does say, "I have a rendezvous with destiny," either very consciously in behavior, or subconsciously in the flashes of thought that are sometimes never crystalized into total awareness. This person considers something beyond the self but doesn't always call that something God, but may call it Mother Nature, the Great Outdoors, Lady Luck, Good Fortune, or a Good Horoscope; there is an attempt to penetrate the meaning and substance of existence and the future. The person may prefer to be called an agnostic, an athiest, or a humanist, but he or she often possesses a more honest inner and secular religion than do many who piously kneel before God. This individual respects the dignity and worth of others, but begins by respecting a personal dignity and worth—by living a life that gives consideration to the foggy bottom of existence, and by living a life that includes time to ponder the spiritual dimensions of existence and whether one's personal life is a contribution to self-development and the enhancement of others.

The expanded person is religious, either in a theistic or in a secular sense. A person thinks and feels, and in doing this, centers both on the self and the relationship with other persons and with the environment. The expanded person does not believe in God as someone with a white robe, a shepherd's staff, and a long white beard, but believes in something beyond the self. There is a spiritual relevancy to this person's existence; a desire to have one's earthly tenure mean something, and this desire, this religious inclination, becomes translated into an essential ingredient of the full life. The expanded person senses personal comfort in the awareness that one's life is an important link in the evolvement of others and of civilization.

In describing the whole person of the future who will contribute to the survival of humanness in our society, Rogers (1980, p. 352) indicates that such a person will be characterized by:

> A yearning for the spiritual. These persons of tomorrow are seekers. They wish to find a meaning and purpose in life that is greater than the individual. Some are led into cults but more are examining all the ways by which humankind has found values and forces that extend beyond the individual. They wish to live a life of inner peace. Their heroes are spiritual persons—Mahatma Gandhi, Martin Luther King, Teilhard de Chardin. Sometimes, in altered states of consciousness, they experience the unity and harmony of the universe.

We felt that we were getting somewhere. Three basic elements had been identified, elements important in the process of expanding the self, elements that sustained the many contented and happy persons who led a personally meaningful existence and who were not in need of professional psychotherapeutic assistance. Yes, such persons engaged in therapeutic human, work, and theistic or secular religious experiences, but was there more to the whole person who had a zest and a passion for life? Was there another dimension to this existence that contributed to the person's psychological fullness?

RECREATIONAL THERAPEUTIC EXPERIENCES

The identification of the fourth dimension of the expanded self occurred on a professional trip to Tucson, Arizona. The trip lasted for just over three days, but it was an expanding experience because it possessed not only therapeutic human, work, and religious experiences, but it possessed a fourth experience in which the person, from time immemorial, had always engaged. It was an experience whose therapeutic value we had never deeply and fully considered as the fourth element in the life of a whole person. The fourth dimension of the expanded self emerged into full conscious awareness at La Fluente, a Mexican restaurant that featured a rollicking Mariachi band. The food was magnificent—it made our hosts and us feel good. The Mariachi band played joyous music that produced among us feelings of elation and euphoria.

But what category of therapeutic experience was this? It was the missing dimension which, because of its simplicity of attainment, we had previously overlooked; it was the fourth category of therapeutic experiences that served to expand the self and to put it into closer contact with the fullness of life: the recreational experience. In our search for another category of therapeutic experiences that contribute to the expansion of the self, we had become too esoteric and complex in our thinking. We had neglected to appreciate fully the therapeutic value of recreation because of its obviousness; while attempting to penetrate the meaning of the forest, we had overlooked the trees at our elbows.

The therapeutic value of recreation is generally not treated by psychological theory builders, but anyone who has observed the essence of the expanded person realizes that recreation plays a vital role in that expansion. Recreation means to re-create; to re-create the self so that it can derive greater relevance and meaning out of life. Recreation contributes to expanding the self by enabling the participant to engage in an activity that can produce psychological relaxation and, sometimes, even a needed amount of tension. Winston Churchill found relaxation in painting—through it, he found expression that enabled him to re-create himself. Henry David Thoreau found naturalistic solace at Walden Pond. Mark Twain was enraptured and psychologically uplifted by the beauty of Hawaii when, as a young man, he was attempting to find his place in the literary sun. John F. Kennedy was psychologically uplifted while sailing a sloop or participating in a game of touch football. Dr. Sol Roy Rosenthal, professor of preventive medicine at the University of Illinois College of Medicine, has accumulated evidence indicating that people who engage in risk-action recreational activities, such as mountain climbing, sky diving, automobile racing, or fox hunting, experience unusual psychological exhilaration as a result of their participation (Furlong, 1969).

As a therapeutic experience, recreation has not received enough serious attention in the literature of psychology because it has been felt that it does not possess enough depth to attract the serious consideration of the scholar. Recreation has been thought to be something irrelevant that is more for the masses than for those inhabitants of the polite and washed world of scholarship. Although Aristotle and Plato acknowledged the value of recreation as an element of the full life, the modern scholar tends to think little of recreation. Perhaps Robert Maynard Hutchins, who became President of the University of Chicago at the age of 27, set the tone for contemporary scholars when he indicated that whenever he thought of exercise, he instead took a nap so that the inclination would pass.

It is interesting to note that scholars who might not publicly acknowledge the therapeutic value of recreation do take vacations, lie in the sun and listen to Beethoven, attend cocktail parties, go fishing and hunting, swim, play squash, shoot billiards, play polo, or recompose themselves by ordering from the top of the menu in the finest of restaurants. Perhaps they do not acknowledge the therapeutic value of football's Super Bowl, drinking beer at the local tavern, stickball, television viewing, or gambling, because if they admit an interest, they will somehow be classified as lowbrows who identify with the common person rather than with the community of scholars.

Although there is a lack of scholarly interest in considering the therapeutic value of recreation, anyone who lives an expanded life and who studies those persons who have a wholeness to their existence will discover that recreation makes a significant contribution to the fullness of that existence. Unto itself, a therapeutic recreational experience cannot produce a fully expanded person; but when linked to and integrated with therapeutic human, work, and religious experiences, recreation becomes the fourth dimension necessary to expand the self toward a personally satisfying psychological balance.

Therefore, if a person's existence is to expand and become more personally relevant, the person should seek out and engage in human, work, religious, and recreational experiences that have therapeutic value and, thereby, enhance the self. The partial life often includes only one, two, or three of the four basic therapeutic experiences. The fourth therapeutic experience, whichever it may be, when it is excluded from our existence, leaves us diminished as persons—and leaves us unfulfilled because of the complementary therapeutic value it provides.

THE PROCESS OF EXPANSION

A person who superficially engages in each of these four therapeutic experiences in an attempt to acquire instant psychological balance will not achieve the desired goal. Such a person goes through the motions, but is not viscerally committed or engaged. This type of person would scurry about looking for another with whom he or she can engage in verbal diarrhea; occasionally stay at work for an extra 20 minutes; say a quick "help me" prayer on the subway; or make sure to get tickets for everybody's favorite play. In order that the self be truly expanded, there must be an ever-increasing and deeper level of qualitative involvement in each of the four categories of therapeutic experiences. The more the person invests in improving the quality of these therapeutic experiences, the more the self will expand and move toward personal adequacy and psychological balance.

The expanding person, however, never expands the self to the fullest degree because today's feelings of full psychological adequacy will not be viable next week inasmuch as personal psychological perfection will always be beyond our grasp; it will always be something that we will only temporarily and partially possess in the process whereby the self evolves. We will never fully possess perfection because we will always desire to expand and go beyond the fullness we now possess; we will never become, but will always be involved in the process of becoming.

The mission is not to attempt to expand oneself psychologically into perfection because accomplishing such perfection is existentially impossible. The best that we can do is to be viscerally motivated to continually expand the self while living with the awareness that personal perfection and full psychological expansion will always be beyond our reach. The expanding person is constantly engaged in expansion, and the only time that one should come close to full and perfect expansion is at the moment before death; at that moment, the person should be all that one can ever hope to become.

Thus, we have attempted to introduce the process whereby a person expands the psychological self, but we have purposely avoided attempting to define the psychological life style of the expanded person. That is the person's business, not ours. We do, however, believe in the relevancy of the four categories of therapeutic experiences that can enable a person to live an expanded existence. A balanced involvement in each of the four therapeutic experiences can lead toward a personally impactful and relevant expansion of the self.

The psychotherapeutic professions can point out the existence of human depersonalization and alienation in our society, and we fully acknowledge the fact of their existence. What we do question is the attitude rampant among some members of the psychotherapeutic professions, an atittude implying that the only way a person can achieve psychological balance is within the confines of the offices of counselors, psychologists, and psychiatrists. To us, this appears to be a narrow view, especially because there is certainly human help being given to human beings by other human beings who exist outside the psychotherapeutic professions.

What the psychotherapeutic professions must admit is that while the services they render to certain people to help those people to live a better balanced psychological existence, the human therapeutic experience they provide is but one of four therapeutic experiences needed by the person in order to achieve a more whole psychological existence. The psychotherapeutic professions must further admit that the human therapeutic experiences needed by the person can and do occur in a variety of settings; they are rendered by people who, though not members of the psychotherapeutic professions, nevertheless possess a genuine empathy for others, an empathy that finds its expression in therapeutically helpful human interactions with members of their families, their friends, their neighbors, and their co-workers.

If one reflects on the four basic therapeutic experiences, one will come to realize that humanity has historically evolved, survived, and managed an environment because there was a psychological inclination to do so—the self was expanded enough so that the person could participate in and contribute to the development of civilization. If we also historically contemplate humanity and consider what has propelled the person from prehistoric times to the present, we will find that whatever wholeness the person possessed emerged because the person engaged in balanced and integrated human, work, religious, and recreational therapeutic experiences through which and by which the self was sufficiently expanded so that it was free to contribute to the well-being and development of others.

If, in turn, one contemplates the future of humanity, one will once again realize that the expanded self is the only hope for advancing civilization and that, in order for the self to be expanded, it must have access and exposure to self-fulfilling human, work, religious, and recreational therapeutic experiences. A person might mistakenly select one or two of these therapeutic experiences that appear to provide a possibility for greater self-emergence than the others; but if a person does this and neglects the other therapeutic experiences, he or she will not possess the personal fullness that is psychologically sustaining over a lifetime. Such a partially realized self eventually erodes because it does not possess the psychological fullness inherent in, and emerging from, an integrating and balancing of the four basic therapeutic experiences available.

EXPANDING THE SELF:
SOME CONCLUSIONS

1. *The self expands because of a balanced, integrated, and continuous involvement in therapeutic human, work, religious, and recreational experiences.* A balanced involvement in the four therapeutic experiences means that one must have contact with one's viscera in order to ascertain the degree of therapeutic balance that exists in one's life. A person must translate this visceral sensitivity into conscious awareness so that the person knows when the balance does or does not exist. When there is balance, the self feels itself expanding and reinforces this expansion. When there is imbalance, the self must be aware of what is causing the imbalance and move toward a particular therapeutic experience that has the potential for creating the desired balance.

An integrated involvement in the four therapeutic experiences is much like the integration that exists among the four climatic seasons. Spring, summer, fall, and winter are distinct each from the others, and yet there is a blending among them. Each season has its own particular refreshing characteristics, but each mingles with the following season to form an integrated whole.

A continuous involvement in each of the four therapeutic experiences indicates that expanding the self is a process rather than an act. Self-expansion cannot occur when a person devotes this hour or this day to a particular therapeutic experience in the hope that there will be a magical result. Continuous involvement means that the expansion of the self never ceases; it occurs continually in the apparently mundane and innocuous experiences of daily living. As a process, it is always flowing, like a brook in search of its lowest level.

2.   *The extent to which the self expands is proportionately related to the degree of qualitative involvement in each of the four therapeutic experiences available.*   Having a balanced, integrated, and continuous involvement in the four therapeutic experiences is the beginning point for expanding the self. The depth of involvement in each of the therapeutic experiences influences the magnitude of self-expansion. Merely to flit from one therapeutic experience to another will leave the self unfilled since such superficial contacts are much like admiring the packaging of a gift without appreciating the gift itself.

In order to expand, the self must immerse itself in each of the four therapeutic experiences in an effort to discover its heretofore unknown depths. The self becomes involved in a search for the hidden value of each therapeutic experience, but there must be a deep desire to seek; a desire to plumb the depths of each therapeutic experience in order to penetrate and absorb its personal relevancy.

A qualitative involvement in each of the four therapeutic experiences will lead the self deeper into personal awareness—a sensitivity to the inner core of a person's existence which influences overt behavior in all phases of life. But qualitative involvement demands not only the desire, but also an investment of time—how much time is relative to the individual—but the investment must be made if there is to be a qualitative expansion of the self. Although we live in a world of instant everything, the qualitative expansion of the self cannot occur with the same quickness. It occurs only when one takes the time to search out the personally impactful elements of each of the therapeutic experiences; and the search is exciting because of the knowledge that today's qualitative involvement can be deepened tomorrow, thus continually affecting the degree to which the self can be expanded.

3.   *The self cannot fully expand by engaging in only one, two, or three of the four therapeutic experiences available.*   Each of the four therapeutic experiences is part of the whole. Unto itself, each of the four therapeutic experiences has only a limited value; but when joined with the others, it is enriched because it becomes integrated with and contributes to the formation of the whole.

When the self limits itself to an involvement in either human, vocational, religious, or recreational experiences, or a combination of two or three of these experiences, it decreases the degree to which it can be expanded. The self becomes more whole, more fully expanded, when it absorbs the inherent value contained within each of the four therapeutic experiences and realizes how each contributes to the fullness of the self.

Whenever the self senses a void in its existence, it is typically due to the absence of one or more of the therapeutic experiences in one's life style. The person who has deeply internalized viable human, vocational, and religious experiences may sense this void because of the absence of the recreative powers of recreational experiences. Another person who has enriched the self through therapeutic recreational, vocational, and religious experiences may sense a void because the person has never engaged in honest and open human experiences. On it goes – psychological voids exist because of the absence of one or more of the four therapeutic experiences in a person's pattern of existence.

The self expands, life becomes more full and personally relevant, when one consciously seeks out a complementary involvement in each of the four therapeutic experiences.

4. *Among the four therapeutic experiences, a person devotes more psychic energy to the one that expands the self more fully than do the others.* To divide the time available for the four therapeutic experiences into quartiles would hamper the expansion of the self. Not all of the four therapeutic experiences have an equal value in the life of an individual, but all should be experienced if the self is to expand. But the four therapeutic experiences cannot be allocated equivalent periods of time with the expectation that equal involvement will insure the expansion of the self.

Among the four therapeutic experiences, one usually has more visceral relevancy than the others and, hence, contributes more to the expansion of the self than the others. When one discovers which of the four therapeutic experiences impacts the self more qualitatively than the others, one intuitively expends more psychic energy when engaging in that therapeutic experience than when engaging in the others. This particular therapeutic experience, when known, holds more promise for expanding the self than the others, and more time is allotted for experiencing it than is provided for the others. Once again, balancing one's involvement in the four therapeutic experiences does not mean devoting an equivalent amount of time to each; it does mean devoting more time to the one that expands the self more fully than the others do, but without neglecting to provide time for becoming involved in the other three therapeutic experiences that also contribute to the expansion of the self.

5. *Involvement in therapeutic human experiences is the catalyst that enables the self to discover the visceral relevancy of therapeutic, vocational, religious, and recreational experiences.* The self that is expanded more fully than others typically experiences more personal relevancy in therapeutic human relationships. These therapeutic human experiences become the base whereby the self feels comfortable enough to project itself toward therapeutic vocational, religious, and recreational experiences.

To feel comfortable with people, to deeply care about the dimensions of their existence, to extend oneself toward others in honesty, openness, and empathy, indicates a willingness to risk the self. This inner feeling of well-being and security enables the self to project itself toward therapeutic vocational, religious, and recreational experiences. Because it has experienced viable human relationships, the self is free enough to penetrate the therapeutic values of vocational, religious, and recreational experiences. The self is free because it does not feel threatened or diminished in human relationships. Such freedom in human relationships must first be sensed and internalized if the self is to gain and be expanded by its involvement in the other therapeutic experiences.

Inner freedom enables a person to be more true, real, and genuine as one engages in therapeutic vocational, religious, and recreational experiences. When the self has been involved in catalytic human relationships that have been enriching and expanding, it possesses the freedom necessary to seek out the therapeutic values contained in vocational, religious, and recreational experiences.

6.   *The self that has been expanded by a qualitative engagement in the four therapeutic experiences will transcend itself and consciously and humanly extend itself toward other persons.*   The self that has expanded itself through an involvement in therapeutic human, vocational, religious, and recreational experiences has a tendency to go beyond itself; since the self feels expanded, it tends toward other persons. A person returns to others when free to do so; when one feels sufficiently fulfilled as a person, one completes a therapeutic cycle by returning to a caring attitude toward others. When the person is fulfilled, he or she is no longer suspicious or distrustful of others. Since the expanded person feels comfortable with the inner self that has been expanded through the four therapeutic experiences, the person in turn feels comfortable in relationships with others, comfortable enough with others to care about what happens to them, comfortable enough so that other persons take on dignity and worth that were previously overshadowed—not because they did not possess inherent dignity and worth, but because the self was so constrained that it was not able to appreciate or to love others.

The cyclical nature of the four therapeutic experiences is, indeed, a phenomenon. Human therapeutic experiences serve as catalysts that propel the self toward expanding vocational, religious, and recreational experiences; and when the self becomes sufficiently expanded through this quartet of therapeutic experiences, it consciously and humanly shapes itself, moves itself, and extends itself toward enriching the existence of other persons.

7.   *The expanded self attempts to replace the tolerance of persons with an empathic sense of unconditional positive regard for persons.*   The expanded self refuses to "put up" with others or tolerate their existence. To tolerate the existence of another person is inimical with the expanded self since to tolerate means, "I'll put up with you, no matter how much I dislike you." The expanded self realizes that the true test of its expansion is its ability to have reverence for the differences among persons. It is relatively easy to have a kinship with people who are like ourselves; but this kinship can produce a neuroticism that has separated and will continue to separate humanity. The expanded self accepts differences; it sees beauty in differences and realizes that the self can be further expanded when it evolves toward an unconditional positive regard for the differences among persons.

The expanded self projects itself toward understanding the basis for these differences, and it discovers that the basis for these differences has been historically created to defend the self rather than to expand the self.

In an effort to protect the self from external pervasive influences, the person has concentrated on accentuating the differences among people and has reinforced separateness. From a base of unconditional positive regard for others, the expanded self sees these differences as artificial and superficial barriers among persons, and attempts to understand them. But the expanded person doesn't concentrate on the differences; he or she looks for the common human elements among people and realizes that, in their humanness, people are more alike than unlike. By having an unconditional positive regard for others, the expanded self seeks a human amalgamation among persons.

8. *The expanding self values the direction of its own expansion but has no inclination to move other persons in the same direction; it respects pluralism because it is evidence of the existence of personal freedom.* The expanded self seeks not to tamper with, manipulate, or convert others. Since the expanded self values its own personal freedom, it does not seek to impose its concept of anything upon other persons. The expanded self realizes that there can be human convergence among people only if the individual is freely allowed to determine personal values. One attempts to impose values on another only when one feels that personal values are superior to the values held by the other person; but the expanded self doesn't feel the need for such a psychological crutch. The expanded self has discovered the values that undergird its existence; but the expanded self realizes that these values are personally relevant because they were freely chosen by the self. In its contacts with other persons, the expanded self doesn't attempt to impose its idiosyncratic value system. Instead, the expanded self creates an atmosphere of communication in which the person can reach toward a crystalization of personally relevant values. When a person discovers personal and motivating values, these values will affect his or her behavior deeply. When one merely transplants the values of another in one's own existence, these transplanted values eventually erode because they were not conceived and implemented in the bowels of the self.

9. *The expanding self has a reverence for the people of the past who have contributed to civilization, is more relevant in its present state of being, and possesses a psychic temperature that insists that a viable legacy be passed on to future generations.* The expanding self knows and values its own existence. The expanding person conceives itself to be a valuable part of humanity in the here-and-now, but is also appreciative of the unknown persons of the past who have contributed to the evolution of whatever degree of humanness exists in the world today. The expanded person has a sense of a personal posterity, a sense that one must contribute to increasing the level of humanness in the world today so that unborn generations will have a more human legacy to inherit. The expanded person knows that the

self is imperfect and that others are imperfect, but also knows that the self has contributed to that imperfection; the expanded person further knows that the self must move to more fullness if it is to contribute to the evolution of humanness – both today and in an unknown tomorrow. The expanded self has a personal *gravitas* that shapes its existence. Because one is an expanded person who realizes that his or her life and existence is important only insofar as it is a contribution to human evolution. The expanded person doesn't want to play games and exist only at a superficial and uninvolved level; the expanded person wants to live and sense the thunder and the rainbows of existence. Why? Certainly for the self, but also for others – the others of today with whom the expanded person shares a meal, a conversation, a laugh – and the unknown others of tomorrow whose world will be better or worse because of the degree of humanness that we express today.

10. *Participation in the four therapeutic experiences is a self-expanding process for all age groups regardless of nationality, race, culture, socioeconomic status, political affiliations, or religious inclinations.* The process of expanding the self is available to anyone who desires to move toward a fuller existence. It is not the preserve of a privileged few on whom Lady Luck decides to smile. A Yugoslavian, a Mongolian, an Italian, a Brazilian, a Russian, an American – each can become engaged in an expansion of the self by a qualitative involvement in each of the four therapeutic experiences. Be the person Black, Oriental, or Caucasian; financially wealthy or impoverished; seven years old or seventy-seven years old; liberal or conservative; Republican or Democrat; Socialist or Communist; atheist, agnostic, or theist – all can expand the self in proportion to the value one places on engaging in each of the four therapeutic experiences available.

Expanded persons in any country or culture do exist, and an investigation of their life styles would reveal that they have qualitatively participated in a combination of therapeutic human, work, spiritual, and recreational experiences. In all countries and cultures, the self can experience personally relevant human experiences, can seek out the intrinsic values in the work being performed, can spiritually link itself to others, and can enjoy itself through recreation. The only barriers that prevent the self from expanding are those self-conceived barriers that one can easily construct. The beauty of the four therapeutic experiences is that they are easily available to all persons but one must sense their value for expanding the self, and must consciously seek out opportunities to experience them.

11. *The expanding self senses an internationally emerging convergence of humanity in various areas of thought; it possesses a deep sensitivity to the psychosocial, philosophical, technological, and biological evolution of humanity and the importance of one's place in that evolution.* The development of sophisticated communications media, especially satellite television programs that have a hemispheric or international scope, have developed among formerly divergent peoples a sense of their commonness, a sense

that they are essentially alike. They cry, feel, debate, emote, love, and fear – together – internationally. People, on an international scale, are beginning to see and sense a commonality in their concern for survival; they see themselves in others when they see the art, dances, culture, and technology of other nations; they sense that among persons, birth and marriage are universally joyous occasions and that death produces sorrow in all of humanity; they realize that intelligence, hope, worship, collectivism, and violence are universal characteristics of people, and they respect all of these characteristics except violence.

This international convergence of humanity is a new and refreshing experience for civilization. For the first time in human history, the person is truly beginning to sense a link between the self and the international community of persons. In the darker periods of our past, some relied on the neurotic need to be devious, to be suspicious and skeptical of those who were different. It is becoming increasingly more difficult to convince the people of nations that they must make war in order to survive, because international satellite television is beginning to draw people closer to people. As this occurs more frequently, it will become psychologically more difficult for persons to want to kill others, because this emerging sense of the international community of persons has affected and will affect a person's positive regard for others.

12. *All educational institutions should make provisions whereby students have qualitative access to each of the four therapeutic experiences.* Within a city, state, nation, hemisphere, or the world, institutions providing their clientele with therapeutic human, work, spiritual, and recreational experiences will make a greater contribution to the wholeness of their clientele. Just as the person who omits one or more of the four therapeutic experiences from existence will be less whole, so, too, will institutions be less whole and less valuable when they omit one or more of these therapeutic experiences from the services they offer to their clientele.

One of the major functions of educational institutions is to produce positive, psychologically whole persons. School settings should make it possible for students to have qualitative human, vocational, spiritual and recreational therapeutic experiences. A school cannot help the self to expand by merely providing cognitive experiences for its students. Within the context of organized education, teaching for knowledge is important, but facilitating the development and expansion of the self is just as important as a primary educational goal. The self is a consequence of experience, and in schools, we provide a host of experiences. Whether or not those experiences enhance the personal growth of students is a question that should be of concern to every educator.

Any institution that hopes to expand the selves of its clientele must make provisions whereby they can become involved in each of the four therapeutic experiences. A particular institution may give greater attention and emphasis to one of the four therapeutic experiences, but it must also be sensitive enough to provide opportunities for involvements in the other three. The specific therapeutic experience featured by a particular institution is buttressed and enriched by the complementary existence of the other three therapeutic experiences.

13. *It is impossible to expand the self into perfection; a person will always be involved in the process of becoming more adequate, but will never achieve full personal adequacy because one's reach will always exceed one's grasp.* A qualitative involvement in each of the four therapeutic experiences will not result in the self becoming expanded in its fullest and most perfect sense. Such perfect expansion is impossible because the nature of a human being is evolutionary; a person progresses, in self-expansion, from one stage to the next, but never reaches an apex, since today's sense of self-fulfillment, no matter how perfect it appears to be, will not and should not be satisfying tomorrow. The goal tomorrow, then, is not only to bring the self to its former level of expansion, but to move the self to the next higher level of expansion. Such an evolutionary expansion of the self never ceases, since it is a process rather than an act. As a process, it is continuous, and the complete expansion of the self can never occur. The struggle is to expand the self beyond the point where it had been previously, to engage the self so that it matures, grows, and develops to its temporary limits, and to realize that these realized limits *are* temporary—that there is an even higher level to which the self can be expanded, and that this higher level can be achieved only in proportion to the quality of involvement in therapeutic human, work, religious, and recreational experiences. But the self can never be perfect. It achieves its highest level of expansion at the moment before it is physically consumed.

REFERENCES

Craig, H. *Shakespeare: A historical and critical study with annotated texts of twenty-one plays.* Glenview, Ill.: Scott and Foresman, 1931.

Furlong, W. Danger as a way of joy. *Sports Illustrated,* 1969, *30,* 52–53.

Montagu, A. *On being human.* New York: Hawthorn Books, 1950.

Rogers, C. R. *A way of being.* Boston: Houghton Mifflin, 1980.

Super, D. E. *The psychology of careers.* New York: Harper and Row, 1957.

Weintraub, S. *Shaw: An autobiography.* New York: Weybright and Talley, 1969.

Zilboorg, G. *Freud and religion.* Westminster, Md.: Paulist/Newman Press, 1964, 31.

INDEX